Lessons from the World

LESSONS
from the
WORLD

◆

A Cross-Cultural Guide to Music Teaching and Learning

PATRICIA SHEHAN CAMPBELL

SCHIRMER BOOKS
A *Division of Macmillan*, Inc.
NEW YORK

Maxwell Macmillan Canada
TORONTO

Maxwell Macmillan International
NEW YORK   OXFORD   SINGAPORE   SYDNEY

Schirmer Books
A Division of Macmillan, Inc.
866 Third Avenue, New York, N.Y. 10022

Macmillan, Inc., is part of the Maxwell
Communication Group of Companies

Maxwell Macmillan Canada, Inc.
1200 Eglinton Avenue East, Suite 200
Don Mills, Ontario M3C 3N1

Library of Congress Catalog Card Number: 90-42513

Printed in the United States of America

printing number

1   2   3   4   5   6   7   8   9   10

Library of Congress Cataloging-in-Publication Data

Campbell, Patricia Shehan.
    Lessons from the world : a cross-cultural guide to music
teaching and learning / Patricia Shehan Campbell.
        p.   cm.
    Includes bibliographical references and index.
    ISBN 0-02-872361-9
    1. Music—Instruction and study.   I. Title.
    MT1.C22   1991
    780′.7—dc20   90-42513
                                                   CIP
                                                   MN

To my parents, my teachers

The [music] profession is indeed carried on by people . . . who have forgotten the human ear. Its pattern of education denies the only logical starting point for a genuinely creative art of music—the ear, and the manifold delights and stimuli that the ear, in conjunction with the experienced mind, can find in the exercise of imagination.

—Harry Partch, "Show Horses in the Concert Ring"

CONTENTS

PART I

Music Learning in the West

PART II

Music Learning in the World

10 TRADITION AND CHANGE:
CROSS-CULTURAL COMPARISONS OF
MUSIC INSTRUCTION IN WORLD
CULTURES   186

Traditional Music Teaching and Learning • Contemporary
Practices in Music Instruction • Summary

PART III

Classroom and Studio Applications

PREFACE

Along with music literacy, performance skills, and musical values, the cultivation of attentive listening and creative expression is a central aim in the education of student musicians. Some of these abilities are partly genetic but all of them can be developed through formal instruction, in informal life experiences, and with the guidance of musician-teachers. Throughout history and across many cultures, the listening ear and creative mind have produced profoundly expressive musical experiences. Competent student musicians today are the result of comprehensive teaching-learning procedures; they are the products of their own well-integrated sensory systems and many dedicated teachers.

Musical growth cannot occur without careful listening, for it is through listening that an individual develops sensitivity to musical sounds. While notation was invented to facilitate the transmission of music as well as to preserve it for the benefit of future generations, it has also become of utmost importance in educating people musically. Musicians develop the ability to translate notation into musical sound and even to hear the notation silently before it is produced. However, the direct link between the sound and the instrument (i.e., that which bypasses the notation) cannot be ignored in a thorough music education. This is the mark of a comprehensive musicianship; to be able to engage the sensory capacities fully and to link the eye, the ear, and the kinesthetic processes.

Music is unique not only for its aural essence but also for its creative potential in that it provides a channel for personal expression. Both creative and re-creative abilities can be nurtured through instruction so that students become as adept in their spontaneous invention of new musical ideas as they are in their interpretation of the musical score. Through their masterful combination of aural and performance skills, intellectual understanding, and personal ingenuity, music becomes for these students a living language that communicates individual feelings and ideas within certain cultural and genre-specific conventions.

This book examines the importance of ear-training and the creative process of improvisation in the history of European art music, in a sampling of world cultures, and in the making of young musicians in contemporary music education settings. It recognizes the value of listening skills without diminishing the importance of notation as a teaching instrument and a memory aid. Moreover, it recommends ear-training and creative experiences that lead to the greater musicianship of students in various stages of their development.

The ultimate aim of these chapters is to recognize improvisation as a key component of music performance, to note the role of aural training in developing one's creative capacity to improvise, and to recommend ways of stimulating the creative musical expression of students. Most music educators and instructors agree that there is more to music than can be notated, but the matters of how to realize the score, how to enliven printed music with personal feeling, and how to invent new music spontaneously are sometimes puzzling and problematic. The extent to which observation, imitation, repetition, vocalization, and solmization are employed in the instructional process is surveyed over time (history) and distance (world cultures); then recommendations are made for the application of these teaching and learning techniques to classrooms and studios. The instructional strategies emphasize aural training and the oral transmission process; along with performance techniques and an understanding of notation as a learning aid, they lead directly to improvisation and a truly creative musicianship.

This volume is intended for music teachers at every level, but in particular those engaged in teaching kindergarten through twelfth grade (K–12) general music, conducting choral and instrumental ensembles, and offering private studio instruction. It should be a helpful addendum to books that present the foundations of music education history, philosophy, and contemporary curricular practices. Its use as an ideas and issues resource in undergraduate methods courses as well as in graduate seminars will inform readers of the nature of music teaching and learning in many contexts.

The description and documentation of teaching and learning procedures in various cultures under a single cover may prove to be the most unique aspect of this volume. While information on cross-cultural processes of music learning is contained in various scholarly writings, much of this is not easily accessible to the music teacher. Those concerned and consumed with lessons, rehearsals, class sessions, student recitals, ensemble concerts, and school assemblies on a daily basis may find this volume to contain a convenient compilation and synthesis of such information.

This book is not an ethnomusicology text, however, nor is it designed for teaching the world's musics. It does not attempt to describe instruments or genres of various world traditions nor to suggest strategies in multiethnic music education; there are numerous volumes that address these matters in detail. Instead, the emphasis in these pages is given to the aural and creative components of music teaching and learning as part of a shared human phenomenon. Historical as well as cultural vignettes provide a sampling of music across time and distance as it is experienced through listening, creating, and re-creating.

The body of the work is presented in three groups of chapters. The first part, "Music Learning in the West" (Chapters 1–5), deals with the nature of aural skills and creativity in the history of Western art music and from historical and contemporary perspectives of American music education.* The relationship of ear training and the creative process is explored through the invention of notation and solmization systems and through the continuing presence of improvisation through the ages. Improvisation and its counterpart, eartraining, have long been accepted and recognized in European classical music as important curricular objectives; music instruction, however, frequently deemphasizes or dismisses the development of aural and creative skills. Theories of music learning and teaching suggest that creativity can be developed through training and that despite culture-specific elements, aural learning is a significant mode of instruction in formal and informal settings.

Chapters 6 through 10 are combined in a second section called "Music Learning in the World" in which music learning and teaching are addressed from cross-cultural perspectives. While no attempt is made to include every music genre from every world culture, traditional practices in the training of musicians are examined through a series of cultural samples representing parts of Asia, Africa, and the West. Issues concerning the techniques of aural learning and imitation, notation and improvisation, vocalization and solmization, and memory strategies are discussed in theory and as they are presently employed; their widespread use suggests that there may be cross-cultural similarities in the way music is taught and learned, regardless of style or culture. The comparison here of traditional techniques of many cultures with current practices in the training of professional musicians in Western-styled schools, universities, and conservatories is designed to present a balance of Western and world tradition and innovation in music education.

* "West and "Western" will be used to refer to European and European-derived art music, while "world" will designate all other art, folk, and popular traditions.

The third part, "Classroom and Studio Applications" (Chapters 11 through 13), offers ways for developing the aural skills and creative improvisation abilities of young musicians. Experiences that emphasize listening, vocalization, and improvisation are adapted to instruction in general music, choral and instrumental rehearsals, and private studio instruction in piano, voice, and various orchestral instruments. While these techniques are sporadically employed by most teachers already, this section recommends ways for a more comprehensive use of them. Furthermore, teachers with an awareness of the ways that listening and creative expression have been integral to music learning in every age and culture may recognize the natural role these techniques play in their own classrooms and studios. The focus experiences are applications of learning and teaching principles for use at various age, grade, and skill levels.

While the first section of the book presents these concepts and techniques as they have existed in the West and as they are considered in educational philosophy and theory, the second section presents a series of cultural vignettes that illustrate their use in other world traditions. These sections are important in providing a rationale to the teacher for understanding music teaching and learning in broad historical and cultural contexts and in lending further support to the wisdom of integrating aural skills and creative improvisation experiences into lessons, classes, and rehearsals. It is the final section, however, that will provide the teacher with useful ideas for the improvement of music education and a validation for the development of the listening ear and the creative mind as essential features of music instruction.

ACKNOWLEDGMENTS

During the past decade, I have developed an awareness of cross-cultural music teaching and learning processes through study, observations, and discussions with musicians, educators, and scholars in the United States, India, Japan, China, Australia, and Eastern Europe. I wish to express my sincere appreciation to those who have guided, informed, and inspired my thinking, in particular William M. Anderson, Terry L. Kuhn, William P. Malm, and Ramnad V. Raghavan. Many thanks also to those teachers and scholars who reviewed portions of the manuscript, providing critical commentary and encouragement to me in various stages: Tilford Brooks, Caroline Card-Wendt, Richard Colwell, George Heller, William Hochkeppel, Jere Humphreys, Orland Johnson, Han Kuo-Huang, Albert LeBlanc, David McAllester, Sara Stone Miller, Terry Miller, Steven Roberson, George Sawa, Carol Rogel Scott, Michael Shasberger, Barbara Smith, Larry Smithee, and Sandra Stauffer. For generous assistance in travel, research, and writing, I give thanks to the National Endowment for the Humanities, the International Research Exchange, the Japan-American Society, and faculty grants from Washington University in St. Louis, and Butler University of Indianapolis. I am grateful to Jonas Svedas, who provided me with my first formal music learning experiences, and especially to my parents, who taught me to learn by listening and to love music. I am indebted to my husband, Charles, who nurtures the student musician in me and is the catalyst for my thoughts. It is his listening ear and good counsel that saw these pages to their finish.

Patricia Shehan Campbell
Seattle, Washington

Lessons from the World

PART I

Music Learning in the West

CHAPTER

1

---◆---

Music in the Curriculum

Music is a human phenomenon. All over the world and throughout history, music has been sung, played, composed, improvised, danced to, and listened to. It is at once cross-cultural as it is also culture-specific: it is universally embraced as a meaningful part of life, and yet its components vary greatly from one culture to the next. Because it is a way of thinking and expressing ideas and feelings, music has appeared as an important symbol of people and culture through the ages.

Like many cultural symbols, music is a learned behavior. Musical understanding, performance skills, and values develop through the underlying social structures set by people from within a culture. There are transmitters and receivers of music in every case, but music learning may be directed and formal, as in the private lesson or the class rehearsal, or informally dictated by conditions placed upon it by a society, as with the mediated music offered by television, radio, and films.

The school music curriculum of contemporary Western society is a premiere example of formalized music learning and teaching. Because people have prized music for its social, moral, and aesthetic values, music has maintained a fairly secure position within the American school curriculum since its inception. But will public support for instruction in music and the arts be continued? Are the methods of instruction employed in the teaching of music working effectively? Will formalized music instruction serve society at large, so that the American public can increase their musical understanding, skills, and values? These are critical issues confronting music teachers in the West today. There is an even more fundamental question: What do we expect to accomplish through school music instruction? Philosophy, goals, and the practices that stem from them require careful thought by the profession. Without periodic appraisal of the function of music education in a society, there is a danger that teaching can become a mechanistic meandering of day-to-day activities that lack true purpose. As a meaningful symbol of culture, music and the means by which it is preserved and transmitted merit our consideration.

A PHILOSOPHY FOR TEACHING MUSIC IN THE SCHOOLS

The place of music in Western society has stimulated considerable discussion since the beginnings of recorded history. Among the intellectuals of classical Greece, Aristotle held music in high regard for purposes of ritual and entertainment and as part of a more comprehensive education. He offered his rationale for learning to sing and play instruments:

> Participation in performing is going to make a big difference to the quality of the person that will be produced; it is impossible, or at any rate very difficult, to produce good judges of musical performance from among those who have never themselves performed. . . . Musical education must include actual performing. . . . What is needed is that the pupil shall not struggle to acquire the degree of skill that is needed for professional competitions, or to master those peculiar and sensational pieces of music which have begun to penetrate the competitions and have even affected education. Musical exercises, even if not of this kind, should be pursued only up to the point at which the pupil becomes capable of appreciating good melodies and rhythms, and not just the popular music such as appeals to slaves, children, and even some animals. (Saunders, 1984, 29)

Music in the West has been viewed variously as the genteel art, the greatest of the social graces, and a cousin of logic, mathematics, and the sciences. During the Renaissance, accomplishments in music and dance were signs of cultivated people. Social embarrassment was best avoided through musical training that included singing, the reading of notation, instrumental performance, and the popular line and couple dances; any or all of these skills were likely to be called upon in a social situation. The opening dialogue from Thomas Morley's *A Plaine and Easie Introduction to Practicall Musicke* offers evidence of musical training among the elite in Elizabethan England and the ostracizing of people who lacked skills:

> Supper being ended and music books (according to the custom) being brought to the table, the mistress of the house presented me with a part earnestly requesting me to sing; but when, after many excuses, I protested unfeignedly that I could not, every one began to wonder; yea, some whispered to others demanding how I was brought up, so that upon shame of mine ignorance I go now to seek out mine old friend Master Gnorimus, to make myself his scholar. (Morley, 1597, 1–2)

American music education had its roots in the need for literate and skillful musicians in the church. The Spanish friars in Mexico and the Southwest and the French Jesuits in Canada succeeded in teaching Native Americans liturgical chant, motets, and masses. English colonists of various religious denominations found their congregations in need of training, and so established the singing school for the development of music literacy and performance skills.

With the growing urbanization of the United States in the nineteenth century came performance opportunities in community choirs and instrumental ensembles. The potential of music in school curricula was eventually recognized for its moral, physical, and intellectual contributions; such training was thought ultimately to increase the pool of singers for choral societies and orchestral ensembles. In 1844, six years after the inclusion of vocal music instruction in the elementary schools of Boston, Horace Mann, secretary of the Massachusetts State School Board, offered this favorable assessment: "Wherever music has been introduced, it has commended itself both to the good sense and the goodwill of all parties concerned" (Mann, 1891, 453). Mann further specified the nature of music's contributions to students and of its promotion of good health through the exercise of the lungs; its intellectual stimulation through the relationship of pitch, rhythm, and harmony to mathematics; and of its influence on the development of character, including attributes of "peace, hope, affection, generosity, charity, and devotion" (p. 456).

Through the nineteenth century, early advocates of school music instruction promoted the Pestalozzian philosophy of learning by doing and of proceeding from practice to theory. The mind, eye, and ear were united in attempts to give all students—and not just the talented—experiences leading to musical understanding and appreciation. Music became fixed as a regular offering in the public schools. Instrumental music was gradually added to the vocal music offerings, and the American public supported music instruction for its moral and physical qualities.

Even in the twentieth century, the philosophy of the Greeks concerning the utilitarian values of music has been reiterated in the statements of superintendents, school board members, principals, and teachers. All were agreed that the aim of education was to train children to become capable and useful members of society, and that music could help to achieve that goal. The Progressive Music Series opened with an introductory statement to that effect: "Music, because of its powerful influence upon the very innermost recesses of our subjective life, because of its wonderfully stimulating effect upon our physical, mental, and spiritual nature, and because of its well-nigh universality of appeal, contributes directly to . . . the fundamental purposes of education" (Parker, McConathy, Birge, and Miessner, 1916, 9).

With the advent of the phonograph, the goals of school music programs were broadened to include the development of an appreciation of the beauty of music. In this century, the drills of the past were replaced by the child study movement's emphasis on the development of individual musical potential in each student. The development of music listening skills, knowledge about music, and musical values complemented the earlier view of school music programs as occasions for performance. By the 1930s, the balanced curriculum in music education included listening, performance, and creative experiences (Mursell, 1936, 521).

While there were underlying beliefs throughout history that guided the extent to which formalized music instruction was advanced within a society, only recently have music educators discovered the importance of developing a philosophy for their practices, one that would uphold the uniqueness of music for its aesthetic qualities. Teaching had been traditionally directed by a series of personally selected goals, and for a long time the profession developed without a common philosophical foundation. Out of the revolutionary period of the 1960s, when changes were rampant and schools were adapting to major social reforms, came the need for music professionals to offer a unified raison d'être. As many societal values, governmental policies, and educational ideals were scrutinized, a philosophy of music education based upon aesthetic—rather than social, moral, physical, or intellectual—principles was shaped. Reimer pointed out the need for clear thinking on the role and purpose of music education:

The profession as a whole needs a formulation which can serve
to guide the efforts of the group. The impact the profession can
make on society depends in large degree on the quality of the
profession's understanding of what it has to offer which might
be of value to society. (1970, 3)

More recently, Reimer expressed not only the "collective con-
science" but also the individual teacher's need for embracing a philosophy: "Individuals who have a clear notion of . . . their aims as
professionals and [who] are convinced of the importance of those
aims are a strong link in the chain of people who collectively make a
profession" (1989, 4). While teaching provides a primary source of
ideas and directions for the development of the profession, reading
and reflection also help to broaden the collective vision. Jorgensen
(1990) warns us of the dangers that anti-intellectualism and restricted thinking pose to the effectiveness of music instruction. She
challenges teachers to read literature in music, education, psychology, sociology, anthropology, and philosophy that will raise difficult
questions and stimulate solutions: "To prevent intellectual fossiliza-
tion, we need to be constantly learning and keeping our minds open
to new ideas, not only in music but more broadly in education" (22).
Through the professional self-assessment of recent decades, American musical education has emerged with a greater and more unified
sense of purpose. Through critical thinking about music and instruction, music teachers may play increasingly prominent roles as transmitters of a significant component of culture.

For the last several decades, the meaning of music as a subject
of study in the curriculum has been associated with the concept of
"aesthetic education." In essence, aesthetic education recognizes that
while extramusical functions of music exist—including music's contributions to entertainment, worship, political and civil events, and
communication—the key role of music education is the development
of students' individual responses to the powerful art of music. To be
sure, music has utilitarian purposes, and the moral, social, physical,
and intellectual outgrowths of music study are widely recognized
today—as they were among the ancient Greeks. The unique manner
in which music conveys feeling through knowledge about its component parts, however, is its greatest gift. Performance, listening, and
creating are means to a single goal: aesthetic experience.

Despite occasional economic setbacks and constantly shifting
social values, music is holding its place as an important entity in
American education. While cultural conditioning occurs today
through the informal listening afforded by Muzak and MTV, school
music instruction makes accessible to all students a means of know-

ing a greater variety of music. Through knowledge, analysis, and creativity; through aural and performance skills; and through music history, literature, and theory, a student learns the elemental components of music and acquires a deeper sensitivity to music's artistic worth. Music in formal education has come to function as an agency for the transmission of society's artistic and sociocultural heritage and for the development of both the talented performer and the informed listener.

FOUNDATIONS OF THE CONTEMPORARY CURRICULUM

"Rationales for the arts carry implications for teaching. In choosing a rationale, we infer the content (curriculum) and methodologies of the arts. Every 'why' means 'what' and 'how.' But what one claims for the arts must be deliverable. Practice must match rhetoric" (Fowler, 1984, 33).

The curricular goals and pedagogical practices associated with philosophy continue to evolve, but the overriding mission of music education in the West is to provide opportunities for students to know music for its artistic merits. The process of music instruction has been reexamined in recent decades through numerous experiments, projects, and symposia. A better understanding of teaching strategies and student responses to them has emerged as a result, along with the clarification of the goals and objectives of music instruction. Of particular interest is the extent to which creativity and musicianship, including ear-training, music literacy, performance skills, and listening were advocated by expert musicians and educators alike.

Composers in the Schools

Educational reform was widespread in the late 1950s and funding was available for innovative projects that could reach to the core of a curricular issue. Math and the pure sciences were the first to benefit, but school music projects with the potential to contribute to the curriculum in distinctive ways were also supported. In providing a means for secondary school students to experience music more intimately as well as offering support for active young composers—those under the age of 35—the Ford Foundation established the

Young Composers Project in 1959. Composers-in-residence were placed in schools, where they wrote music for performance by student ensembles and solo musicians, exposed students and teachers to the subtleties of contemporary music, and nurtured the creative talent of young student composers. Further support by Ford came in 1963 with the institution of the Contemporary Music Project for Creativity in Musician Education, as composer residencies were continued under the title Composers in Public Schools, and again in 1968 when Professionals-in-Residence to Communities was established. Creativity was at the core of these projects, which provided professional opportunities for composers and encouragement to students for developing their own creative musicianship through association with and guidance by composers.

The Yale Seminar

Among the significant influences of contemporary American music education were the recommendations of the Yale Seminar on Music Education. Although the seminar included few music educators, thirty-one professional musicians, scholars, and professors met at Yale University in June 1963 to examine musical materials and musical performance. The Yale musicians looked at music instruction throughout the country and said:

1. It is of appalling quality, representing little of the heritage of significant music.
2. It is constricted in scope. Even the classics of Western music—such as the great works of Bach, Mozart, Beethoven—do not occupy the central place they should in singing, playing, and listening. Non-Western music, early Western music, and certain forms of jazz, popular, and folk music have been almost altogether neglected.
3. It stunts the growth of musical feeling because it is so often not sufficiently interesting to enchant or involve a child to whom it is presumed to be accessible. Children's potentials are constantly underestimated.
4. It is corrupted by arrangements, touched-up editions, erroneous transcriptions, and tasteless parodies to such an extent that authentic work is rare. A whole range of songbook arrangements, weak derivative semipopular children's pieces, and a variety of "educational" recordings containing music of similar value are to be strongly condemned as "pseudo-music." To the extent artificial music is taught to children, to that extent are they invited to hate it. There is no need to use artificial or pseudo-music in any of its forms.
5. Songs are chosen and graded more on the basis of the limited tech-

nical skills of classroom teachers than the needs of the children or the ultimate goal of improved hearing and listening skills. This is one of the causes of the proliferation of feeble piano and autoharp accompaniments and "sing-along" recordings.

6. A major fault of the repertory of vocal music stems from the desire to appeal to the least common denominator and to offend the least possible number. More attention is often paid to the subject matter of the text, both in choice and arrangement of material, than to the place of a song as music in the educational scheme. Texts are banal and lack regional inflection. (Lowens, 1971, E-4)

The consensus of the Yale participants was that music programs seldom included representative examples of contemporary music, early Western music genres (including medieval and Renaissance works), or non-Western musics. Despite the creative works of contemporary composers, the research findings in early music by musicologists, and the international scene that was affecting other aspects of society and school subjects, many music programs were seen as insular, remote, and guilty of recycling materials that were used at least a generation earlier.

Criticisms were balanced with recommendations for the improvement of teaching in performance ensembles and general music classes. A summary of ten recommendations in the report is given below.

1. The primary aim of K–12 music education programs is the development of musicality, to be accomplished through vocal and instrumental performance, movement, *creativity through composition and improvisation, ear training and listening.*

2. The repertory of school music programs should include the best representative examples of Western, non-Western, jazz and folk musics from all cultures and periods.

3. A continuous sequence of *guided listening* experiences should be provided at the elementary and secondary school levels.

4. Performance opportunities should include a variety of experiences in orchestral, band and choral ensembles, chamber ensembles, and keyboard instruction. *Basic musicianship* and theory should supplement performance instruction.

5. Advanced courses in theory and literature should be available for the motivated and musically gifted, and should allow students occasions for discovery and analysis of musical components in the literature and their possibilities in *original compositions.*

6. Visiting musicians, composers, and scholars should be placed in residence in schools in order to cultivate the musical interests and understanding of students.

7. Music resources in the community should be called upon to expand and enrich school music programs.

8. Opportunities for advanced study in music, art, drama and dance, including at performing arts high schools, should exist throughout the country, and not just in select metropolitan areas.

9. Greater use of recordings, films, radio and television should be made to illustrate performance techniques and music in ancient and distant cultures.

10. Teacher education programs should be improved and enriched through a series of workshops addressing new curriculum content. (Palisca, 1964, 53–56)

Although the attainment of music literacy was not belabored in the seminar proceedings, the assumption was that experiences in performance ensembles and advanced theory and literature classes require it. Beyond an understanding of notation, ample training in aural skills (ear-training) was recommended as a component of musicality and as a supplement to performance. Along with providing experiences in performing and listening to the best available art and folk music, teachers were encouraged to nurture creative expressiveness through composition and improvisation. The Yale Seminar made educators aware of the potential of music education to contribute to a more musically knowledgeable society while it underscored deficiencies that were long overdue for change.

Several immediate reactions to the Yale Seminar had a direct effect on public school music instruction. In response to the report's second recommendation, the U.S. Office of Education supported the Juilliard School of Music in collecting songs from all periods of Western art music and from various folk music traditions. The Juilliard Repertory Project, as it became known, was a collaboration of composers, scholars, and teachers who compiled and then tested the collected songs in realistic classroom settings. The resulting high-quality and authentic vocal and instrumental songs, 230 in all, were published as the Juilliard Repertory Library.

The Yale Seminar also stimulated a reform in music teacher education, which appeared partly through the activities of the Contemporary Music Project for Creativity in Music Education. A four-day meeting, the Northwestern University Seminar on Comprehensive Musicianship, was held in April 1965 as a means of improving teacher education programs. Attending music educators, performers, composers, theorists, and musicologists reviewed the organization of college and precollege music instruction. They decided that the development of comprehensive musicianship in students required the integration of music history, theory, and applied music courses; this integration and resulting musicianship then became the goal of experimental programs at thirty-six schools and universities.

The CM (Comprehensive Musicianship) Approach

Comprehensive Musicianship or the CM approach defined music education as a total approach to learning through the common elements of music. An understanding of melody, rhythm, texture, form, and dynamics was recommended through experiences in performance, perceptive listening and analysis, and creative composition and improvisation. Students assumed three roles in a CM class: performer, listener, and composer; sometimes they functioned in several roles simultaneously (i.e., the composer-listener and the performer-listener). The active involvement of students in musical experiences was central to the CM approach and discovery learning was suggested as key to a meaningful grasp of music concepts. Despite the depletion of supportive funds from the Ford Foundation in 1973, the goals of Comprehensive Musicianship continued to have an impact on school music programs through the 1970s and 1980s.

Manhattanville Music Curriculum Project

At Manhattanville College of the Sacred Heart in Purchase, New York, a landmark creativity project was originated in 1965; its task was to develop curricular materials for sequential instruction in music from grades three through twelve (Thomas, 1970). Although the Manhattanville Music Curriculum Program (MMCP) was independent of the Yale Seminar, the expectations of its participants of how learning would best occur were similar to those of the Yale Seminar. Both groups believed that learning required experimentation with the components of musical sound. Discovery learning was encouraged through free and guided exploration, through the imitation of musical ideas of others in group settings, and through planned and "premeditated" improvisation. Through a series of problem-solving experiences that built on sequential music concepts introduced through the grade levels, the aural, dexterous (performance), and translative (notational) skills of students were shaped. A five-year examination of ninety-two MMCP-modeled music programs followed, and the relationship of creating, thinking, and feeling processes in students' development of musical sensitivity was noted.

The Tanglewood Symposium

Another impact on the music curriculum was the Tanglewood Symposium. As a response to the vast changes of American society in the postindustrial age, the purpose and role of music education was defined and in some ways redesigned. Questions were raised concerning "music of our time" and contemporary music; the meaning of aesthetic education as a peak experience; the nature of music creativity in the music classroom; and the potential of technology as a means of acquiring knowledge about music, the arts, and the world at large. An evolutionary course of music and music education was posited, and a utopian vision of what music could mean to society in the year 2000 was proposed.

A representative sampling of American society attended the symposium held at Tanglewood, Massachusetts, in the summer of 1967. Included in discussions with music educators were musicians, sociologists, educators, members of the corporate world, scientists, labor leaders, and government officials. A unified call was voiced for the placement of music at the center of school curriculum as a means of providing for aesthetic, nonverbal encounters with the traditions and charges of American society and the world at large.

Eight summary statements were delivered in the Tanglewood Declaration, which laid the foundation for the progress of music education in the years to come.

1. Music serves best when its integrity as an art form is maintained.
2. Music of all periods, styles, forms, and cultures belongs to the curriculum. The musical repertory should be expanded to involve music of our time in its rich variety, including currently popular teenage music and avant-garde music, American folk music, and the music of other cultures.
3. Schools and colleges should provide adequate time for music programs ranging from preschool to adult or continuing education.
4. Instruction in the arts should be a general and important part of education in the senior high school.
5. Developments in educational technology, educational television, programmed instruction, and computer-assisted instruction should be applied to music study and research.
6. Greater emphasis should be placed on helping the individual student to fulfill his needs, goals and potentials.
7. The music education profession must contribute its skills, proficiencies, and insights toward assisting in the solution of urgent social problems such as those in the inner city or other areas with culturally deprived individuals.

8. Programs of teacher education must be expanded and improved to provide music teachers who are specially equipped to teach high school courses in the history and literature of music, courses in the humanities and related arts, as well as teachers equipped to work with the very young, with adults, with the disadvantaged, and with the emotionally disturbed. (Choate, 1968, 139)

Implications for the music curriculum were addressed by a committee of music educators, and standard programs of music instruction for elementary, junior high, and senior high school students were studied. Four areas of music instruction were recommended for the elementary level: (1) understanding many types of music through *guided listening* or performance; (2) studying music through singing, playing instruments, moving to music, or a combination of these; (3) *arranging and composing* music for instruments and voices; and (4) understanding and using music notation (Choate, 1968, 136). Suggestions were made for the improvement of secondary school general music courses, often thought to be of poor quality and irrelevant to adolescents; these recommendations included an emphasis on participatory and performance activities that build musical skills and knowledge.

Issues concerning the nature and nurture of creativity were addressed as fundamental to the profession by another Tanglewood committee. Professional and personal qualities of teachers, including the acceptance of *divergent thinking* and occasional nonconforming behavior, the flexibility to adapt to the needs of students as individuals, and the ability to excite and motivate new ways of thinking about music were seen as critical to the *development of creative musical expression* in students. Statements of symposium speakers led to the committee's prediction that students would one day be taught music comprehensively in a laboratory setting, performing, composing, analyzing, and discussing music in a way that would nurture creative thinking in music.

Still another committee examined the place of technology in music instruction in the 1960s and its future role in the coming decades. The function of the computer as a storage and retrieval machine was discussed, along with specific instances of its use by composers and theorists in the analysis of musical structure. Mechanical teaching machines and programmed instruction booklets invented or inspired by the reinforcement theory of B. F. Skinner were expected to be replaced by computers, so that students might be offered experiences in *ear-training*, the development of notational skills, and *composition* at their own speed of learning. The committee praised the potential of computer-assisted instruction as a means of teaching theory and music history.

A follow-up to the Tanglewood Symposium was the establishment of the Goals and Objectives Project (GO Project) in 1969 by the Music Educators National Conference. Task forces were created, and within a year, two major goals were proposed: (1) a vital musical culture, and (2) an enlightened musical public. Thirty-five long-range objectives, which reflected the statements of the Tanglewood Symposium, were specified for study and implementation by music educators in their school settings. While curricular content was clearly "under fire" in terms of which musical styles belonged in the school programs, the learning process and particular instructional techniques were also carefully considered. The Tanglewood Symposium and the GO Project pointed to the importance of creative musical expression through school experiences in composition and improvisation, and suggested that the new technology to come could advance the development of students' musical skills and knowledge, including aural skills and basic music literacy.

The Ann Arbor Symposia

A decade after the Tanglewood Symposium, the Ann Arbor Symposia were conducted in the summers of 1978, 1979, and 1982. The aims of the meetings were to search for underlying psychological processes on music teaching and learning and to consider means for interpreting and implementing these findings. Problems pertaining to auditory perception, motor skill development, cognitive skills, memory and information processing, affect and motivation, and child development were addressed by psychologists and music educators (Music Educators National Conference, 1981, 411).

Because motivation and creativity were thought to be "of great current interest to music educators," Ann Arbor III offered an occasion for psychologists to share with music educators their research findings on these two constructs (Music Educators National Conference, 1983, i). Motivation and creativity were seen as inseparable, and therefore closely linked to one another in classroom practice. In a summary of the symposium proceedings, the following were viewed as necessary components for stimulating music creativity in students: the setting of challenges by the teacher, the provision of opportunities for student choice in the events of an activity, the function of the teacher as a role model, and the use by the teacher of encouragement and constructive criticism rather than inappropriately administered praise or continuous reproof (McKeachie, 1983, 61–62). Symposium speakers defined creativity as innovative and nonconformist behavior and appealed to teachers to encourage divergent thinking in music analysis, listening, composition, and improvisation.

These events of the past several decades helped shape the status of contemporary American music education, providing goals and a clear direction for its future. The seminars at Yale and Tanglewood were opportunities for practitioners and observers to challenge inappropriate, incorrect, and outmoded curricular methods and materials, and to recommend curricular content based solidly on musico-aesthetic goals. Other events were experimental projects in interpreting the goals of musical sensitivity and creativity. In many of these, musicianship was defined as a combination of aural and listening discrimination skills, psychomotor skills, music literacy, and the creative capacity to compose and improvise as a measure of musical understanding. While the foundations of the contemporary school music curriculum were laid through these efforts, further advances in computer-based instruction, technology and the media, and research findings in music and cognition can be expected to continue to affect views on music teaching and learning in the West.

THE CONTEMPORARY CURRICULUM: PHILOSOPHY IN PRACTICE

A rich history precedes the contemporary kindergarten through twelfth grade (K–12) music curriculum, and the current goals that define music instruction have been carefully considered. Performing ensembles and general music classes are governed by professional statements of philosophy and goals, but variations in practice result from socioeconomic factors, students' needs, and teachers' skills; these factors affect music instruction in the private studio as well. The instructional techniques that teachers employ are testimony to their educational philosophy, as they are also the means for achieving pedagogical goals.

What is the current state of music learning and teaching in American schools? What practices are commonly found, and how do they reflect the goals of aesthetic education? How do these practices mirror the successes of recent curricular projects? Recall that in the context of aesthetic education, the purpose of music education is to provide opportunities for students to experience music at its deepest level through performance, listening, and creative activities. Music is fundamental to life itself, and music as aesthetic education offers ways for students to know music's structure, its expressiveness, and its styles in history and across cultures. Music humanizes us and touches us profoundly, and while our responses may be nonverbal, they are nonetheless enlightened through study. Despite the contributions of school music programs to social and athletic functions, the development in students of responses to music that are impassioned and deeply felt remains at the heart of the professional mission.

When one observes teaching and learning behaviors in classes, rehearsals, and lessons, the realities of the music instruction process emerge. Music reading and the performance of notated music in solo and ensemble settings appear to be important practical goals of school music; if not the only avenues, they are at least critical components of a sequence that leads to aesthetic experience. Other important factors include the development of aural discrimination and listening skills, solmization and vocalization, opportunities for creative expression, and a knowledge of music in historical and cultural contexts. The attainment of a comprehensive musicianship—music literacy in its broadest definition—requires the combination of all these components.

Performance Skills

From their earliest occasions for private study or participation in performing ensembles, students are introduced to exercises that develop psychomotor skills. Similar to the athlete, the music student strives to develop the strength, agility, and flexibility that are the foundation of the performer's art. Scales, arpeggios, patterns, and phrases are performed to "warm up" the fingers, hands, arms, lips, and vocal cords and to develop and maintain the skills of earlier exercises. Through repetitive learning, motor schemas are developed and voluntary actions become unconscious reflex actions. Students can then concentrate on other tasks, such as responding to conductor cues, sight-reading new music, and addressing the expressive components of the music. The development of performance skills is probably the most visible outcome of school music programs and one which often justifies to the public the place of music in the curriculum.

Music Reading

Teachers have long viewed music reading as an important but extremely complex achievement. Theoretically, music reading occurs through a multimodal progression, from sound to symbol to sound again: (1) aural—the student's initial experience with the sound itself and the eventual ongoing ability to develop aural images; (2) visual—the recognition of the notational symbol for the sound; (3) mental—the translation of the symbol to the neural network which then initiates a physical gesture; (4) kinesthetic—the actual generation of the sound on the instrument; and (5) aural—the student's reception, analysis, and evaluation of that sound. Music reading is a sophisticated process that incorporates a variety of sensory modes. In a developmental view of music learning, there are preparatory expe- riences in listening, singing, and movement that offer an acquaintance with music as an aural art before notation is introduced. Experiences in Dalcroze eurhythmics and Orff's chants, songs, and instrumental music, for example, are introductory prereading encounters with music that lead to an understanding of music notation.

Aural Skills

Listening is a meaningful part of the development of a student musician. Guided listening to the architecture of a masterwork is one interpretation of "aural skills," and general music classes provide occasions for such experiences through call charts and listening grids. But even more than this, listening discrimination is the training of the ear to perceive the relationships of pitches and rhythms that are sung, played, and heard within the context of a larger work.

Aural learning through imitation is an efficient avenue for the introduction and retention of musical phrases and patterns; it can be appropriately applied to various learning settings. Students listen as the teacher models a melodic or rhythmic phrase, performance technique, or stylistic nuance. While notation provides some of the details of the musical work, musical intricacies can be presented efficiently through the teacher's performance or through the teacher's singing or chanting of a phrase. Demonstration and its corresponding imitation are useful learning tools, and the student's aural skills can be sharpened through the occasional use of the techniques.

In reality, music instruction in schools and private studios may be providing only occasional opportunities for ear-training. The capacity to hear what is printed in the score, to listen for groupings and configurations, or to refine intonational inaccuracies is not often nurtured through the contemporary curriculum. Instead, listening tends to be passive; thus, the student has difficulty in attaining an independent musicianship. Aural skills can provide students with a "seeing ear" so that they can perceive phrases, shapes, and contours that are inherent in music. Ear-training and its cousin, sight-singing, are essential to a thorough musicianship; the ability to sing with the ear and hear with the voice are signs of an all-inclusive music literacy, a truly comprehensive musicianship.

Solmization and Vocalization

Aural skills are nurtured through solmization, the process of singing the solfège syllables of a melody, and through vocalization, the act of singing a melody on a neutral syllable or chanting a rhythm in any number of syllable systems. Students can become acquainted with the tonal and rhythmic content of a song or musical work through singing and chanting exercises that establish particular patterns in their ears. The choice of solfège system—whether Movable Do, Fixed Do, or some combination—may not matter so much as the mere opportunity for students to sing what they will later experience in a more complete musical context—as listeners, performers, and composers. Instrumentalists who sing and chant phrases they would ordinarily (and eventually) play, experience their music in intimate and personally expressive ways. While vocalization can occur through imitation of the teacher or by reading notation, solmization is associated with and motivated by the music score or staff. Both are important for increasing aural perception and for leading the student toward music literacy.

Creativity

Few would deny the association of music with creativity, and the term *creative* has been extensively applied to teachers, lessons, and programs. All too rarely is creativity associated with student activity, however; students have few occasions within their lessons or classes to produce and develop original musical ideas. Despite models such as the Manhattanville Project, composition and improvisation experiences are often avoided by teachers who may have difficulty knowing where to begin or who would prefer structure and stability to the chaos and unpredictability of a "creative atmosphere."

Still, music is considered one of the creative arts, along with the visual and literary arts, dance, and drama, and could be treated as such in the instructional process. Students possess untapped expressive ability and, with guidance, they can learn to conjure up a musical phrase, and retain, refine, expand, and vary it within a framework. In the past, composers have needed to master notational skills before beginning to create, but today's electronic technology makes it possible

for students with little or no knowledge of notation to produce finished musical compositions with the flick of several switches.* Improvisation, on the other hand, is not usually recorded or preserved
intact. It can be utilized by students at any level of experience or
training to produce musical sounds spontaneously within set parameters.

The development of creative ability requires opportunities for
students to learn through trial-and-error experiences, by exploration,
and with the encouragement of the teacher. It also requires time
within already tight schedules, and yet the result of creative experiences can be more musically expressive performers and intelligent
and discerning listeners. Composing and improvising measure musical understanding because all prior learning can culminate in the
student's personal expression of earlier-accumulated musical ideas.
As he or she selects and rearranges familiar fragments in new ways,
the student is creating music that holds personal meaning and value.

Comprehensive Musicianship

While music instruction has traditionally focused on reading
and performance skills, aesthetic education offers a more comprehensive view of the instructional process. Performing ensembles, general music classes, and private lessons are vehicles for developing
listening discrimination and aural acuity and for stimulating in students the motivation and means for creative musical expression.
Comprehensive musicianship is all-inclusive music literacy, which
can be defined as music reading and much more: an understanding of
music aurally, structurally, historically, and culturally. It is the ultimate musicianship, and those who have acquired it understand and
enjoy music to its fullest potential.

SUMMARY

Music instruction can be interpreted in a variety of ways, and
many methods and materials serve as guides toward musical goals.
For schools to succeed in realizing the goals of the contemporary

---

* While technology has provided shortcuts for the amateur, music reading and writing
are still prized tools of the composer of Western art music. The development of notational skills is useful and recommended for composers of any genre, including popular
music, because of their contribution to a broader understanding of the musical art.

K-12 music curriculum, however, the philosophy must be translated into practices that are feasible in the real world of the schools. Music as aesthetic education must take into account the interdependency of cognition, performance, listening, creativity, and affect. Students gain a thorough understanding of music through the development of reading, writing, aural, and performance skills, and through the most personal of encounters that come with composing and improvising musical ideas.

American school music programs have evolved and matured since their beginning over 150 years ago when their initial aims were more streamlined and straightforward: to teach singing and music reading. The addition of instrumental performance brought about the tradition of school orchestras and bands and an even greater need for music reading. The phonograph added to the curriculum the goals of music appreciation and understanding through listening. Since mid-century, the study of music as an academic discipline, and finally for its aesthetic qualities, has called for a broader set of components. If comprehensive musicianship and a thorough music literacy are to occur in formal educational settings, the effort will require the combination of aural, kinesthetic, and notational skills along with provisions for creative expression. Music education will then be fully realized and will fulfill the philosophical goals that have been established through history and in the contemporary curriculum.

CHAPTER
2

◆

Ear-Training and the Creative Process in European Art Music 1: The Development of Notation

Just how important to the musician are aural skills and creative talent? After all, notation preserves in print the inventions of composers through the ages. We who depend upon notation cannot imagine a time or place without it. Yet, notation came slowly to the West, a world in which aural learning and improvisation were once firmly entrenched.

Historically, the ear and singing voice of a student were trained before he or she learned performing techniques for various instruments. Instruction was based on the student's observation of the musician-teacher who used few words but many demonstrations. Formalized training of performing musicians existed among the ancient Greeks and Romans and continued through the ages. In seminaries and convents, in church schools, in orphanages, later in conservatories, and in private and public schools, music instruction established a tradition of ear-training that blended well with the use of notation. Only in universities was music once viewed theoretically rather than primarily as a performing art.

Notation preserves musical ideas as they were originally conceived, but in many genres of European art music, notation has been intentionally skeletal. As early as the Middle Ages and throughout the Renaissance, ornamentation, improvisation, and the application of stylistic nuances required a keen ear and a watchful eye. In a sense, an oral tradition was partially maintained even as notation provided the musical framework. By listening to the teacher and other performers, the young musician gained a sense of style that he could call upon in improvisation.

From the Middle Ages onward, however, attempts to establish systematic approaches for reading music notation have been documented. Music instruction featured solmization practices that sought the coordination of the ear and eye in learning the staff and the musical phrases that would later appear in notated works and in improvisation. Even before 1600, the most skilled performers of European art music were historically products of the balance between music reading and aural learning. They had the ability to listen, remember, and apply musical ideas through personal expression, interpretation, and improvisation experience.

THE ANCIENT GREEKS AND ROMANS

Music in the West was originally preserved by rote memory. Before the invention of notation, music was transmitted orally by the teacher to the student, who recalled these melodies in later performances, either intact or as a basis for creative improvisation. Notation-prone cultures developed their systems only after the formation of a script for language; such was the case in the West. The cave paintings of the Cro-Magnon man, the hieroglyphics of the Mediterranean region, and the alphabetic script of the ancient Greeks provided visual means of exchanging and preserving ideas. Like the writing of words, musical notation developed gradually, and only after a long history of oral transmission did literacy become an important aspect of a musician's education.

Music was subject to much debate during the first Classical Era, that of ancient Greece. Music was viewed as broadly inclusive of several arts, and singing or instrumental performance was but one small facet of a musical education. Aristotle believed in the value of music instruction, but often spoke of music's function as entertainment rather than as enlightenment. Plato, however, reasoned that an ideal education should include music and gymnastics, of which dance was also a part. He viewed training in music as a potentially intellectual experience that contributed to the development of moral character. According to Plato, when students "have learned to play the lyre . . . they become more civilized, more balanced, and better adjusted in themselves and so more capable in whatever they say or do, for rhythm and harmonious adjustment are essential to the whole of human life" (Hamilton and Cairns, 1961, 322). The Greeks maintained the doctrine of ethos, believing that music was thought to affect moral character. Since the aim of education was to develop citizens of good character, music was carefully scrutinized so that only "good" music in particular modes and rhythms was presented to students.

While there were systems of notation among the Greeks before the sixth century, none were significant in the process of applied music education. Later, in the Hellenic Age, musicians learned their performance art on the *kithara*, *lyre*, and *aulos* through the techniques of imitation and repetition so characteristic of the Greek ideal of education. Private instruction was the rule for instrumental music, and those of considerable talent spent their childhood and youth with master musicians responsible for their total education, including music.

The training of young voices was a group experience, as singers learned aspects of vocal production and repertory while preparing for performances at religious festivals. This practice of choral instruction was a precursor to the development of schools, in which groups rather than individuals were called together for the more efficient use of the teacher's time.

From the fourth century B.C. and through the Greco-Roman period, music became increasingly associated with arithmetic, geometry, and astronomy. The curriculum for training young men as leaders contained a brief period relegated to exercises in notation (and theoretical relations of music, mathematics, and the universe—"music of the spheres") and a minimum of applied lessons on lyre. But as the Golden Age faded, so did the interest in performance as Plato and outspoken statesmen reacted against the excesses of virtuoso music competitions. The late Greek model of education was continued during the period of the Roman Republic. Musical performance was regarded as an avenue of passive enjoyment; the well-bred listened while slaves performed. The interest in theoretical aspects became an obsession for educated Romans, with the mathematical principles of pitch treated as an abstraction entirely removed from sound. The evolution of the quadrivium (the four interrelated subjects of arithmetic, astronomy, geometry, and music), which originated with the Greeks, was continued by the Romans and became more firmly established in the Middle Ages.

THE MIDDLE AGES

Music instruction in the Middle Ages occurred in monasteries, *scholae cantorum* or schools for choristers, the courts, and, after 1100

A.D., the universities. The Roman statesman Boethius reinforced the thoughts of ancient Greece on the relationship of music and mathematics. He further divided musical studies into distinctive experiences, declaring that "there are three kinds of people who are considered in relation to the musical art. The first type performs on instruments, the second composes songs, and the third type judges the instrumental performances and composed songs" (Bower, 1967, 103). A contemporary interpretation might rename these "music-types" performers, composers, and music critics. Boethius described performers as slaves to their instruments and noted that playing and singing required no thought or reason. Composers, he said, also used little thought but were guided by a certain natural instinct. It was the third type that Boethius held as the ultimate goal of a musician, in that judging modes and rhythms required the intellectual analysis of music. This evaluative capacity was the result of a solid education in the scientific and philosophical aspects of music, to be acquired at the universities of Salamanca, Paris, Prague, Cologne, Krakow, and Oxford in the later Middle Ages.

The First Choir Schools

Even while the seeds for the scientific study of music as theory took root, there was a strong interest in the formal training of performing musicians. The Schola Cantorum established at Rome in the fourth century A.D. was a model of the singing and grammar curriculum later found throughout Europe.* Psalms and hymns were taught to choirboys, who furnished music for services in cathedrals and monasteries. Instruction followed the oral tradition, but the reading and writing of neumes and notes were taught as they were gradually developed. The training of young singers may have been harsh at times, according to observations in the Lateran Palace, the setting of Pope Gregory's period as choirmaster prior to his election to the papacy: "[There] are venerated the couch from which he gave lessons in chant, [and] the whip with which he threatened the boys" (Treitler, 1974, 338).

Early Developments in Notation

The transformation of an oral tradition to a literate one directly affected the process of music learning in the West. The gradual de-

---

* Early Christians were at first opposed to music, especially instrumental music, due to its association with the pagan Greeks. They changed their minds early on, though, and decided that music could be an aid to worship.

velopment of the Western notation commonly used today began in the Christian era through the work of Pope Gregory the Great in the sixth century A.D., and extended for nearly a millennium. Two motivations brought about its use in the transmission of liturgical chant, both of which were didactic in nature: the need for a memory aid for later reference after the lesson, and the need to communicate the music across time and distance.

During his drive for the political unification of Europe under his throne, Charlemagne enforced a condition first sought by the Pope: the standardization of chant music. This standardization process was possible only through a system of notation. The variant performances in churches and monasteries throughout Europe were subsequently made uniform when melodies became codified through the symbols of notation. Charlemagne waged an open campaign against the Franks and Gauls so that a standard and uncorrupted view of singing, based on Rome's version of the chant, was eventually adopted. Charlemagne then demanded that the clergy develop schools in which religion, reading, writing, arithmetic, and music—including psalms, notation, and the chant—were taught. Clergymen were advised to "learn the Roman chant thoroughly, and employ it in the correct manner at the night Office and the day Office, just as our royal father, King Pippin, decreed when he suppressed the Frankish chant, out of unanimity with the Holy See and peaceful concord in the Church of God" (Mark, 1982, 69).

The progress of notation can be traced from the earliest accent markings indicative of pitch or stress, to the setting of text at different heights, to the system of neumes, to the development of graphs, including the staff on which neumes were placed (figure 2–1). Not until the thirteenth century were issues of time value resolved with the rise of mensural notation. Performers and teachers of music enthusiastically accepted notation as it helped them retain a greater musical repertory than they could hold in memory, and it allowed them to learn without being directly in contact with the composer (Rastell, 1983).

In a real sense, the early notations served as mnemonics (aural cues for recalling pitches and rhythms) for melodies the singers had already learned by rote. The earliest "score" of text with accent markings triggered the memory so that a melody could be reconstructed within the constrictions of the text as a result of the singer's experience with the musical idiom. That experience was developed over many years, and learning was one of the mechanisms of oral transmission: from the first exposure to chant as a choirboy, the singer was assimilating melodic principles and patterns, the vocabulary of the musical performance. The early neumes were nonspecific memory

A

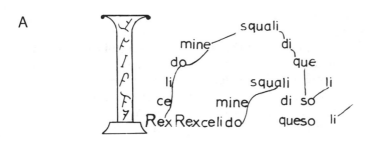

B

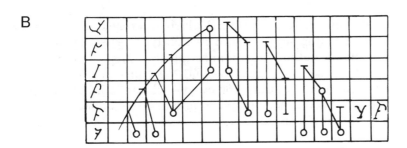

C

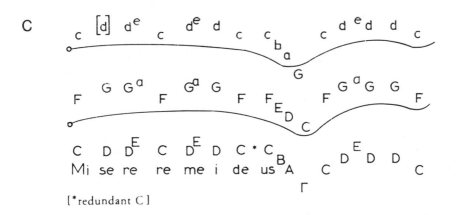

[*redundant C]

D

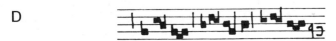

FIGURE 2–1 Early examples of European notation, sixth–tenth centuries A.D.

From Richard Rastell, *Notation of Western Music*, London: J. M. Dent, 1983. Reprinted by permission.

cues; these did not encode information about the size of the interval. As Treitler observed, "That information, or better, the competence to supply it, would have come from the singer's mastery of the grammar of the modes and melodic types (1982, 245). The evolution of notation from less to more specific in its designation of pitch information was motivated "by the need to represent non-traditional matter, and also by the need to represent even traditional matter for singers who were not as well–versed in the tradition" (Treitler, 1982, 261).

Odo and Guido

Medieval choirmasters were particularly interested in how they might train their young singers more efficiently. They experimented with the ingenious methods for connecting the musical sounds to signs and symbols, so as to move beyond the time-consuming rote method of instruction necessary for every melody. Odo, the tenth-century abbot of Cluny, described the function of the monochord in a system of his design that used letters for pitches:

> The letters, or notes, used by musicians are placed in order on the line beneath the string, and when the bridge is moved between the line and the string, shortening or lengthening it, the string marvelously reproduces each melody by means of these letters. When any antiphon is marked with the same letters, the boys learn it better and more easily from the string than if they heard some one sing it, and after a few months' training, they are able to discard the string and sing by sight alone, without hesitation, music that they have never heard. (Strunk, 1950, 105)

Clever as the monochord method was, it was criticized for its simplicity of procedure that suited only beginning readers of notation. The eleventh-century Benedictine monk, Guido d'Arezzo, called it "childish," and proceeded to establish a system of solmization as a memory aid for learning to read new music. He was widely respected as a scholar in the theory and pedagogy of music; because of his reputation he was called to the papal court at Rome to explain and demonstrate his solmization practice. He used the text of a famous hymn to St. John, "Ut Queant Laxis," as a memory aid. In this hymn, the first syllable of the first six phrases began on a successively higher degree of the major scale from *c* to *a*, or *ut, re, mi, fa, sol,* and *la* (figure 2–2). This hexachord was used to assist the learner's memory in teaching chant. Guido explained the system further, contending that

> if, therefore, you wish to commit any note or neume to memory so that it will promptly recur to you . . . you must mark that

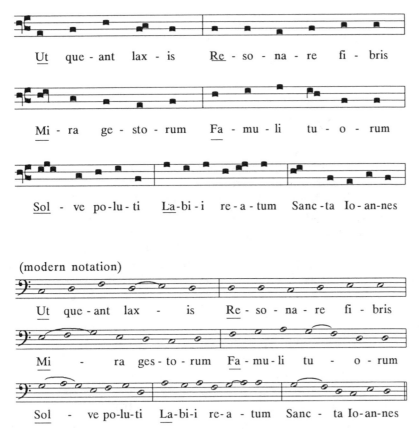

Ut queant laxis / Re-so-na-re fi-bris
Mi-ra ge-sto-rum / Fa-mu-li tu-o-rum
Sol-ve po-lu-ti / La-bi-i re-a-tum / Sanc-ta Io-an-nes

(modern notation)

Ut queant lax - is / Re-so-na-re fi-bris
Mi - ra ges-to-rum / Fa-mu-li tu - o-rum
Sol - ve po-lu-ti / La-bi-i re-a-tum / Sanc - ta Io-an-nes

FIGURE 2–2 "Ut Queant Laxis," Hymn to St. John (under-lined letters are the syllables that Guido used to indicate scale tones).

note or neume at the beginning of some especially familiar melody; and to retain each and every note in your memory, you must have at ready command a melody of this description which begins with that note. . . . To sing an unknown melody competently as soon as you see it written down, or, hearing an unwritten melody, to see quickly how to write it down well, this rule will be of greatest use to you. (Strunk, 1950, 124)

Guido is credited with numerous other contributions to music theory and the learning process, including the placement of staff lines to indicate intervals of a third, and the use of the hand as a visual and tactile reference to the pitches of a song or scale. The "Guidonian hand," on which each syllable or pitch is assigned to a finger joint or fingertip, may actually postdate him (Miller, 1973). Still, the use of the hand to clarify church modes and individual chants originated during his era and was a popular aid to solmization through at least the seventeenth century (figure 2–3).

Medieval Choirs

In the professional training of medieval choristers, rehearsals occurred about twice weekly for the full choir. The boys met daily, however, in order to learn the music that the men already knew. The cantor, or precentor, who was responsible for the performance of music in the church, was often assigned teaching duties; these usually consisted of demonstrating the sound of chant vocally while using a variety of hand signals. Although the rote system of learning was eventually abandoned for notation, the development of reading skills required considerable time and effort. Because parchment was expensive and printing by hand time consuming, notated music was rare until the fifteenth century, and group sourcebooks rather than individual performing copies were used. A large-sized collection of notated chant and liturgical songs was placed on a lectern. The teacher would keep the beat with one hand while pointing to the music on the stand with a stick.

The conversion of much of the West into a musically literate society was of major consequence, and while oral transmission persisted for many centuries, the emerging process of preserving music paved the way for the new musical products. With notation came the beginnings of polyphonic music, the complexities of which would have been difficult to cultivate without a system for recording its multiple layers of melody. But despite the enthusiastic acceptance and use of notation among musicians, they did not immediately abandon the related concepts of orality and improvisation. From the medieval period onward, notation often provided the only framework for creative improvisation by the performer. Even polyphonic pieces were often the result of improvisation practice: organum, discants, and motets were created by adding one line at a time to the notated melody.

Apprentice Musicians

In the area of secular music, aspiring young minstrels learned their trade through a seven-year apprenticeship, and only small portions of their repertoire were laid out in notation. Mostly through an osmosis program, apprentices learned by example from the master minstrels, committing tunes to memory and improvising on them. A

FIGURE 2–3   The Guidonian Hand.

Milan, Bibliotecca Ambrosiana, MS D.75.INF.

troubadour's song was not precisely fixed but was rather a living musical and textual idea flexible and free to be varied at the whim and will of the singer. Van der Werf described the oral transmission process of a troubadour's song to its written version: "First, a troubadour 'found' his song without the help of pen and ink; others learned the song from him by rote and passed it on to subsequent generations; finally several scribes, independent from another, wrote down the song as it was known to performers in different locales" (1984, 4). Once the apprenticeship was completed, the expansion of the minstrel's repertoire was as likely to occur from actual performances, such as "conventions" at which minstrels occasionally gathered, as from deliberate and formal teaching sessions.

THE RENAISSANCE

University trends through the Middle Ages continued during the Renaissance: music as scientific study was held constant in the quadrivium while the performance of music was cultivated in collegiate-associated settings, especially in churches and cathedrals. By the late fifteenth century, there were several perspectives on the place of music in the university, indicating both conservative and progressive trends: the integration of music with other philosophical studies, the emphasis on music as an artistic practice, and the association of musical studies with the humanities, including Greek and Latin literature. These humanistic influences were noted in Renaissance treatises that addressed the Greek musical ethos, the explanation of Greek terminology used in music, and the relating of musical to poetic meters.

Academies and the University

There was a growing emphasis on *ars musica* at the European universities throughout the sixteenth century. In Italy, applied voice and instrumental lessons were taught privately in academies under the auspices of the university. In the university proper, *musica speculativa* was put to the service of *musica prattica* as performance practice began to direct the course of theoretical discussions and writings. In France, England, Germany, and Italy, works devoted to the problems of instrumental music performance appeared during this period, so that along with the occasional treatise came the printing of instruction books in organ, lute, harp, and violin (Carpenter, 1958, 327).

Although informal conditioning, aural learning, and the oral tradition continued to contribute to the training of musicians, musical skills were increasingly derived from formal instruction. These systematic efforts were manifested in the establishment of academies in which the concern gradually shifted from a general education offering a balance of many subjects to music learning in particular. The academies were concerned with practical matters of performance and the development of music literacy; solmization was thus emphasized as an aural and oral foundation for all musicians regardless of their eventual specialization. Italy led Europe in the development of academies during the Renaissance, although some were also known in France and Germany.

Music Instruction during the Reformation

Music instruction during the Reformation in Germany was a reaction against earlier educational practices that were thought to be unrealistic and superficial. Lutherans and Calvinists advocated an education that combined the liberal arts, including the science of music, and the practical art of music. Lutherans supported the study of vocal and instrumental music for worship, while Calvinists emphasized vocal instruction, often to the exclusion of instrumental study within the curriculum. Luther's attitude toward music in general education served as a guide toward the organization of the elementary and secondary curriculum. His remarks offered strong support for music education: "A schoolmaster must know how to sing or I would not allow him to teach" (Sternfeld, 1948, 105) and "If I had children and were able, I would have them learn not only languages and history, but also singing and instrumental music and the whole course of mathematics" (Sternfeld, 1948, 99).

Since students were important in community performances such as church services, weddings, funerals, and banquets, music was a vital part of the curriculum. At the age of eight, boys began instruction in singing and music theory which they continued through the age of eighteen. Daily music exercises were viewed as an avenue for lifting one's heart to God and for the fulfillment and integration of the physical, spiritual, and intellectual self. Great care was given to accommodating music and singing instruction for the hour following lunch, with the intention of tuning the mind for further academic study in the later afternoon.

Psalmbooks served both religious and musical functions and were used to guide students toward musical literacy. Theoretical issues were briefly addressed in music classes, but the emphasis was on repertoire and techniques of singing. Parrish (1966) described the

Enchiridion Utruisque Musicae Practicae (Handbook of Both Kinds of
Musical Practice) authored by Georg Rhau, a printer and pedagogue
of the Reformation period. Solmization and notation were featured
in the handbook, but the long-winded discussions of hexachords, mutation, *musica ficta*, and mensural proportions were conspicuously
absent. Instead, actual exercises in singing were inserted as demonstrations of the meaning of theoretical principles.

Solmization practices, including the "Guidonian hand," and the
mnemonic system of solfége based upon the pitches of the hexachord
continued through the Renaissance. The expansion of the hexachord
to include "una nota super la," the B♭ or B♮, resulted in experimentation and invention of new solfége syllables. As they learned to sightread melodies, students also learned to write counterpoint and to
improvise melodies over a cantus firmus. Major theorists such as
Zarlino and Glareanus made few references to solmization, although
it is generally believed that this omission may have been because
medieval solmization practices were not significantly changed during the sixteenth century.

In Elizabethan England, the art of singing was only partially
cultivated. Illiteracy was commonplace, and the lining out of psalms
was the typical procedure in church services. There, a precentor first
sang one phrase of the melody, followed in imitation by the choir or
congregation. Seldom did members of the British working class have
time or money to devote to the serious study of music, and many may
never have heard the madrigals of Morley nor the ayres of Dowland.
For those privileged few members of the upper class where music was
viewed as a genteel accomplishment, lessons were offered at home by
private arrangement. In seventeenth-century England, only cathedral, collegiate-church and choir schools—and not universities—
emphasized the study of skills in note-reading, vocal production, and
part-singing (Woodfill, 1953, 222).

Instrumentalists were still trained through the guild system,
which remained prominent in Germany until the nineteenth century.
Boarding schools were maintained for apprentice musicians, and students' experiences in playing with their masters in formal performances was viewed as an effective learning strategy. Because guilds
were private organizations, the training of instrumental musicians
was rarely described in writing; thus, their methods remain secret
even today.

Improvisation and the Virtuoso Musician

Throughout the earlier eras of Western music history, displays
of virtuosity and improvisatory skills were widespread, attesting to a

European heritage of aural learning and spontaneity in performance. Medieval musical forms, including the discant, organum, and motet, were created by adding melodies to previously worked-out melodies. The *fauxbourdon* of the fifteenth-century Burgundian composers Dufay and Binchois, and the English practice of improvising a parallel third (gymel) or thirds and sixths (discants) above a printed melody were evidence of the relationship between composed and improvised music in the early Renaissance.

When the practice of writing out all the parts first became current in the sixteenth century, improvised music was distinguished from the composed and finished work called *res facta* by its looser construction in the matter of cadences and rhythmic motion. The Renaissance motet and Ordinary of the Mass, for example, were composed works, while the antiphons, graduals, and introits, retained the practice of melodic improvisation over the longer notes of the traditional cantus firmus.

Instrumental performers improvised dance pieces through the medieval and Renaissance periods, and extravagant embellishments on traditional melodies were the rule of the day. Performers learned musical ideas for improvisation first by listening and singing, and later transferred their vocal melodies to their instruments. Keyboard notation and tabulatures offered sacred and secular songs upon which florid countermelodies could be added. Free forms based on fugal imitation became commonplace by the middle to late sixteenth century. The prelude or intonation was a type of free-form keyboard improvisation, an extemporaneous performance that set the mode and mood for vocal or instrumental pieces that followed.

Virtuoso instrumentalists during the Renaissance developed a repertoire, partly learned and stored in the memory, which became a foundation for their improvisation. These ornamented and embellished performances were transcribed on paper and published for amateur and student musicians to follow. The music of Willaert, de Rore, Palestrina, and Marenzio offered examples in the art of ornamentation as well and were often held as models for students to emulate. Representative pieces by these and other composers were compiled within the didactic manuals for aspiring vocal and instrumental performers. As described by Ferand, these manuals were notable "in their pedagogic aim of providing performers with models of ornamentation and ornamented compositions, to save them the trouble of inventing the embellishments themselves" (1966, 154).

The concept of one authentic performance did not exist during the Renaissance, just as the reading of notation was only gradually becoming the standard by which all musicians were directed in their musical performance. In the universities and academies, and in the

elementary and secondary school curricula of church and choir
schools, there was a growing shift of interest from music theory to
performance. Distinctions between folk and art music were more
clearly delineated by the close of the sixteenth century, so that trained
performers of art music were more likely to be literate than were folk
musicians and thus to base their partly improvised performances on
written scores. For Renaissance musicians, music instruction was
more often than not a matter of practical experience in solmization,
vocal and instrumental techniques, rehearsal in a growing repertory
of notated music, and finally, their own personal expression through
improvisation.

SUMMARY

European art music was shaped through many centuries. What
began as an oral tradition of entertainment music by the Greeks and
Romans, then developed into ecclesiastical chant, liturgical hymns,
and instrumental dance pieces, later became a notated music that
could be performed by professionals and amateur alike at various
times and places throughout the continent. From the Greco-Roman
period onward, master musicians transmitted complete musical
ideas without the aid of notation, and students who aspired to the
profession developed keen listening skills. Interest in theory followed
performance, and music soon found a place in the formal curriculum
alongside logic and the sciences. Beyond the theoretical study of music offered in medieval universities after the sixth century, the training of performing musicians in church-related schools and in guilds
continued to emphasize aural skills. With the development of notation, solmization practices were introduced so that students would
understand the logic of the staff and acquire skills for reading music
on their own. Improvisation was a key component of music among
the Greeks and Romans and throughout the medieval and Renaissance eras; the marks of an outstanding musician were not only his
ability to read notation but also the musical sensitivity to add a
personal interpretation to what was contained in manuscript form.
The ear, the eye, and the creative mind were exercised in lessons and
actual performances of European art music from the earliest recorded
history.

CHAPTER
3

◆

Ear-Training and the Creative Process in European Art Music 2: Improvisation and Solmization since 1600

By 1600, staff notation was largely in place and European art music could thus be conveniently preserved and transmitted. Still, there was a compelling need for musician-teachers who could instruct in performance techniques, ornamentation, and the extent to which the score could be personally interpreted. Through the Baroque and Classical periods, and in the nineteenth and twentieth centuries, improvisation and an expressive interpretation of notated music continued to be marks of the well-trained musician.

Throughout Europe, schools, academies, and conservatories were established for the study of applied music and theory. After rigorous training, including ample occasions for refining aural and reading skills, students were guided toward interpreting the musical score. By the nineteenth century, music instruction was an accepted curricular offering for commoners—the general public—rather than only for the talented or wealthy. Music literacy was deemed an important goal of general education, and solmization emerged as a principal feature of instruction. In this way, ear-training and sight-reading were closely linked.

Through the last four centuries, European art music has emerged as a sophisticated tradition with a myriad of styles and genres to offer performers and listeners alike. The brilliance of Bach, Mozart, Beethoven, Brahms, Schoenberg, Bartok, and Stravinsky—to name just a few— is preserved in staff notation for future generations to realize. There is, however, an element of the oral tradition in even the most carefully preserved music when the student's trained ear catches the musical nuances in the teacher's demonstration. The art of classical music in the West thus encompasses not only the composer's genius but also the performer's gifts of listening and expressing creatively. In studios and classrooms, music literacy, ear-training, and the development of creative expression are the ultimate goals of music instruction in the West.

MUSIC INSTRUCTION 1600–1795

Music instruction in Europe during the seventeenth and eighteenth centuries occurred in a number of settings and in ways that increasingly resembled the study of music in schools, universities, and conservatories of western Europe and North America as it is practiced today. The position of music in education was strengthened during this period so that children and youth in parochial schools received regular instruction in the theory and performance of music. Universities continued to uphold the philosophical and theoretical tradition in music study that the ancients had established. The church choir schools of the Middle Ages and the Renaissance guilds of instrumental musicians were forerunners of the conservatories in which students were trained as professional musicians through lessons conducted by master musicians in private settings. Music instruction as a formalized process was coming of age, developing as swiftly as the music itself. During this time matters of intonation were resolved, great musical genres were being formulated, and instruments of the modern orchestra were evolving; paralleling these developments was an increasing interest in the pedagogy of music— its techniques and methods.

Music among the Aristocracy

In aristocratic families, the amount of leisure time available to members was good reason to procure teachers who offered lessons in singing or on various instruments. Music masters were hired as permanent staff members in major households. Method books were printed that would expediently lead sons and daughters of the wealthy to performances of art and popular music of the time. Those materials that promised technical proficiency on an instrument or the development of a pleasing voice in "ten easy lessons" were widely sought out.

In these families, boys only occasionally studied an instrument or developed sight-reading skills for informal community sings, but girls were encouraged to develop performance skills as one of their chief social graces. Singing lessons were commonly offered to girls, who hoped that developing a pleasant voice would add to their desirability as marriage partners. In England, reason was not thought to be a feminine attribute, and thus the theoretical study of music was not advised for young women. Rather, the performance of music was viewed as an "agreeable" art that would win a husband, attract a circle of friends, and nurture the offspring (Kassler, 1972, 215).

Music Instruction in Parochial Schools

In church-related parochial schools throughout the continent, the concept of musical training in the total education of students was held even more firmly in place during the seventeenth century than during the Renaissance. In the Lutheran church schools, there were systematic efforts to develop music literacy in students. Solmization techniques were directed toward providing experiences in hearing and then seeing in notation pitch and rhythm patterns common in the art and folk traditions of the time. Not only formal music instruction but also recreational music activities were advocated; social singing, dance, and the performance of folk and popular music were permitted and encouraged as extracurricular activities.

From Guilds to Conservatorios

Music guilds, whose function was to train performers on various instruments, were scattered throughout Europe. Like the unions of carpenters and painters, their purpose was to facilitate the learning of a trade: how an instrument was played, designed and constructed, repaired and maintained. Specialized training of the voice, on the other hand, continued to occur in academies, boarding schools, and church schools. In Italy, homes for poor, abandoned, and homeless children were the scene of sometimes rigorous music learning activity. Their programs were designed to include a full-day schedule of vocal exercises, solfeggio, ornamentation, and the theory behind the practices. These orphanages, called *conservatorios*, and guilds were the earliest stages in the development of the modern conservatory.

Venice and Naples became centers for providing a music education to homeless children through state-supported conservatories. Fee-paying pupils were eventually also admitted to alleviate the financial difficulties the schools were experiencing. The emergence of the conservatory as a self-supporting institution, coupled with its astounding products—the high-quality musicianship of its young graduates—led to widespread acclaim and emulation of this teaching institution throughout Europe during the eighteenth and nineteenth centuries.

Conservatories for vocal and instrumental music were eventually developed in cities such as Prague, Leipzig, and Berlin, but the learning arrangement at the Paris Conservatory is particularly notable. Following attempts to establish an academy for the opera and an institute to train wind musicians, the National Conservatory of Music and Declamation, later the Paris Conservatory, was opened in 1795. It featured several novel concepts: it provided instruction in both voice and instruments under one roof; its aims were secular rather than clerical; and it had the ability to provide instruction for talented students throughout the nation. Students between the ages of eight and twelve were admitted to classes by examination and audition, progressing through stages devoted first to solfége, then to singing and playing instruments, and finally to theoretical knowledge and the history of music.

Performance was the principal aim of instruction at the Paris Conservatory, at other European conservatories, and in the American conservatories modeled after those in Europe during the nineteenth century. Teachers were drawn from the area's orchestras and opera houses, in the belief that performers could teach through their modeling and demonstration. This practice was vital to preserving aspects of performance style from earlier musical eras that were not clearly indicated through notation.

IMPROVISATION IN THE BAROQUE ERA

While music notation had been established for several centuries, the cornerstone of Baroque style—improvised embellishment—offered performers an independence and expressive freedom. The score provided the essential melody, but it was assumed that the musician would add cadential trills, appoggiaturas, and passing tones. The Baroque period was distinguished by improvisatory performance practices that developed from three sources: an awareness of emerging national styles, which varied greatly from Italy to France, England to Germany: the interest of performers in conveying certain emotions in expressive ways; and the development of the *basso continuo* style that required chordal improvisation over the score's figured bass. The emergence of an independent instrumental style, including the rise of the violin as the premiere solo instrument in the seventeenth and eighteenth centuries, and the development of opera were accompanied by the profusion of ornamentation and improvisatory passages that distinguish the music of the period.

The Basso Continuo

By early seventeenth century, the techniques of basso continuo had become a skill highly desired in players of harpsichord, organ, and lute. Through inventing a chordal part completely free of the score (unfigured) or with the guidance of scale-tone numbers under the bass line (figured), performers offered strong harmonic support to the melody. Donnington described the more common figured bass as "a continuo to which accidentals and figures have been added showing the main intervals required" above the bass-line pitches (1974, 289). The distribution of intervals was not shown, but the performer was directed to produce certain harmonies with varying degrees of thoroughness; each realization was likely to be different from another. A premium was placed on spontaneity, and a fresh and buoyant quality was more important than a deliberate and polished working-out of the accompaniment.

The art of the basso continuo was an outgrowth of the Renaissance practice in which stringed instruments doubled the notes sung by singers of secular and sacred music, but it became freer and more creative over time. Skilled performers of basso continuo learned their practice largely by ear, and their increasing familiarity with the musical style brought them greater ease in the invention of lively accompaniments. In reference to the lack of signs in the use of unfigured bass, Giovanni Piccioni referred also to the process of learning how to translate a single notated melody into a full contrapuntal sound:

> I have preferred not to set any sort of signs, such as sharps, flats, and figures, over the notes, as many do, since to unskillful organists, they are confusing rather than otherwise, while to the knowledgeable and expert, such signs are unnecessary, for

they play them correctly by ear and by art. (Donnington, 1974, 291)

The further development of the thoroughbass practice was a type of piece known as *partimento*. While figured thoroughbass scores provided a bass line and a melody, and unfigured bass offered a melody only, the partimento presented only a bass line and figures. It was the responsibility of the performer to realize the melody, inner voices, and of course, ornamentation. This practice resulted in highly improvisatory pieces in the late Baroque period, such as toccatas, preludes, and fugues.

Ornamentation and the Virtuoso Musician

From one country to the next, improvisation during the Baroque period was widespread. Instrumental improvisation was flourishing in England at this time. The earlier Renaissance virginal style was influential in the improvisations of stringed and wind instrument players during the seventeenth and eighteenth centuries. Variations on popular and folk songs were common and the technique of melodic and harmonic improvisation on a ground bass was perhaps the single most celebrated aspect of English Baroque music.

In France, the melodic embellishments of the vocal genre known as *air de cour* were less flamboyant than developments in the keyboard style. Couperin's music is evidence of French Baroque style of improvisation; the performer was expected to know the style well, as ornament signs are used sparingly. A concentrated period of listening and experimentation was the pathway to knowledge of the improvisation practice of French Baroque genres. The measure of performance freedom was considerable, and while learning the practice through an instruction manual was not often successful, "even the *vive voix*, the live demonstration of a teacher" was barely capable of teaching the style (Neumann, 1965, 5).

In Italy, the *opera seria* and solo violin were the focuses of improvisatory style. Adagio movements were likely places for embellishment; here the tempos were slow enough to provide ample opportunity for ornamentation. The *da capo* aria offered another opportunity to improvise, sometimes at great length, so that the return to the first section was a true test for the listener in distinguishing the original melody. Identified also as "the varied reprise," this practice was prevalent through the eighteenth century. C. P. E. Bach noted its appeal to audiences in 1760:

> Variation upon repetition is indispensable today. It is expected of every performer. The public demands that practically every

idea be repeatedly altered, sometimes without investigating whether the structure of the piece or the skill of the performer permits such alteration. It is this embellishing alone, especially if it is coupled with a long and sometimes bizarrely ornamented cadenza, that often squeezes the bravos out of most listeners. (Ferand, 1957, 141)

Some of the great composers of the Baroque period—J. S. Bach, Handel, Sweelinck, Frescobaldi, and Buxtehude—were performers who improvised complete pieces, some of which were eventually notated while others were lost forever after that single musical event. J. S. Bach's improvised ornamentation represents a culmination of two centuries of embellishment. In the works of most other composers, the open spaces in their notation and the long durations were the skeletal structure for ornamentation and improvisation by the performer. In Bach's scores, the staves are crowded with the elaborations of the melody and supporting voices, all carefully worked out and notated by the composer himself.

The works of Handel, Telemann, Corelli, and Vivaldi, among others whose notation is not complete, can be performed in the practice at the time by applying the principles of Bach's style found in his fully notated works. Aldrich described in some detail Bach's use of appoggiaturas, trills, turns, and mordents; the free melodic figures called *passagio*; the dissolution of longer notes into shorter rhythmic values; and the variation of a repeated or sequential passage (1949, 32–33). The potential for ornamenting Baroque music may lie in an understanding of Bach's "notated improvisations," which provide completed versions of what other composers left as only musical frameworks.

Despite the obvious focus on solo improvisation or improvisatory melodies with complementary accompaniment of the basso continuo, there was also ensemble improvisation. Especially in the early to middle seventeenth century, performers on groups of instruments performed embellishments of the vocal line with a careful balance of independent invention and restraint. Sometimes in the score for vocal works for which instrumental accompaniment was expected, neither the specific instruments nor a suggested number were designated by the composer. In the early operatic scores, choruses often had no written accompaniment. Given only a few measures of continuo in the score, an instrumental ensemble might have improvised extensively. The type and number of instruments and the thematic material or the development of a given theme were decisions to be made by the ensemble director. Agazzari advised that to maintain a semblance of civil order and musical sense, ensemble improvisation should proceed with caution:

> All this must be done prudently: if the instruments are alone in
> the consort, they must lead it and do everything; if they play in
> company, each must regard the other, giving it room and not
> conflicting with it; if there are many; they must each await
> their turn and not, chirping all at once like sparrows, try to
> shout one another down. (in Rose, 1965, 389)

As amateurs became enamored of music making as a leisurely activity and as students attempted to learn the style, treatises were written to explain the art of spontaneous embellishment and variation. By the middle of the eighteenth century, a large variety of instruction manuals had been written by composers, theorists, and performers such as Tosi, Quantz, Tartini, Hiller, C. P. E. Bach, and Leopold Mozart. The advice to novices in these books was that the art of ornamentation and improvisation was to be reserved for those who had first studied well the art of composition and who had developed the talent and taste for creating melodies more beautiful than the original ones.

IMPROVISATION IN THE CLASSICAL PERIOD

The improvisation of Baroque performance practice was not completely abandoned in the music of the Classical composers, although changes were clearly evident. While virtuosic displays continued during the second half of the eighteenth century, there was also a growing tendency toward classical simplicity. Freely improvised embellishments became increasingly rare, and figured bass was relinquished as carefully worked out inner voices were notated by the composer. The gradual restriction of spontaneous expression may have reflected dissatisfaction with performers whose interpretation and improvisations did not meet the style expectations of the composer. Composers developed a more precise notation that indicated their intent more accurately and introduced a greater sense of finality in the score.

Appoggiaturas and Cadenzas

Mozart himself was a brilliant improviser, but while the performance of many of his works requires considerable display of virtuosity, nearly all of his music is written out. Still, the performer has license to make improvisatory additions to the written score, including grace notes, slides, turns, and trills as well as larger insertions of two distinct types: the *eingang*, or lead-in at the fermata, and the *appoggiatura*.

On the fermata at certain cadential points, the performer improvised a brief passage, thus providing a transition between sections. These fermata embellishments, called eingang, served the function of an elongated anacrusis, anticipating the next section while linking it to the previous one. Mozart also continued the convention of the vocal appoggiatura which had been in practice for nearly 200 years: accented syllables were to be placed on the strong beat and sounded on a consonant pitch, even though the score frequently indicated a violation of the rule.

The appropriate filling in of the "white spots" in Mozart's manuscripts was the performer's choice but also his greatest challenge. Mozart advised against the extravagant embellishments of the time, pleading instead for moderation befitting the simplicity yet elegance of his music. At times, the empty spaces were meant to remain empty and devoid of flourishes, so that silences were occasionally used by Mozart as powerful points of expression. In other instances of melodic austerity and static orchestral accompaniment, the pianist was well within stylistic reason to add ornamental flourishes. The second movement of Mozart's D-minor concerto, K. 466, provides an example of the type of ornamentation the composer might have suggested had he prepared the work for publication (figure 3–1).

The cadenza was another improvisatory device that flourished in the seventeenth and eighteenth centuries. While Mozart's music featured some of the most brilliant examples, the cadenza's development spanned about three hundred years from the Renaissance to the early operas of Verdi. As the popularity of virtuoso singing increased during the seventeenth century, final improvisatory passages became common near the end of a concerto movement or aria. The appearance of a fermata over a tonic 6–4 chord was the soloist's cue to begin an expressive passage of ornaments, arpeggios, and scales. As many performers made these cadenzas quite lengthy, some composers and theorists recommended that they last no longer than a performer could hold his or her breath. By the time of Mozart, cadenzas were frequently written and only modest embellishments were inserted.

The use of thoughtful and well-researched improvisation and ornamentation was and is vital to the performance of music of the classical period. The music of Mozart, as well as that of Haydn and Beethoven, requires a certain improvisatory reserve that is learned through much directed listening. When in doubt, the listener can refer to a general rule offered by Eva and Paul Badura-Skoda (1962, 204): "Too little is better than too much." Likewise, Neuman (1986)

FIGURE 3–1   Notation and possible execution of Mozart's
D-minor concerto, K. 466, 2nd movement.

From Frederick Neumann, *Ornamentation and Improvisation in Mozart*, Princeton,
N.J.: Princeton University Press, 1986.

suggests that "even a Mozartian skeleton or sketch will be preferable
to an attempt at completion that carries the danger ... that one is
destroying rather than reconstructing" (p. 255–256). Still, the realization that the classical music so commonly believed to be thoroughly contained in print is in reality partially improvised offers
another example of music as a creative art form. In addition, it underscores the limitations of notation in preserving the musical sound.

MUSIC EDUCATION FOR THE COMMON MAN

The continuing rise of the middle class brought with it a demand for equality in education and government-sponsored social services. Learning was viewed as the right of all and not merely a
privilege of the aristocracy. For those who were seeking the liberation

of a broadened education, the study of music was supported for its social and psychological benefits, and its incorporation into the education of the common man was considered throughout Europe.

Among the philosophers active during the era of educational reform was Jean-Jacques Rousseau, who paved the way for including music as a curricular offering for all children. The French philosopher Rousseau suggested that no children were too young to be exposed to musical experiences. He noted that "each age and condition of life has a perfection and maturity of its own," and that children could learn music through experiences designed for their own musical involvement (Boyd, 1952). The development of the literate musician was to proceed from extensive childhood experiences in listening, singing, playing, and creating. Rousseau regarded music reading and writing as theoretical matters, and he advised against emphasizing literacy skills until the student had had sufficient listening and participating experiences.

There were other views that were less supportive of musician education. The philosophical radicalism of John Locke, the British philosopher, proposed that music was a waste of a young man's time and that it deserved the last place in a curriculum. In a system of education whose goal was to instill principles of religion and morality, music served no utilitarian purpose. Music instruction that did exist in the scattering of grammar schools and private seminaries of Locke's England was deplorable:

> The music master devoted five or ten minutes each to individual students at the keyboard, during which time the other pupils awaited their turn. Classroom instruction of this sort kept the master busy but the pupils idle. Such a situation prompted some musical pedagogues to devise ways in which to employ more usefully the hours of their students. One such means was the method of teaching by question and answer, where a textbook, called a "catechism," was employed. (Kassler, 1972, 221)

There were also tremendous incompetencies in the British way of exposing students to notation and facts that were removed from the musical sound itself. Rainbow describes the attempts of local teachers and organists in the late eighteenth century:

> In an age when most teachers interpreted their task as packing a child's head with facts, the same technique was automatically applied to the music lesson. It was commonly assumed that once the rigmarole of staves, clefs, crotchets and quavers, sharps and flats, and the rest had been explained and memorised, the child would be competent to employ them. (1982, 20)

The church was more likely to have been the impetus for music teaching than were the schools, and some church directors continued the medieval practice of learning music and its theory by rote. The rationale for studying a particular theoretical concept and the theoretical concepts themselves were set in verse, to be committed to memory by the student through repetition of the teacher's chanting. The *Complete Psalmodist*, a manual for singing psalms published in 1741 by John Arnold, presented many examples of this strategy for learning the rules of music notation. Among the couplets which the student heard and then memorized were the following:

> Therefore, unless
> Notes, Time and Rests
> Are perfectly learned by heart,
>   None ever can
>   With pleasure, scan
> True Time in MUSIC'S Art
>
> Under each flat the half note lies,
> And o'er the sharp the half doth rise.
>   (Rainbow, 1982, 17, 18)

Despite the urging of John Locke to emphasize only those courses that would serve a useful purpose in life as well as the prevailing attitude that music should be taught at home or in church settings, Rousseau's ideas were influential in England and throughout Europe into the nineteenth century. Out of decadence came reform: education, formerly reserved for the elite, eventually became available to the common people; music, for a time viewed as peripheral to academic subjects, was made a focal point of the curriculum; and didactic teaching, long the standard, yielded to an interest in heuristic learning. The close of the eighteenth century promised a revolution in music instruction; evidence of these changes was seen and heard in the conservatories and schools of Europe and North America.

THE NINETEENTH CENTURY

The cultural changes of the Industrial Age transformed the Western world. European towns and villages grew into urban areas during the nineteenth century as tradesmen's shops were replaced by factories. Farming became more efficient and lucrative through the invention of machines that sowed and reaped great expanses of fields with far fewer laborers. Transportation systems linked cities to one another, as railroads and steamships became major enterprises. By late in the century, women increasingly left their sewing circles for salaried positions, a shift that affected the traditional structure of the family. The middle class continued to rise in prominence and its voice became important in political policy throughout much of Europe.

Musical conditions in the cultural capitals of Europe were in a state of transition through much of the nineteenth century. The patronage of composers and performing musicians by the courts and nobility, so widespread in the Baroque and Classical eras, was no longer the common practice. The professional musician was often left to his own resources for survival, a condition clearly demonstrated by the career of Beethoven early in the century. With the decline of aristocratic patronage came the rise of "salon music" and popular songs that suited the taste of the rising bourgeoisie. The prospects of the artist-teacher in Vienna were bleakly painted by a critic writing for the *Allgemeine musikalische Zeitung* in 1800:

> Without steady employment, only a pianoforte player may perhaps earn a decent livelihood—and even so, he must possess enough self-denial to serve willingly the houses that support him, furthermore give lessons morning, noon, and night. . . . Music lessons are not nearly as profitable as they once were, since dilettanti can always be had for trifling fees. ("A Sketch of the Principal Features of Contemporary Musical Life in Vienna," in Weiss and Taruskin, 1984, 325)

Bel Canto and the New Virtuosity

The replacement of the traditional elite by the broad middle class encouraged the growth not only of salon music but also of particular styles of opera and concert music. Virtuosic musicians appealed to the tastes of the new masses—and thrived. Highly accomplished violinists and pianists became social phenomena, stunning their audiences with their technical accomplishments. Niccolo Paganini, the greatest violin virtuoso of the century, created a sensation in performances throughout Europe with his unprecedented instrumental effects, fanciful improvisations, and extreme liberties of interpretation. One account describes the performance of the *allegro maestoso* movement of Paganini's own sonata: "He would leap to a height beyond all height, with notes of desperate minuteness, then flash down in a set of headlong harmonies, sharp and brilliant as the edges of swords; then warble again with inconceivable beauty and remoteness, as if he was a ventriloquizing-bird" (Houtchens and Houtchens, 1969, 274).

Despite composers' use of precise notation throughout the nineteenth century, there were occasions for performers to insert their creative expression and personal interpretation through ornamentation, cadenzas, improvised preludes, and free improvisation (chiefly by keyboard players). The simplicity and refinement of music in the Classical era had aroused the romantic concern for expression, so that a certain freedom in "going beyond the written notes" was fashionable and acceptable within limits. Ornamentation consisted of conventional diminutions of single notes as indicated by symbols above the staff, of variation of melodic phrases, and of the insertions by the performer of additional material as with cadences and improvised preludes.

Virtuoso singers were a compelling part of Italian *bel canto* opera, and their variations and diminutions of original melodies or addition of entirely new melodies was excessive when compared to eighteenth-century standards. The length of an opera's run and the challenge of holding the attention of an audience that became quite familiar with arias over time were reasons for the considerable freedom performers took in their interpretation of the score. In the 1830s, Rossini and Bellini began to write out the ornamentation in their operas. By the time of the mature Verdi operas, *bel canto* and its decorative lines had given way to dramatic opera, in which ornamentation was often inappropriate and singers were less likely to have been trained in its performance.

Tonic Sol-fa and Solmization

Similar to performance practice, music instruction at conservatories, academies and schools were also in the midst of transition and reform. Europeans were actively engaged in searching out methods of solmization that would develop the ear and lead to literacy. The English Tonic Sol-fa system, known first as the Norwich Sol-fa system, and in contemporary practice as Movable Do, was first developed by Sarah Glover in the 1830s, to be later popularized by John Curwen in the 1840s.*

---

* Movable Do refers to the relative system by which the tonic of any key is "do." By contrast, Fixed Do is absolute in its designation of pitches, so that C is always "do" regardless of whether it serves as the tonic (as in C major), the subdominant (as in G

As a Sunday school music director, Glover observed the illogic of teaching children notation before they had had singing experiences. She stated in her philosophy that "in teaching children music, I think it is best to instruct them on the same principle as they are taught; *viz* by deducing theory from practice rather than practice from theory" (Rainbow, 1967, 50–51).

In her *Scheme for Rendering Psalmody Congregational* (1835), Glover devised a seven-note syllable series that eliminated the problem of mutation between hexachords present in earlier systems, from Guido d'Arezzo onward. Her movable form of sol-fa syllables (*do, re, mi, fa, sol, la, ti*) permitted the same correspondence of syllable to scale degree regardless of the key. The staff was abandoned, as notes were set from left to right on a page in the way that words were set in books. An acute accent (´) over a solfége letter indicated the octave above the unaccented letter, and a grave accent (`) signaled the octave below. Rhythmic notation was conveyed through the spacing of letters and the use of the colon, period, and comma to mark durations of the one beat, a half beat, and quarter beat. Hyphens followed pitch letters for longer durations. An excerpt from Glover's *The Sol-fa Tune Book* (1839) is found in figure 3–2.

John Curwen's (1901) notation system owed much to Sarah Glover. Capital letters were replaced by lower-case letters, and superscript and subscript strokes were substituted for accents to designate the octave of the pitch. Curwen's modifications moved toward greater simplicity and clearly designated solfége symbols that would eventually lead to the staff notation of common practice. An example of Curwen's system from his book, *The Standard Course in the Tonic Sol-fa Method of Teaching Music*, appears as figure 3–3a. A familiar tune, "America," is shown in the Tonic Sol-fa symbols in figure 3–3b. For the teaching of rhythm patterns separate from songs, a mnemonic system was developed that formed the basis of the "Kodály" syllables in current use today.

While the British formulated their Movable Do, a different solmization was already in practice on the European continent. In the Italian solfeggio and in the French solfége, Fixed Do was the common system of ear training and sight-reading. The older pitch syllables were largely retained in naming the scale: *ut re mi fa sol la si ut* in France, with the substitution of *do* for *ut* in Italy to facilitate singing on the open vowel. The syllables designated for pitches did not change with the key as in Movable Do; regardless of the place-

---

major), or any other function within a scale. (For a more complete discussion refer to Bridges, Doreen. "Fixed and Movable Doh in Historical Perspective." *Australian Journal of Music Education* 30 (1982).

(Sarah Glover, *The Sol-fa Tune Book*, 1839, p. 18)

FIGURE 3–2   Sarah Glover's Norwich Sol-fa.

ment and function of the pitch in a key, the pitch maintained its association with the same syllable.

Based on a figure notation first suggested by Rousseau in 1742, a modified numerical system was developed by Pierre Galin, Aimé and Nanine Paris, and Emile Chevé, and was readily accepted into the pedagogy of music in France by the middle of the nineteenth century. Numerals 1 through 7 were applied to the scale degrees in a Movable Do method, with the tonic always designated as 1. With a range of three octaves for vocal music, pitches of the highest octave were marked by dots above the numbers, with dots placed below the numbers for the low octave pitches. For noting rhythmic values, horizontal lines similar to the note flags used to show eight and sixteenth values in notation were placed above the numbers, and longer notes were shown by large dots liberally spaced to the right of the number. When singing, the performer used the solfége syllables rather than the numbers. This French "Chevé" notation was a purely pedagogical device intended to help the student understand the staff. The relationship of numbers to staff notation was gradually phased in, in a manner similar to that illustrated in figure 3–4.*

Rhythm was approached by the Chevé system by chanting aloud the onomatopoeic syllables for each duration. The system was widespread throughout Europe by the end of the century and was used in

* Following the path of French colonialism, the Chevé system is still practiced in parts of Southeast Asia and Africa.

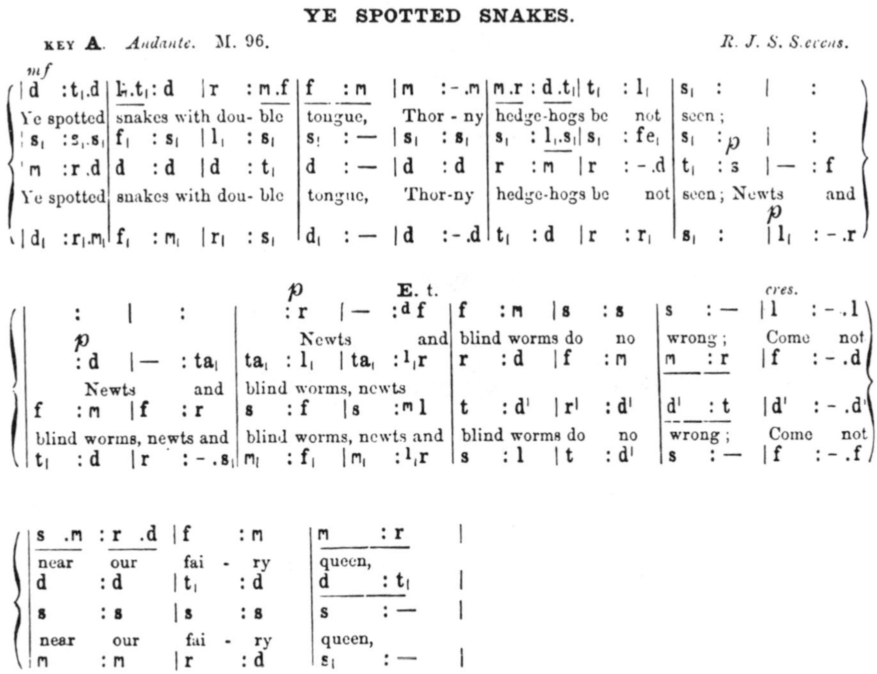

YE SPOTTED SNAKES.

KEY A. *Andante.* M. 96.   *R. J. S. Stevens.*

mf

|d :t₁.d|t₁.t₁: d |r : m.f|f : m |m :-.m|m.r : d.t₁|t₁ : l₁ |s₁ : | :
Ye spotted| snakes with dou- ble | tongue, | Thor - ny| hedge-hogs be | not | seen ;
|s₁ :s₁.s₁|f₁ : s₁ |l₁ : s₁ |s₁ : — |s₁ : s₁|s₁ : l₁.s₁|s₁ : fe₁ |s₁ :*p* | :
|m :r.d|d : d |d : t₁ |d : — |d : d |r : m |r : -.d|t₁ : s |— : f
Ye spotted| snakes with dou- ble | tongue, | Thor-ny | hedge-hogs be | not | seen ; Newts   and
|d₁ :r₁.m₁|f₁ : m₁ |r₁ : s₁ |d₁ : — |d : -.d|t₁ : d |r : r₁ |s₁ : |l₁ : - .r

p   E. t.

        : | : |:r |— :d f|f : m |s : s |s : — |l : - .l
p   Newts   and| blind worms do | no | wrong ; | Come   not
:d |— : ta₁ |ta₁ : l₁ |ta₁ : l₁r|r : d |f : m |m : r |f : - .d
Newts   and| blind worms, newts
f : m |f : r |s : f |s : m l|t : d¹ |r¹ : d¹ |d¹ : t |d¹ : - .d¹
blind worms, newts and| blind worms, newts and| blind worms do | no | wrong ; | Come   not
t₁ : d |r : - .s₁|m₁ : f₁ |m₁ : l₁r|s : l |t : d¹ |s : — |f : - .f

|s .m :r .d |f : m |m : r |
near our fai - ry | queen,
d : d |t₁ : d |d : t₁ |
s : s |s : s |s : — |
near our fai - ry | queen,
m : m |r : d |s₁ : — |

FIGURE 3–3a   John Curwen's Tonic Sol-fa.

America

Key G

| d :d :r | t₁ :-d :r | m :m :f | m :-r :d |

| r :d t₁ | d :- :- | s :s :s | s :-f m |

| f :f :f | f :-m :r | m :fm rd | m :-f :s |

| lsf :m r | d :- :- ‖

FIGURE 3–3b   "America" in Tonic Sol-fa.

teacher-training institutes and private schools in Switzerland, the Netherlands, Russia, and parts of England. The so-called Kodály rhythm syllables were thus first established by the French and later adapted into the Hungarian method. The similarities between the older French and the Kodály syllables are striking (figure 3–5).

The German system of solmization discarded the sol-fa syllables altogether, and used letter names for absolute pitches instead. They

FIGURE 3–4 French Chevé notation, and its realization on the staff.

| French: | ta | | ta | té | ta - fa - té - fé | ta |
| Kodály: | ta | | ti - ti | | ti - ri - ti - ri | ta |

FIGURE 3–5 Rhythm mnemonics of Chevé and Kodály systems compared.

extended the Movable and Fixed Do systems by specifying sharps and flats, adding to each letter "is" for sharp and "es" for flat; for example, G-sharp became "gis" and D-flat became "des." This solmization practice allowed every note of the chromatic scale to be represented in a vocalized exercise.

Composers, performers, and teachers of music in the nineteenth century were clearly concerned with the preparation of musicians who were thoroughly trained in the theoretical aspects of their art. The great interest in evolving a logical system for teaching sight-singing stemmed from the assumption that the ability to "solfége" scales and melodic passages was directly related to the development of aural skills. A keen ear was considered an essential tool for the performing musician, as audience expectations throughout much of the Romantic period set high standards for the performer's expressive application of "parlando rubato." With appropriate training in music reading, solmization, ear-training, and of course, performance technique, the performing musician of the nineteenth century was at some liberty to interpret the score within the boundaries of the style.

THE TWENTIETH CENTURY

The twentieth century has been witness to a blend of change and tradition in music as a performing art and in the pedagogical devices for training young musicians. The development of musicianship and the encouragement of greater musical creativity in school programs have been professional issues in Europe and in North America, along with the concern for musical literacy. While reading notation is maintained as a critical component in a solid music curriculum, aural learning through imitation continues as well, a natural occurrence when one is dealing with the aural art form of music. The development of a student's aural skills and the expressive capacities to compose and improvise music are widely acclaimed as significant aims of contemporary music education.

Precision versus Chance

Today's teachers of Western art music seek the "infallible method" for developing a thorough musicianship in their students, and carefully study different approaches to ear-training and note-reading to discern their particular benefits. Some teachers are concerned with issues of the historical rote-note controversy (See chapter 4). So, too, are contemporary composers compelled to choose between a precise or a vague notation of their musical ideas, and between standard and invented notational symbols. The graphic notation of music by composers has taken on new looks in recent decades, wavering between attempts at greater precision and efforts meant merely to suggest a musical image for improvisation. From aleatoric "chance" music to notation that features new symbols for new timbres, European (and Euro-American) art music of the post-1950s has shifted and stretched to satisfy the minds and ears of the late twentieth century. Advances in technology have been influential in music's sound, its notation, and in its means of preservation and transmission. The current era has given the Western world a new view of music, but its contemporary place in society bears an immediate relationship to its past.

The question of creativity in the musical works of twentieth century composers is often a matter of *whose*: the composer's or the performer's. After the extensive allowances in the nineteenth century for virtuosic improvisation in the *bel canto* style of opera, in cadenzas, and in the virtuosic performances of instrumentalists, composers were increasingly inclined to write out their musical thoughts, a practice that restricted the performer's creativity. Some neoclassical composers of the twentieth century, including Poulenc, Hindemith, and Stravinsky, reacted to the Romantic concern for "expression" by stipulating in the score that the music was to be performed precisely as written and without personal expression. Some composers avoided the human element altogether and wrote works for player pianos, tape recorders, synthesizers, and electronic devices. Until the middle of the twentieth century, improvisation was largely abandoned in favor of the re-creation by the performer of the musical notation as it was preserved in print.

Perhaps the emergence of jazz rekindled the interest in improvisation among composers of art music. The likelihood was greater, however, that spontaneously created music resulted as a reaction against the exacting nature and absolute governance of the musical score. Symbols had been invented and instructions for performance inserted to portray the sound more precisely: Alois Haba's quartertone notations, Olivier Messiaen's added dots for an otherwise normal metrical rhythmic group, paragraphs or new terms as explanation of the intended musical outcome, and the attempts of numerous composers to symbolize the sounds of new instruments or new techniques on traditional instruments. In the art music of the avant-garde, improvisation may have been a way to free the performer from the restrictions of too many symbols.

Freedom for Composers and Performers

Improvisation is characteristic in the realization of all printed music, and a visual representation of musical sound is typically inadequate, observed Cope, who also noted that "it has taken centuries for the music world to develop a set of symbols that serve to carefully isolate the creative mind from his audience—symbols, the inadequacy of which cannot begin to represent the significance of a Mozart, a Brahms, or a Beethoven" (1976, 146).

Nonetheless, some composers present less information than others to the performer. In the composed music of the 1950s and 1960s, particularly, the performer often acted as composer; scores frequently contained such minimal information that completely extemporaneous performance was the only remedy. The aleatoric or "chance" music of John Cage was perhaps the clearest example of nearly uncontrolled works of music; in these, soloists and ensembles created music without restrictions and almost entirely independent of the score or of the performance of other musicians.

The concept of group improvisation was devised by the American composer Lukas Foss as a means of allowing selected performers an opportunity to express their own musical intuition. Still, it was grounded in a communal feeling and mutual understanding of the nature of the work. Foss called it 'Action-Music.' " Chamber improvisation lays the emphasis on the 'performance' resulting from the situation, and puts the responsibility for the choices squarely on the shoulders of the performer. It by-passes the composer. It is composition become performance, performer's music" (Schwartz and Childs, 1967, 333).

In a return to the issue of notation, some twentieth-century scores appeared as graphic designs that disregarded the conventional staff notation completely in an attempt to stimulate the spontaneous creativity of the performer. Bussotti's "Five Pieces for David Tudor" (1949) appears as snarled lines and blotted ink figures on the staff, while Earle Brown's "Folio" is reminiscent of the visual artist van der Leck's "Geometrical Composition of 1917." "Music for Telly" (1973) by Elliott Schwartz combines traditional notation with graphic designs and verbal instructions to lead performers to the composer's intended realization of the score (figure 3–6).

The responsibilities of composer and performer to a musical work require the interaction of the two. Stravinsky relayed his thoughts on the nature of performance as the realization of sounds to symbols:

> It is taken for granted that I place before the performer written music wherein the composer's will is explicit and easily discernible from a correctly established text. But no matter how scrupulously a piece of music may be notated, no matter how carefully it may be insured against every possible ambiguity through the indications of tempo, shading, phrasing, accentuation, and so on, it always contains hidden elements that defy definition. . . . The realization of these elements is thus a matter of experience and intuition, in a word, of the talent of the person who is called upon to present the music (1985, 299).

The balance of notation and improvisation is a delicate one, pursued by composers through the ages of Western art music. The performance of contemporary music is a demanding task that requires the discipline to understand notation that may include mathematically complex rhythms and spatially disoriented pitches. The works often require as well the performer's inventive and free spirit, with the clever combination of musical experience, imagination, and logic to interpret the unconventional score in expressive and musically satisfying ways. The shifting sands of musical style will lead to further developments in this and the next century, but the matters of creativity and literacy will likely continue to figure prominently in the training of performers who can realize the musical score.

SUMMARY

An overview of the development of European staff notation as well as the parallel pedagogical changes that occurred through history help one to gain a comprehensive picture of contemporary music education practices. For Western art music, the oral tradition of

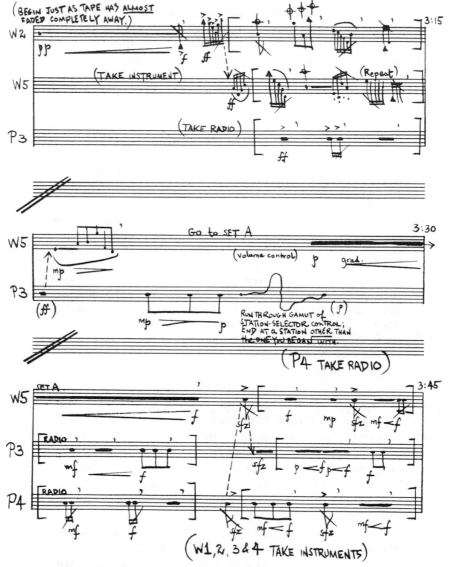

FIGURE 3–6 Excerpt from Elliot Schwartz, "Music for Telly."

Courtesy of Elliott Schwartz.

learning solely by listening was supplanted by the development of skills in music reading, ear-training, and solmization. Aspects of the older transmission process were continued through vocalized mnemonics that could be delivered by teachers to students (as in the case of rhythm), and through solmization systems that offered a refinement of aural skills. The expression of the performer's creative self was guided by the stylistic parameters of the time which changed through the course of history, but it was through study with a musician-teacher that the appropriate techniques for improvisation or ornamentation were learned. While the European invention of notation has provided an efficient means of learning music for performance, and one which has provided a model for an expedient approach to music learning throughout the world, the subtleties of music as an expressive and interpretive art underscore the absolute need for training the ear.

CHAPTER

4

◆

Music Teaching and Learning in the New World

Methods of music instruction in the West have shifted from rote to note and back again. With the settlement of the New World came the adaptation of many European philosophies in American schools and society. For several centuries, standards of the Old World guided the training of musicians in the United States and laid the foundation for the inclusion of music in the public school curriculum.

At the time of colonialization, Western art music had long been preserved through notation. As models of music training, European conservatories emphasized music reading so that students could realize music from scores. At the same time, conservatories kept alive the training of musicians in the skills of ornamentation, embellishment, interpretation, and improvisation. The performance of music required the combination of aural and reading skills.

In colonial America, music education was advanced through the singing school movement and through the publication of tunebooks. The entrance of music into public school curricula in the nineteenth century furthered earlier efforts toward the shaping of an American musical culture. Devices such as the American shape notes, cipher (number) notation, rhythm mnemonic syllables, and various solmization systems were experimentally introduced in schools and communities and evaluated for their effectiveness in developing reading and

60

performing skills. By the end of the nineteenth century, a principal goal of education was for students to have knowledge of music's fundamental elements, including the ability to read notation, to sing in tune, and—for some—to play an orchestral or band instrument.

Music education in the twentieth century saw the diffusion of public school music throughout the country and the broadening of the music curriculum. Performance opportunities in choirs, bands, and orchestras were increasingly available, and general music programs were organized according to the concepts of the progressive education movement begun by Dewey. Some educators maintained that music learning was synonymous with the attainment of literacy skills, while others saw it as a synthesis of performing and listening experiences for the development of literacy, aural skills, and creativity.

Since the beginnings of American public school music programs, the rote-note controversy has influenced teachers in their choice of music and teaching methods. Many educators saw the gray, in-between area rather than the contradiction and sought a natural balance through the combined use of the ear and the eye. For some, European-derived solmization practices appeared to be an appropriate means for training the ear while also teaching the staff. While the development of music creativity was sometimes viewed as a method in itself (and the basis for musical understanding), it was more frequently seen as a peak experience to be achieved only through the accumulation of (1) literacy, (2) performance, and (3) aural skills.

THE UNITED STATES TO 1800

The church was an important factor in the music that was performed in the New World and in the way it was taught. In Central America, in Canada, and in New England, attempts at formal and informal music education occurred under the direction of the clergy, mainly with the purpose of improving music for worship.

Early Missionary Efforts

Spanish friars were probably the first European music education in the Americas, offering music instruction to Native American Indians in Mexico and in the southwestern United States. Fray Pedro de Gante, who was actually Dutch by birth, described some of his pedagogical experiences among the Aztecs in letters written during the years 1529 through 1558 (Heller, 1979). He taught the Indians to read, write, and sing the music of leading European composers of the medieval and early Renaissance periods, organizing them into ensembles that provided music for liturgical services. His school, the first on the North American continent, was modeled after the European cathedral schools and provided an opportunity for the sons of Aztec chiefs to become musicians and teachers who would spread their knowledge of European music throughout Mexico. De Gante was sensitive in his teaching to the rich ceremonial celebrations of the Indians, setting verses from the Catechism to their familiar melodies and in their Nahuatl language. Other Franciscan friars active throughout Central America and in the southwestern regions of Arizona, New Mexico, Texas, Colorado, and California were influenced by the work of Fray Pedro de Gante.

In the Great Lakes region and in Canada, French priests provided music lessons for the Indians as early as the seventeenth century. A school was opened in Quebec for French and Indian boys in 1632 where Jesuits taught the singing of sacred music. Father Paul le Jeune recalled the aural-oral process by which the boys were taught: "I carefully pronounced the Pater or the Credo which I had arranged in verse for them to sing: they followed me word by word learning very nicely by heart" (McGee, 1985, 7).

New England Psalm Singing

Perhaps the best known early music education efforts were among the New England colonists. These included the Puritans and other Protestant church people who kept their worship services alive with the singing of psalms first learned in their native England. The Ainsworth version of the *Psalms of David* provided poems for the Puritans, to be sung to traditional melodies; there was no notation. Out of this manual grew the first published songbook (and the first book of any type) in America, *The Psalms, Hymns, and Spiritual Songs of the Old and New Testament*, commonly known as *The Bay Psalm Book of 1640*. Still, the *Bay Psalm Book* had no notation until the ninth edition in 1698. Only thirteen melodies were printed for 159 psalms, a paucity that reflected the general decline in the quality of psalm singing, the decrease in participation by the congregation, and the growing musical illiteracy in colonial America.*

* The ability of Puritans, Pilgrims, and other early colonists to read music was a gradual process; this led to the first known singing schools around 1710 and to the first tunebooks in 1721.

The practice of "lining out" or "deaconing" took hold in the New World as it had in England and Scotland. In this practice a church deacon or precentor was designated to set the pitch and chant the tune line by line, followed in imitation by the congregation. Since the precentor sang the psalm tunes from memory, he frequently varied them, and in time there was often little similarity between the original and the sung tunes.* The congregation further contributed to the corruption of the originals by inaccurately imitating or intentionally decorating the tunes. The number of tunes sung decreased as well, and by the early eighteenth century, there were only five or six tunes in common use (Eaklor, 1985, 89).

Ministers in England and in the New World protested the decoration of psalm tunes by both the precentor and the congregation. In 1711, an English clergyman complained of one parishioner's song style:

> What gives us the most offence is her theatrical manner of singing the Psalms. She introduces above fifty Italian airs into the hundredth psalm, and whilst we begin "All people" in the old solemn tune of our forefathers, she in quite a different key runs divisions on the vowels, and adorns them with the graces of Nicolini. (Rainbow, 1982, 11)

In 1720, Reverend Thomas Symmes similarly complained about the precentors of his Massachusetts church: "Every Leading-Singer would take the Liberty of raising any Note of the Tune, or lowering of it, as best pleas'd his Ear, and add such Turns and Flourishes as were grateful to him (Hitchcock, 1974, 5). Symmes was concerned that the orthodox psalmody would be replaced with an indigenous folk style of singing. To help prevent this he became part of a growing movement to revive formal music instruction (Britton, 1958, 200).

Tunebooks and Singing Schools

A number of solutions were considered for the removal of improvisatory or plainly inaccurate singing from music used for worship. These included silencing the congregation and forming select choirs of trained readers, the use of musical instruments (largely disapproved by those with Calvinistic beliefs), and the development of music-reading skills for all the congregation. The last, music lit-

* The lining-out practice is preserved today in some African-American denominations, particularly in the South, and in Gaelic churches of the Scottish Highlands.

eracy, was heralded as the key to the future of music's preservation and transmission.

Instruction manuals were created to provide a means of singing psalms syllabically by note as they were originally intended. Hundreds of tunebooks were published during the eighteenth century. Most of these contained a section on the rudiments of music that was intended to teach staff notation. They also held a collection of psalms, hymns, and spirituals to be used in practicing the theoretical knowledge gained from the first section. By 1800, there were at least 154 published tunebooks, and over a thousand more appeared during the course of the nineteenth century. The tunebook compilers were singing school teachers, many of whom were also composers of the distinctive "early American" hymns included in the books (Britton, 1958, 204).

Thomas Walter's tunebook, *The Grounds and Rules of Musicke Explained* (1721), was the first American music textbook (Gates, 1988, 190–191). It contained "rules for tuning the voice," instructions for reading music, warm-up exercises for the voice, and musically notated examples of scales, intervals, pitches, and rests. On the unprinted pages of the second half of the book were penned staff lines and notation of the hymns to be learned for singing in the church. John Tufts's fifth edition of *An Introduction to the Singing of Psalm Tunes* (1726) is musically identical to the earlier tunebook, except that special fasola syllables (discussed in the next section) were placed on the staff as a substitute for standard notation.*

The publication of tunebooks paved the way for the American phenomenon known as the singing school. The first such school was established about 1710 in Boston; many others followed throughout New England, the mid-Atlantic states, and the South well into the next century. People convened in a church, in a school house, or in the homes of church members to learn to read music and to study sacred music that could later be performed in church. An itinerant singing master could come to town for a month or more, and students would enroll in his weekly class sessions. The course of the meetings was guided by the tunebooks so that music fundamentals and songs for worship were learned. Vocal production and accuracy of rhythm and pitch were stressed with the intention of improving the quality of students' singing as well as raising their level of music literacy. The singing lessons culminated in a choral concert for the church or town assembly.

* Fasola is the name given to a solfege syllable system which applies the syllable "fa" to the first and fourth degrees of the scale, "sol" to the second and fifth degrees, and "la" to the third and sixth degrees. The leading tone, or seventh degree, is sung as "mi."

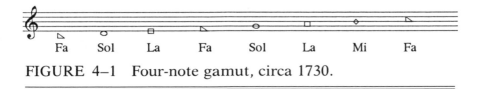

FIGURE 4–1   Four-note gamut, circa 1730.

Exposure to tunebooks and singing schools produced note-reading congregations. As the more proficient singers began to realize that their singing was enhanced by proximity to one another they began to sit together in groups, a practice that marked the beginning of the American church choir. Despite early resistance by some in learning to read notation, "singing by rule" or "regular singing," aided by tunebooks and the singing master, were important to the growth of music education as well as to church music. Rather than remaining with the strict rote transmission system of the past, amateur and professional musicians, through tunebooks and singing schools, had an efficient way to learning music by reading notation.

Fasola Notation

Using the fasola system of syllable notation popular in England at the time, New England manuals which the singing masters followed often began with the presentation of a major scale as the basis for sight-reading melodies in the second half of the book (figure 4–1). The four-note gamut of the fasola system provided the means for learning the songs, which were first taught through imitation of the syllables sung by the instructor. Only after the syllables were thoroughly learned were the words added. The learning sequence progressed from the gamut, or scale, to proportional durations of pitches and rests. The importance of the leading tone, *mi*, was stressed through rules and drills; knowing its unique function and placement in the scale put all other pitches in proper perspective for the singer. Three- and four-part songs were learned one line at a time from the singing master, who sang them while pointing to notation that illustrated each sound.

Before the singing classes began, the singing master would likely have tested each student's voice individually. One student of Moses Cheney, a well-known New England master, recalled his own nerve-wracking experience in pitch-matching and his student role as a keen observer of the singing master:

> "Well, my lad, will you try?" "Yes sir." I looked him in the mouth, and as he spoke a note, so did I, both up and down. I

did not wait for him to call the note First; I spoke with him. Now by watching him so closely, and observing how he spoke the notes, but would come so as to speak with him. The master turned away, saying, "this boy will make a singer." I felt well enough. (Keene, 1982, 24)

Shape Notes

From the beginning, various methods were sought to simplify the reading of music in the tunebooks published for use during singing school sessions. The placement of fasola on the staff by John Tufts in 1726 was one of the earliest American simplifications (figure 4–2). Eventually, the European fasola system of solfége was modified so that a different shaped notehead was assigned to each syllable. Known also as "buckwheat" notation and "dunce notes," the syllables and their shapes were depicted in a manner that became widely accepted (figure 4–3).

William Little and William Smith's *The Easy Instructor* (1801) was the first book to use shape notes. It was followed by Andrew Law's *The Art of Singing* two years later: in this book the *fa* and *la* shapes were exchanged (figure 4–4). A seven-shape system was also devised, following the European assignment of one syllable for each pitch in the diatonic scale. The advantage of the shape notes was that

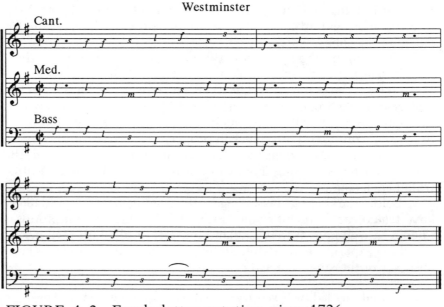

FIGURE 4–2   Fasola letter notation, circa 1726.

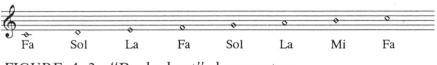

Fa　　Sol　　La　　Fa　　Sol　　La　　Mi　　Fa

FIGURE 4–3　"Buckwheat" shape notes.

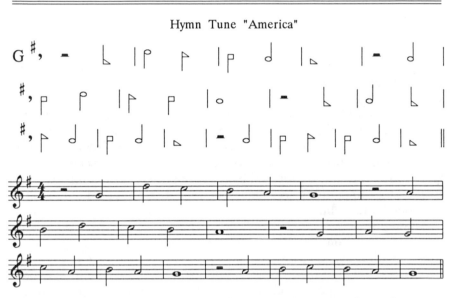

Hymn Tune "America"

FIGURE 4–4　Andrew Law's shape notation, with realization on staff.

the singer could immediately recognize the pitches they symbolized, so that a staff was unnecessary (although it was more often used than not). The emphasis was on designating pitch rather than rhythm, which in most hymns was likely to consist of even quarter notes, and occasional half and whole notes (Cobb, 1978).

　　Tunebooks using shape notes to aid in the singing of religious hymns appeared in many regions of the young American nation; among these books were *Kentucky Harmony, Christian Harmony, The Southern Harp, Sacred Harmony,* and *Missouri Harmony.* In the first half of the nineteenth century, more music was published in the United States in shape notes than in regular notation.* Despite its

* In some areas—for example, the Blue Ridge region of Virginia—singing schools featuring the shape-note method continued until 1900. Today, denominations such as the Primitive Baptists, who continue the song style, rely upon oral transmission for the music, reading pocket-sized collections of hymn texts but supplying melodies and harmonies from their own collective memory of "shape-note tunes" (Sutton, 1982, 11–26).

apparent effectiveness as a means of teaching music, the shape-note system was never adopted by early music educators in their classrooms, possibly because of its association with folk music and country people (Ellis, 1957).

The Decline of the Singing School

Some of the urban singing schools developed into singing societies in the late eighteenth century. These groups were devoted to the performance of the choral masterworks but were nonetheless nurtured by the activities of the singing school. Rather than teaching for an understanding of notation, directors sought to bring music to the public, and thus the focus was shifted from learning the fundamentals of music reading (which was assumed) to the refinement of the music through interpretation. Not only sacred but also secular songs were rehearsed and performed by singing societies; this music often included compositions by Bach, Beethoven, Handel, Mendelssohn, Schubert, and Schumann.

Singing schools began to fade by the second or third decade of the nineteenth century. With their demise came the development of music academies, for those who sought private instruction on musical instruments, and the growing interest and finally the integration of music into the public school curricula. With the advent of a more secular society, the church was no longer the centerpiece of community activities. Music education in the United States was finding its way into the school curriculum.

PUBLIC SCHOOL MUSIC IN THE UNITED STATES: THE EARLY YEARS

The industrialization of the United States brought factories into the cities; these workplaces were believed to harbor ignorance and poverty, requiring only menial labor skills. Those who worked in these factories, however, the descendants of early settlers and the masses of immigrants arriving on the eastern shores of the United States, saw promise for the future through education, and gradually America began to fulfill that promise. As American society adapted to increasing urbanization, a massive social reform was begun through the establishment of a system of public education. Jean-Jacques Rousseau and Johann Heinrich Pestalozzi enlightened Europeans and Americans with their views of human development, which they said began in the critical stage of childhood. It was the recognition by

Americans of the learning potential of children, as well as their perception of education as a way of rising above society's problems that helped to bring about the public school system. The eventual inclusion of music in the curriculum was a recognition that the arts are essential in a truly broad and comprehensive education.

The extent of European influence in America on matters of educational theory and practice intensified in the nineteenth and twentieth centuries. The musical repertoire selected for performance, listening, and analysis in American school programs was largely European in style or had been composed by those trained in the tradition of European art music. Also, the American process of music education for the young had been greatly affected by the developments that had occurred in Europe during the preceding two centuries. Contemporary elementary and secondary curricula are a result of the exchanges between the Old and New worlds.

Pestalozzian Influences

The Swiss educator, Johann Heinrich Pestalozzi, set the scene for a system of education that schooled children through participatory experiences. He advocated learning through the involvement of the senses, and consequently, the intellect. Pestalozzi held the teacher responsible for opening up the sensory avenues of their young students and in connecting these sense impressions step by step from simple perception to complex conceptual understanding.

Pestalozzi was in favor of providing children with a musical education. This preference was noted by Horace Mann, educator and secretary of the Massachusetts Board of Education, who, on observing Pestalozzi's school in Switzerland, reported that

> music was everywhere in evidence. The teachers were masters of vocal music and they played upon one or more instruments as well. One was as certain to see a violin as a blackboard in every room. Singing was taught not only as an accomplishment, but as a means of recreation and socialization. (Reisner, 1930, 206)

While Pestalozzi was not himself trained as a musician, he urged Michael Pfeiffer and Hans Nageli to write a book on singing that would incorporate his principles. Just as Pestalozzi's own book, *How Gertrude Teaches Her Children*, was influential in the formulation of school programs in the early to mid-nineteenth centuries, Pfeiffer and Nageli's *Method of Teaching Singing According to Pestalozzian Principles* impressed early pioneers in American music education. Aside from the exercises in rhythm and melody and the collection of unison songs, the chief contribution of the book was the gradual introduction of musical concepts and skills using a sequence that blended aural experiences with notation.

Among many music instructors in the nineteenth century, there was a strong anti-rote sentiment. Still, the Pestalozzian idea of sound before symbol was advocated in conference presentations, in publications, and especially in practice. Joseph Neef, a Swiss educator often credited with bringing "music instruction according to Pestalozzi" to the United States, proposed an outline for teaching music that underscored the merits of extensive aural experience, including the imitation of the teacher by the student, before the reading or writing of notation was initiated. American educators William C. Woodbridge and Elam Ives were also among the trailblazers who advocated a place for music in the schools, and both promoted Pestalozzi's ideas as effective techniques (Keene, 1982).

Lowell Mason and Public School Music

In 1838, with the establishment of music as a bona fide curricular offering in the Boston public schools, Lowell Mason introduced there aspects of the Pestalozzian tradition of learning through sensory experiences. He acknowledged the Swiss master's educational theory in his famous *Manual of the Boston Academy of Music, for Instruction in the Elements of Vocal Music on the System of Pestalozzi.* In fact, the manual was only marginally Pestalozzian in content and method, and was probably plagiarized from a nonpertinent source (Pemberton, 1985, 108–109).* Mason practiced the approach of student imitation of the teacher, and his classes would often progress without the use of books or notation. He justified the practice of rote singing and demonstrated his awareness of the realities of classroom teaching when he stated that

> there is no objection at all, to learning tunes by rote, under the direction of a judicious teacher. It is only objectionable when in consequence of singing the syllables appropriate to solmization, the pupil is led to suppose that he is singing by note, while his voice is guided solely by others. (Mason, 1834, 7).

* Pestalozzi's name was used commonly to refer to educational systems of the time, and Mason may have found the prestigious name useful in the promotion of his own method. (See Efland, A. "Art and Music in the Pestalozzian Tradition." *Journal of Research in Music Education* 31 (1983): 165–178).

Mason's own teaching of vocal music was filled with experiences intended to increase the ability of the student's ear to discriminate pitches and rhythms—their patterns and phrases—and to cultivate the voice. For people who had learned to read music in the singing schools or in the homes, strategies that included music learning by imitation, through the use of a Movable Do system, and through the use of familiar patterns as a bridge to the unfamiliar, were commonly employed. Mason added to the rote versus note controversy that was to gain momentum through the century, and which continues to be the topic of heated discussion today.

Following the Civil War, teachers were divided between those who followed Lowell Mason's ideas on rote teaching in initial stages and those who preferred to introduce music notation from the beginning of formal music instruction. While Mason preferred that singing experience through specific pattern exercises precede the learning of notation, others of the "rote" school later used the singing of songs themselves as the foundation of eventual note-reading. In either case, however, those who adhered to the rote imitation process postponed music reading until the student had achieved a certain familiarity with the sounds.

Textbook Approaches to Vocal Instruction

As various approaches to solmization were developed in Europe, the debate between rote and note instruction continued in the United States. There was general agreement in the late nineteenth century as to the importance of music reading, but the relative proportion of rote songs and reading exercises a teacher included in his or her classroom was indicative of which side of the philosophical debate the teacher favored. Luther Whiting Mason, whose popular National Music Course of instructional song books and charts was published in 1870, articulated the role of rote singing in the development of children's musicality, noting that correct rote singing "leads to a discrimination between a musical and unmusical style" of singing and that children learn to sing best if they have "the right examples at the start" (Mason, 1870, iii). Hosea Edson Holt led the revolt against the rote approach, and his instruction series, the Normal Music Course of 1883, provided the sight-singing exercises and songs that were expected to develop music reading skills in just a few years of school music classes. Twenty-four exercises in the first-grade book, for example, were devoted to the performance through reading of just the first two notes of the scale (Birge, 1939).

Decade after decade, the focus in music classrooms fluctuated from music reading to singing for its own sake. Music education in American schools had matured considerably in its first sixty years. The issue at the close of the century was no longer whether music was vital to the curriculum—it was; the major concern had become how to shape musicianship in students who could then be both musically literate and aurally attuned.

TWENTIETH-CENTURY APPROACHES TO AMERICAN MUSIC EDUCATION

The issues of creativity and music literacy were addressed through various movements and approaches to music education in the twentieth century. Ensembles and instrumental classes stressed performance and reading skills; general music classes experimented with music appreciation and creative experiences in music. The matter of ear-training, although invariably acknowledged as a curricular objective, was often peripheral rather than central to the daily music class, rehearsal, or lesson.

Child Study and Progressive Education

The child-study movement of the late nineteenth and early twentieth centuries placed importance on the observation and analysis of children's behaviors and abilities and led to modifications in approaches to teaching. Social Darwinism, a perspective influenced by Darwin's *Origin of Species* (1859), suggested that the growth and development of individuals correspond to the evolutionary development of the human race. Children matured physically, intellectually, and emotionally in a way that traced the development of the human race through the ages, from its primitive beginnings to the present.

The prominent American psychologist, G. Stanley Hall, attempted to link child study with educational practice and the developmental stages of children. Hall's "recapitulation theory" of Social Darwinism was paraphrased in music textbooks and became the beacon of good hope for the solid music instruction of children. Applied to music education, the theory held that children progressed through a "primitive period" in which rhythm is the focal point of the musical experience [ages three through eight], to the "simian and historic" periods of growth in musical skills [ages eight through twelve], to the appreciation of music in adolescence (Humphreys, 1985, 82). Both the developmental psychology of children and their musical responsiveness were considered by curriculum planners.

According to Hall, the purpose of school music programs and the method by which music was taught were most clearly manifested in adolescence. Beginning at age thirteen, the individual's more mature intellect and character were capable of shaping values subconsciously, values that were "developed through years of rote singing" in early and middle childhood (Rideout, 1982, 146). The child-study movement reinforced the nurturing role that schools could play in guiding children toward realizing their intellectual, emotional, and musical potential. Through the advocacy of proponents like G. Stanley Hall, music achieved a more prominent status in the schools.

In the early years of the twentieth century, the progressive education movement gradually replaced the child-study movement. American educator John Dewey advocated the discovery method, in which students utilized problem-solving skills rather than mere memorization of information through formal exercises. The artistic creativity of children blossomed in special programs and was heralded as demonstrative of the "child-centered" thrust in education. Ideally, the interests of the children determined the curriculum, and the practice of fixing a curriculum without full knowledge of student abilities and interests fell into disuse. As a result of Dewey's ideas on the school's efforts to accommodate children's individual intellectual and artistic pursuits, some teachers emphasized student-active and teacher-passive behaviors in their classes.

Growth of Performance Ensembles

Performance became an increasingly important goal of school music programs. From the success of elementary vocal music programs came secondary school choir programs in the nineteenth century. Instrumental music arrived later, with the organization of the first high school orchestras around 1900 and the first bands within the decade. The greatest expansion of instrumental music education occurred in the 1920s, partly because manufacturers of instruments saw their community band markets drying up, and partly because bandsmen were returning from World War I in search of jobs. Former community band leaders and military trained musicians took teaching positions in the public schools. Contests and festivals brought school music to the attention of the public, who took great pride in and offered considerable support for their school ensembles.*

Attempts to develop music reading skills continued throughout

* See chapter 12 for a more complete account of the emergence of ensembles in public school education.

the century and were most closely paired with instrumental instruction and performing ensembles. Singing in the elementary school or in high school choirs was alternately viewed as an activity to be directed through rote or note procedures; band and orchestras, however, became the principal training grounds for reading notation. Choral ensembles were less successful in preparing literate musicians and in many cases, the nineteenth century rote-to-note approach was preserved intact. Despite current Deweyan thought, elementary music instruction was too often mistaken as an activity in recreational singing rather than music learning, and rote learning without directed listening was the rule rather than the exception.

European Approaches to Music Instruction

Instructional styles in American music education, especially at the elementary level, were strongly influenced by the thoughts of several prominent musicians and pedagogues from abroad. In Europe, the artistic and educational climate at the turn of the century brought about a creative commingling of music with dance. Émile Jaques-Dalcroze formulated his eurhythmics at the Geneva Conservatory as an avenue of rhythmic training, and its introduction to the United States established movement as vital to music learning, especially for children.* Rudolph von Laban founded his Choreographic Institute in Zurich in 1915 at the same time that Martha Graham and Ruth St. Denis were pioneering the art of modern dance. Carl Orff, once a student of an experimental music, theatre, and dance project with Jaques-Dalcroze, established with Dorothee Gunther in 1924 a school for gymnastics, dance, and music. The interest in rhythmic training as expressed creatively through movement had developed as an important thrust of music educators by the 1930s (Campbell, 1990).

Toward a Contemporary Curriculum

While an educational trend toward objectivity through the evaluation of musical intelligence, skills, and knowledge occurred early in the century, other projects emphasized the more subjective nature of creativity. In the 1920s, Satis Coleman designed a curriculum that encouraged children's creative musical expression on their own

---

* See Chapter 11 for a discussion of several approaches to music learning including those of Jaques-Dalcroze, Kodály, and Orff.

homemade instruments. From 1937 to 1945, Donald Pond and Gladys Moorhead directed the Pillsbury Project, which allowed young children free reign with instruments, space, and time for the exploration of musical sounds. In the late 1950s and 1960s, such programs as the Ford Foundation's Young Composers Project, the Comprehensive Musicianship Seminar, the Yale Seminar, and the Tanglewood Symposium encouraged the development of the creative musical potential in each student. The emergence of the Orff approach in the United States during the 1960s, with its emphasis on exploratory experiences in rhythmic speech, song, instrumental performance, and movement, was seen as another viable tool for developing music creativity at the elementary level. Yet, despite these and other experiments, a didactic approach to music instruction has remained the most prevalent method—and as many maintain, the most manageable one for ensemble settings and group instruction in music.

Beginning in the 1950s, music learning began to be associated with theories of educational psychology, and creativity through improvisation and compositional activities was included in curricular goals with increasing frequency. Jerome Bruner's emphasis on the natural intuition of the child and his or her ability to solve problems when given the opportunity, underscored the importance of heuristic learning. Similarly, the humanistic psychologist Carl Rogers advocated a child-centered educational process in which the teacher was to be a facilitator of learning, so that the student might encounter ideas, experiment with them directly in a participatory fashion, and evaluate them for their potential use. When these theories are applied to classroom practice, many students are stimulated to perform, compose, analyze, and think about music more creatively. The Manhattanville Music Curriculum Project and the Hawaii Project interpreted these theories for the music classroom, infusing improvisation and experiments in sound as means of teaching performance skills and knowledge* (Mark; 1988).

Jazz emerged as the all-American musical contribution to the world, and with it gradually came another opportunity for creative musical expression in the schools. Not until the 1950s were jazz and stage band ensembles established in the schools, however, and even more recently and rarely do genuine vocal jazz ensembles appear in music programs at the secondary level. Their presence, though, provides students with opportunities for independent musicianship and improvisation within the parameters of an ensemble.

With the spread of the Hungarian method to North America in the 1960s, a sequence for reading and writing music notation was

* See Chapter 5 for a discussion of theories relevant to music learning and creativity.

introduced. Based on the English Tonic Sol-fa and the Chevé mnemonic rhythms, the pedagogical techniques of Zoltan Kodály have
been employed in elementary classes and occasionally in secondary
choral ensembles as well. The use of the voice as the natural instrument for learning musical concepts increased Kodály's relevance in
the vocal music program. The Hungarian view of music reading and
writing as a principal goal throughout the nation's educational system had led Kodály to develop the system for the Hungarian schools.
Music educators who recognized the significance of music literacy
through solmization saw the value of adopting Kodály's technique in
American schools (Choksy, 1988).

Other approaches to an understanding of music notation were
developed, and for teachers of instrumentalists, perhaps Japanese
violinist Shinichi Suzuki's practices have been the most widely modeled. The Suzuki method exploded onto the American scene just three
decades ago, and its basic tenets of listening, performance technique,
and motivation have remained intact ever since. The image of pint-
sized violins has been associated with Suzuki, but his philosophy
runs much deeper: his establishment of Talent Education declared
the goal and means of nurturing natural musical ability. The "Mother
Tongue" method recognized repeated hearings of the music to be
learned as the most important facet in music learning, and the young
musician was not introduced to notation until sufficient imitative
aural learning had been provided, often after several years. The transfer of the method by Suzuki and his proponents from violin to piano
to the various instruments of the orchestra has been possible, while
the underlying series of listening, imitating, and repeating behaviors
has been continued. Likewise, the "listen and play" approach has
been used successfully with intermediate and advanced students, in
private lessons and in groups. While learning notation is a prominent
goal in Suzuki-styled music instruction, extensive aural experiences
and opportunities to play by ear precede the development of notational skills (Kendall, 1984; Wickes; 1982).

Among the most recent advocates of an aural learning mode of
instruction is Edwin E. Gordon, who developed his music learning
sequence in the 1970s (Gordon, 1984). Similar to the hierarchical
learning theory of Robert Gagné (1977), Gordon's theory compares
learning music to learning a spoken language, as a progression from
first simply perceiving and responding to sounds to the advanced
levels of problem-solving and conceptual understanding. The student
develops basic discrimination skills through aural and oral techniques; he or she learns to read and write notation only after aural
experiences. Student imitation of the teacher's singing of tonal patterns and chanting of rhythm patterns is an aid to understanding the

symbols. Stages of inference learning, including generalization, improvisation, and theoretical understanding, come after the synthesis of musical sounds and symbols.

Pedagogical approaches to music learning in American schools of the twentieth century are many and varied. Assorted projects in creativity have provided guidelines for the musical development of children, and exposure to jazz performance in secondary school ensembles has allowed students to cultivate skills in improvisation. Techniques to train students in listening skills are apparent in selected ensemble exercises and warm-up routines, and through experiences suggested by the classic European methods of Dalcroze, Orff, and Kodály. Listening is also basic in the rote approach advocated by Suzuki and Gordon to provide an aural foundation for music reading. Common themes are shared by several of these methods: it appears that the view of music as a creative and partly aural art has not been entirely relegated to the historical past.

SUMMARY

The chronological history of "rote versus note" in the New World was not an absolute and unequivocal progression from one to the other; rather, the development and widespread use of notation in American schools brought about the modification of an earlier oral approach to music instruction. For many in the profession, rote learning was not completely abandoned but found its place as a useful technique in the making of the young musician.

As a means of linking the ear with the eye and of developing aural and reading skills simultaneously, solmization was embraced by many teachers, particularly at the elementary level and in choral ensembles. Conferences, symposia, and special projects have focused much attention on the significant contributions aural skills and creativity can make in developing the comprehensive musicianship of students (see chapter 1). The history of music teaching and learning in the New World has been a colorful one, replete with experimentation and attempts to respond to the needs of American society. The future role of music in American culture may be partly dependent on the willingness of teachers to promote its potential as an avenue for personal expression and to connect carefully the symbols of staff notation with their musical sound.

CHAPTER

5

◆

Theories of Music Learning

Music teaching and learning are complex processes. Various disciplines have converged in an effort to understand how people perceive music, think about music, respond to music, and behave musically as performers and composers. In the field of music education alone, there is a substantial body of literature on the development of listening discrimination, creative and analytical thinking, conceptual understanding, performance skills, and affective responses. Teacher-student interactions have been assessed, and the influences of instructional strategies and styles have been closely observed and evaluated. Research efforts in such disparate fields as acoustics, aesthetics, anthropology, education, ethnomusicology, musicology, neurology, psychology, and sociology are leading to even broader perspectives on music teaching and learning.

Psychologists and anthropologists, along with music educators and ethnomusicologists, have had a significant impact on our understanding of music learning processes. The systematic study of child development, first undertaken by psychologists to explain the origins of adult behaviors and thought processes, has blossomed into the distinct discipline of developmental psychology that concentrates on cognitive development from birth through adolescence. Social anthropologists were only peripherally interested in childhood until the 1930s, when Mead (1932) focused her attention on children as the essential element of cultural interpretation. Through an increasing number of ethnographic case studies that combine these disciplines, the developmental stages of childhood in various cultures are becoming more fully understood. Occasionally, such investigations illustrate musical thinking and performance behaviors of children (Blacking, 1967; Booth, 1987); more often, they provide the basis for cross-cultural comparisons in music.

Contemporary theories of learning are based largely on principles established by Western psychologists in this century; many of these theories have been applied to music. Some explain the sequential unfolding of children's responses to music and recommend processes for teaching music to children and adolescents that correspond to the students' developmental stages. Some provide a rationale for learning through discovery and exploration while others explain the benefits of teaching didactically. Music reading, motor skills, and the practice behaviors of performers have been examined in theory and practice, and the learning and teaching modalities of students and teachers have been analyzed. Still other theories offer insight on the nature of creativity and prescribe ways for nurturing the expression of original music ideas in children.

The interdisciplinary contributions to the knowledge base in music cognition, teaching, and learning are still largely Western oriented, yet the urge to generalize across cultures is tempting. After all, the ear, brain, and neuromuscular system are human faculties that do not vary greatly from one individual to the next. There are common features in the musical thought processes of individuals from one culture to the next, but just how large a role does culture play?

Piaget (1952) once regarded his ideas on child development as psychobiological and thus universally valid. Indeed, not until his conversations with Margaret Mead in the 1950s was he impressed with the potential of social influences to shape cognitive development; this realization then inspired him to undertake extensive cross-cultural testing of his theory. In the application of Piaget's theory among people who had had little previous contact with Western values, the findings often did not match the results produced by Piaget at his laboratory in Geneva (Modgil, 1974).

Culture plays a considerable role in psychological processes, including musical thought. Bronfenbrenner described the impact of culture on behavior in a broad sense, but the ramifications for music learning are clear:

> Seen in different contexts, human nature, which I had previously thought of as a singular noun, became plural and pluralistic; for the different environments were producing discernible differences, not only across but also within societies, in talent, temperament, human relations, and particularly in the ways in which the culture, or subculture, brought up the next generation. (1979, xiii)

Environmental factors in the shaping of musical talent may be considerable, as musical development is a result of both psychological and sociocultural factors. While it would be erroneous and shortsighted to imply that the sequence and strategies of music learning and teaching are wholly transferable to other cultures, there may be some cross-cultural components. Future investigations by specialists in a variety of discipline may show that certain aspects of musical thought and behavior are widespread, although probably not universal.

How can music learning be defined in ways that are fitting for genres and styles across cultures and historical eras? Are traditional folk music and classical music learned in similar ways? Can learning theories explain the way music is formally taught by teachers to students and informally transmitted in the environment? What is creativity in music, and how is it developed? The strategies so commonly employed in classrooms and studios—ear-training, vocalization, and improvisation—may become better understood by examining them as they relate to theories of learning.

MUSIC, LEARNING, AND ENCULTURATION

Music is a significant form of human behavior and a means of satisfying the unique human need for aesthetic expression (Gaston, 1968; Merriam, 1964). In every world culture, there are those who perform and create music, and those who listen and respond to music. The elements of melody, rhythm, texture, and form in a musical style are combined in ways that are dictated by the people themselves, and the resulting sound becomes a definition of a specific culture. The transmission process also distinguishes one musical tradition from the next. Yet, however varied the regional differences, there may be certain similarities in music learning that extend across many traditions.

Merriam (1964) proposed that learning occurs in three ways: *enculturation, training* and *schooling*. Through the process of *enculturation*, a set of experiences within the culture is shared by every member. As we learn to behave and think in particular ways, we are learning our culture. Society shapes our views, our tastes, our manner of dress, food, and etiquette. From birth through old age, the individual is exposed to values, attitudes, and information through an informal means of social learning. The child's cognitive system is organized through cultural learning—the observation and imitation of the established society; the maturing individual develops perspectives that reflect those of the culture.

Musical taste is a natural outgrowth of enculturation. A national style of folk music, with its inherent tuning system, scale, and rhythmic and textural traits, is likely to be more favored by members of the culture than by nonmembers. The prevalence of the music within the environment makes it familiar, a trait that in turn often generates preference. Enculturation is also demonstrated by the ability of young children to learn songs on hearing them, even when no instruction is provided. Transcending all cultures, there appears to be some "natural" skill in the building of a song repertoire, with children informally learning and committing to memory an extensive set of songs without the aid of a teacher.

Learning occurs in directed ways as well, so that specific information and skills are transmitted by family members and in formal school settings. *Training* involves the conscious efforts of teachers and students in the acquisition of knowledge through experiences relegated to some, but not all, members of a culture. Along with professional teachers, parents may serve as teachers of their children, initiating activities with an instructional intent. An essential aspect of training is that the individual consciously seeks information and is presented with avenues by which to attain knowledge and skills. *Schooling* is a more restricted and formal type of cultural learning, a type of training that occurs in specific locations removed from the home environment. Merriam (1964) discussed these learning types as they appear in Bali, Ghana, Australia, and Sierra Leone.

Others have also discerned differences in types of learning, or music learning in particular. Smith (1987) made distinctions among several familiar labels, offering the most commonly used "music education" to refer to the teaching of music in elementary and secondary schools and to collegiate programs that prepare teachers for the profession. "Education in music" concerns the learning of music as performance as well as its historical and theoretical aspects; this type of learning occurs in formal educational settings including conservatories and university schools and departments of music. The phrase "music learning" is given a broader connotation that encompasses formal and informal contexts and in which the emphasis is placed on the learner rather than the teacher. The influence of Merriam's learning types is evident and is acknowledged by Smith.

Formal and informal education, its characteristics and effects, have been examined by Greenfield and Lave (1982). In these different settings, the contrast in the role of teacher and learner is considerable. The teacher is responsible for imparting knowledge and skill in formal settings, while informal education holds the learner responsible for obtaining information. Learning occurs through verbal interchange, questioning, and explicit pedagogy and curriculum in formal education, as opposed to teacher demonstration, student observation, and imitation so common in informal settings. Informal education can include enculturation, and in many cultures, training, while formal education can be best equated with schooling, whether in conservatories, public schools, or private studio.

Bateson (1972) defined three broad dimensions of learning in which each level is a continuation of the previous one. These types were related to music learning by Ellis (1986). Learning I occurs without effort, rather unreflectively; in this phase music within the environment is absorbed by the individual. The music must be experienced through participation, which is largely a matter of imitating others who perform. Children's game songs and congregational singing are examples of this type. In Learning II, thinking is combined with experience and the student expends efforts to become a competent performer. Concentrated periods of practice occur in the development of coordination, strength, agility, and speed. The beginning student of trumpet, voice, or violin may represent Learning II, which is in effect the process of learning to learn. The ultimate phase is the performance experience that communicates to the performer more than technical skills; it is an expression that is personal, joyful, even religious. Learning III offers an aesthetic experience that reaches beyond the grind of the practice room, the contests, and the competitions. While Learning I may be associated with enculturation, the second and third types can occur through formal or informal processes, training, or schooling. Ellis (1986) considered these learning types as they applied to practices in an Australian aboriginal community, but they can also be applied to music learning in other cultures.

Returning to Merrian's learning modes, while enculturation in music can span one's entire lifetime, music training in the West generally begins in middle childhood. A typical example of music training is found as a child begins piano lessons, taught either by a musical parent in the home or by a person hired on a weekly basis. Schooling may begin with basic literacy and aural skill development as well as simple performance skills that are developed in an elementary school music class. Music instruction in studios and in school programs have as its principle objective the development of musicianship in students. As a consequence, specialists are employed and curricula are designed to use the allotted time in the most educationally efficient manner.

Training in music is often the result of parental involvement. A mother might teach nursery rhythms, counting tunes, or seasonal carols to her child. In the traditional Balkan cultures, mothers share songs with daughters who work beside them in the fields and factories (Shehan, 1987) while fathers invite sons to learn the art of improvisation in epic song at all-male gatherings that last well into the night (Lord, 1960). In Laos, young boys are challenged to learn the performance of the *kaen*, a bamboo free-reed mouth organ, by their father and the elder men of the village (Miller, 1985). During puberty rites in Australian aboriginal culture, boys are taught their family ties through genealogy chants sung to them by their fathers, older brothers, uncles, and other related kinsmen (Jones, 1980). Young girls in the culture learn from their mothers didactic songs that instruct them in methods of preparing food, keeping house, and raising their own children (Waterman, 1971). While most traditional societies provide for the training of their own young in the customs of their culture, schooling is a more recent phenomenon in many parts of the world.

THEORIES OF LEARNING AND CREATIVITY

Educational and psychological theories of learning and cognition have contributed much to our understanding of how music is learned and taught in the West. Music teachers have adapted theories in their attempts to provide plausible explanations for their students' musical responses and to guide themselves in more efficient presentations of concepts to students. A number of learning theories warrant consideration, particularly those pertinent to aural learning, creativity, and environmental issues—including learning through enculturation. The discussion that follows is not intended to be a comprehensive review of the extant educational and psychological literature on learning and instructional theory, but it does consider those theories that address issues supporting the refinement of aural skills and the development of the capacity for creative improvisation. Aspects of cognition, developmental psychology, sociocultural influences of and behavioral approaches to transmission, teaching, and learning, and the illusive nature of creativity are examined. Some theories have been tested for their relevance to music instruction and enculturation; however, their implications for cultures outside the West are mostly conjectural at this time.

Cognitive Psychology: Learning, Retaining and Restructuring

Cognitive psychology has contributed much to our understanding of how sensations and experiences are perceived and how knowledge is gained and remembered. Since the turn of the century,

psychologists Wertheimer, Kohler, Koffka, and later, Lewin described their "Gestalt" approach as arising from an interest in the
process by which meaning is attached to sensory experiences. The
Gestaltists sought to explain the individual's perception of new information as it relates to past experience and as it contributes to the
individual's composite (whole) self. Perception was thus thought to
be a continuous process of forming and responding to relationships
with people, places, and objects. Early on, cognitive psychologists
viewed the individual's environment as more than simply the sum of
its parts. The Gestalt theory explains learning as a basic reorganiza-
tion in the individual's perceptual field, with consequent changes in
knowledge, skills, attitudes, and values (Wertheimer, 1959).

Contemporary cognitive psychology emphasizes the mental operations that people employ in perception, thinking, memory, learning, and skill development. Cognition is seen as similar to a
computer's information-processing system, in that the processes that
come between the stimulus (input) and response (output) are the
mental strategies that people employ to understand their environment. The encoding and adapting of new information to the old, the
selective filtering of experiences, and the storage and later retrieval of
information are the substance of research in cognitive psychology
today; the implications of these activities for learning and instruction
are considerable (Bourne, Dominowski, and Loftus, 1979; Andre and
Phye, 1986).

Knowledge of the nature of mental structure, including sensory
registers, short-term and long-term memory, and the process by
which information is accessed, may lend a fuller comprehension of
the learning potential of students, and of the interventive and inter-
active strategies of the teacher. Research-based knowledge of changes
that occur in cognitive structures of students as a result of instruction
offers potential for the development of teaching technologies and
testing procedures for students with typical and special abilities.
While traditional studies in experimental psychology focused on the
description of cognitive processes, current interest in the acquisition
of knowledge and in development of mental structures may
strengthen the relationship between cognitive psychology and educational practices (Andre and Phye, 1986).

Among the cognitive strategies employed by musicians, the ability to acquire and retain musical ideas has particular relevance for
understanding music learning and creative improvisation. The preservation of information for storage in the memory is what cognitiv-
ists call "chunking," or the organization of information into easily
retrievable units of information (Miller, 1956). Chunking is a part of
the involuntary cognitive structuring of new information by students;

it is also one of the most useful instructional devices a teacher can master. As teachers present student musicians with melodic or rhythmic patterns (rather than single sounds) to be sung, chanted, and played, these phrases are internalized by students for later use. Complete phrases or subphrases are stored in the ear, the mind, and the appropriate neurophysiological pathways, to be recovered at a moment's notice for use in the act of improvising. The most creative musicians possess the capacity to perceive and process this musical information from the teacher or other sources within the environment, to organize it into aural and kinesthetic chunks, and to reshape it in new and inventive ways. This storing-retrieving-synthesizing ability may be one of the most meaningful cognitive strategies the performing musician can develop.

Instructional theories deriving from early descriptive studies of cognitive processes (through the mid-1960s) include those of Bruner, Ausubel, and Gagné. Of the three, Gagné's *Conditions of Learning* (1977) is the most specific in its description of the progression of sensory information from perception to concept formation. Gagné suggested that the teacher's role becomes particularly prominent in arranging the learning environment for the final problem-solving phase of the hierarchy. It is at this point that the student is presented with opportunities to apply previously acquired information creatively to new shapes and configurations. The bits and patterns of musical information are thus subject to retrieval and reshaping into new musical expressions during the problem-solving act of improvisation.

Cognitive views of learning and instruction such as Gagné's conditions begin to reveal the internal processes of learning and creativity as they relate to external behaviors and to the environment that first triggered them. Continued experimentation in laboratory and instructional settings outside the West may provide a better understanding of those mental processes that may in fact be psychobiological in nature and a part of the human phenomena of thinking musically and creatively.

Developmental Psychology: The Piagetian Perspective

The stage-dependent theory of Piaget offers a model of cognitive development that is supported by an extensive body of literature. Piaget's four stages of thinking through which children pass are widely known and provide the basis for the musical development of children addressed earlier. These stages are the sensorimotor (ages

0–2), learning though direct sensory experience; preoperational (ages 2–7), learning through the manipulation of objects, noting the consequences, internalizing them for the future, thus transforming stimuli to symbols; concrete operations (ages 7–11), viewing objects in concrete, tangible, and systematic ways but not abstractly; and formal operations (ages 11 through adulthood), learning abstractly and with logic and deductive reasoning.

The stages suggest that children be given many opportunities to listen, sing, play, and move to music in their early years. Stage-dependent theory implies—although it does not specifically state—that children should be exposed to music of the dominant culture and to representative pieces from various music styles in order to build their vocabulary of musical sounds. Exploratory experiences with musical instruments can provide occasions for musical expression, allowing children to internalize the function, timbral effects, and performance techniques of instruments. The introduction of staff notation should occur only after preliminary experiences; like Pestalozzi, Piaget would appear to recommend the sound-before-symbol approach.

Various tasks have been devised to apply Piagetian theory to music (Pflederer, 1967; Zimmerman, and Sechrest, 1967). The aural perception of musical elements, in particular the identification of music as one of its parts is altered, has been of particular interest. It is during the years of middle childhood, during the stage of concrete operations, that the concept of conservation emerges. Children develop the capacity to recognize the invariant aspects of an object as other dimensions of that object are altered. The child conserves, or realizes, the invariance of one musical element when another is altered; for example, he recognizes a melody even when it has been sung in a minor instead of a major modality, or in triple rather than duple meter. Conservation is one of the major breakthroughs or passage points in the intellectual development of a child. Conservation of tonal and rhythmic patterns is improved through maturation, although the child may need instruction to show significant improvement.

In a series of investigations that applied Piagetian theory to the development of children's music thinking capacities, Serafine found that "the majority of cognitive processes are not in evidence until age 10 or 11" (1988, 227). Eight-year-olds were quite capable of identifying timbres, discriminating among random melodies, and perceiving structure in simple melodies, but they were less successful at perceiving motivic transformations over the course of a longer composition. Nontemporal processes that concerned perception of tonality, cadences, and transformations of a musical theme have been demonstrated by some children as young as six, but the perception of texture as a simultaneous dimension of music develops much later. Serafine concluded that the hearing capacity may be the same for children as for adults, but that "it is the difference in cognition that distinguishes how different a composition is for the child and for the adult" (p. 233).

No other learning theory has been replicated in so many cultures as Piaget's, and yet due to differences in language, experience, and cultural values, the interpretation of results has been problematic. Cross-cultural studies that apply Piagetian theory to music may answer questions about common features in the development of music cognition and skills throughout the world. Experimental controls will be necessary, however, before we can safely make generalizations about the developmental music learning process across cultures.

Behavioral Approaches: Reinforcement from the Environment

Reinforcement theory of the behavioral school of psychology offers a compelling approach to instruction, child rearing, and the development of interpersonal relationships. Stemming from the observation and analysis of specific behaviors, behaviorism and the closely linked theory of associationism are combined to examine the environment for its role in providing reinforcers as stimuli that evoke specific responses. Behaviorists are concerned with the association of stimulus to response to subsequent stimuli as the network that defines learning behaviors. Learning is thus described as the partnerships formed between stimuli and responses, and behavior is seen as externalized thought—a manifestation of stimulus-response coupling. Psychologists Watson, Guthrie, Hull, Thorndike, and Skinner contributed to the extensive literature on environmental influences in the modification of behavior (Bower and Hilgard, 1981).

Skinner's theory of operant conditioning is at the heart of procedures for behavioral change, whether for naive children or sophisticated adult learners (1971). Stimuli operating in the young musician's environment—the vibrant sound of an instrument as it is played, the lavish praise of a teacher, the acceptance by peers, audience, or expert musicians—are responsible for changes in behavior. According to Skinner, reinforcement can shape musical skills, concepts, and values. Society itself provides informal exposure to music and musical behaviors which it deems of value, and formal training further reinforces particular musical traditions as well as the techniques necessary for their performance.

The Skinnerian technique of successive approximation, or the shaping of behavior by reinforcing each progressive step toward an ideal, is one of the most commonly practiced techniques in the training of performers. Shaping requires that teachers accept less-than-perfect renderings of a musical passage, and dispense approving remarks for responses that are similar to, or that approximate, the desired performance behaviors. The decision of which behaviors merit reinforcement at any given time may be difficult, but shaping techniques provide a useful guide for teaching new performance skills and repertoire. As an environmental agent, the teacher focuses the student's attention on one attainable goal at a time, and performance techniques gradually begin to approximate those of the master.

The components of Skinner's operant conditioning theory, including reinforcement and shaping practices, guide the student through the learning process. These and other behavior management principles help students to acquire information, and some of the external forces of the environment that earlier encouraged learning behaviors (e.g., the teacher's praise) are eventually faded; the student accepts these behaviors and their associated ideas as part-and-parcel of his or her "modus operandi." Still, the teacher as environmental agent, dispenser of approval, and model of appropriate behavior is recognized by behaviorists as a premiere influence of learning.

Bandura's (1977) social learning theory offers a provocative view of the potency of persons within an environment to serve as models of behavior that are later replicated by the observer. Children and students of all ages frequently target individuals within their environment whom they will later emulate; these individuals may or may not be formally designated as teachers within the culture. Observations of models are then mentally organized according to images or descriptive words and thus are more easily memorized. As the student recalls the visual or verbal codes and practices the behaviors first demonstrated by the model, the processes of environmental influences and social learning are played out.

The discovery learning theory of Bruner (1960) and the field theory of Lewin (1951), while cognitive rather than behavioral in orientation, nonetheless explain learning as environmentally affected and less a matter of biological change than a nurturing by people and an influencing by events within the environment. Lewin, a leading Gestalt psychologist, was particular concerned with the life space, the expectations, abstract ideas, beliefs, and memories that influenced the individuals's thinking and behavior. Lewin's concept of life space suggested that the individual is attracted or repelled by aspects of his environment, and that learning occurs when favorable environmental factors motivate the child. The mere presence of music in the home and community is likely to influence the developing musicality of the student; a pleasant learning experience or a kind and sympathetic teacher can also contribute to an attractive musical life space.

Environmental agents such as teachers, parents, and siblings facilitate learning throughout childhood. In homes where parental attitude is positive and involvement in music is extensive, music achievement is likely to occur or to advance more quickly than in homes with little or no live or recorded music (Brand, 1986). Shuter-Dyson and Gabriel (1981) reported several factors in the home environment that may be related to musical ability, including the number of instruments in the home, the frequency with which recorded music is played, parental singing and playing of instruments, and the music interests of brothers and sisters. In a comparison of six-year-old children of Polynesian and European descent, Buckton (1983) reasoned that the greater vocal accuracy of the Polynesian children may reflect the value that family and community place on singing at an early age. In Western and other cultures, environments that provide musical opportunities are beneficial—if not critical—to development.

Learning Modes: Aural, Visual, and Kinesthetic Channels

An important concern of music teachers in the formal instructional settings of schools and studios is the manner in which they present musical concepts to their students. In his modes of representation, Bruner (1966) suggested that there are three teaching and learning strategies: enactive, learning through a set of actions; iconic, learning through images and graphs; and symbolic, learning by going beyond what is immediately perceptible in the environment. To some extent, these modes parallel Piaget's developmental stages, but Bruner's levels can be applied to learners of every age and intellectual stage. A sequential process of learning to read notation is a clear-cut example of the three modes, which may begin with arm and body movement to represent the ascending and descending contours of a melody, followed by line graphs or maps that trace the melodic contours, and culminating with the reading and writing of notation itself on the staff.

Related to modes of representation and central to music instruction is the concept of learning modality, the subject of much research and a theoretical explanation by Barbe and Swassing (1979). There are three modalities or sensory channels through which individuals receive and retain information: aural, visual, and kinesthetic. Each person can claim a dominant modality through which he or she processes most efficiently as well as secondary modalities that complement the dominant channel. As there are differences between individuals, there may also be cultures that emphasize one sensory channel more than another. An exploration of modalities will require extensive ethnographic study, but such efforts may lead to a greater understanding of cognition from cross-cultural perspectives.

The application to music of learning modalities as well as Bruner's modes of representation is fascinating and may assist the teacher in selecting appropriate instructional approaches. Visual learners learn by seeing, reading notation, and observing demonstrations by others. Those who are auditory learners benefit from verbal instructions and from musical examples presented by the teacher, another student, or recordings. Kinesthetic learners develop knowledge and skills by feeling, participating, and becoming directly involved with music in a physical way. The goals for all students are to learn to read music and to develop aural sensitivity; still, there are various avenues for their attainment.

The expectation that students sample music through all three modalities may actually bring about a strengthening of the weaker two sensory channels while also serving to integrate preferred with less-preferred modes. For those who are visually oriented—and this is the greatest proportion of students, due to their consistent exposure to television, video, and films—the task of careful listening to music before seeking its symbolic representation may be the most challenging mode of all. However, in exercises that require the student to listen to musical patterns, to hear repetitions and development of these patterns, and to be aware of their interpretation by various media, the development of aural sensitivity is inevitable.

Creativity: The Intellect and the Personality

While psychologists had recognized the importance of the creative process for at least a century, few had ventured very far from the psychology of concept and skill acquisition by the mid-1900s. Perhaps, as Guilford (1967) maintained, theorists and experimentalists had lacked the courage to tackle the complexities of creativity and concerned themselves instead with simpler thinking and learning processes. By the 1960s, however, a growing number of psychologists had laid the foundation for an understanding of creative thinking. In particular, Guilford (1959) and Torrance (1966) sought to define creativity operationally and to provide theoretical models and measurements of creative thinking.

As the first dean of creativity research, Guilford based his theory of creativity on a taxonomy of factors of intelligence (Guilford and Hoepener, 1971). All the factors, according to Guilford, consist of levels or categories, each representing a dimension of his cubelike Structure-of-Intellect (SI) model (figure 5–1). Of the 15 operations in the SI model, that of divergent production, or the generation of many possible solutions to a problem, was analyzed for its obvious connection with creative thinking. Guilford posited the elements of fluency, flexibility, originality, elaboration, redefinition, and sensitivity as critical to creativity and thus intelligence. It was Guilford's view that these elements would provide valid measures of creative ability.

Torrance developed a series of measurements, based on Guilford's SI model, that were called the Torrance Tests of Creative Thinking. The open-ended format of the tests provided an opportunity for the subject to express qualities of divergent thinking in verbal and

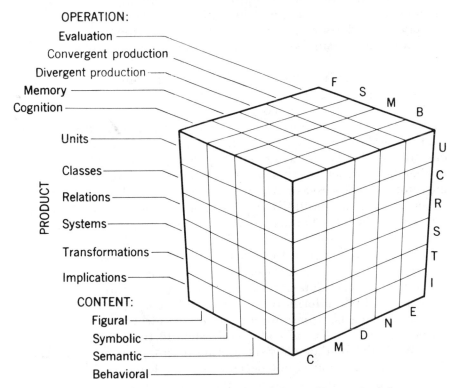

FIGURE 5–1　Guilford's Structure-of-Intellect Model.

From J. P. Guilford, *The Nature of Human Intelligence*, McGraw-Hill, 1967. Reproduced by permission of McGraw-Hill Publishing Company.

nonverbal operations. The tests were translated into many foreign languages, including Hindi, Hungarian, Punjabi, and Japanese, and numerous studies were undertaken to examine the effects of maturation, gender, socialization, and socioeconomic factors on creativity. Torrance (1966) was particularly interested in the relationship between creativity and intelligence, and noted that in individuals with an IQ score of more than 120, creativity is more important in predicting school achievement than any other factor.

Maslow's hierarchy of needs (1954) is unique in its view of personality development of the individual and may in part explain the development of scientific discovery and artistic expression. The hierarchy suggests a progression from basic physiological needs of all humans, such as food and water, to the level of self-actualization, the realization of human potential and talent. This last level is the fulfillment of self and is interpreted to include creativity and personal expression. Maslow's self-actualized individual can think and act spontaneously, originally, and inventively. As applied to music instruction, the development of the capacity to compose, create, and interpret music from the score characterizes the self-actualized musician.

Among Bruner's many contributions to learning is the concept of intuitive thinking, the focus of which is the encouragement of risk taking, guesses, exploration of student-initiated hypotheses, and student discovery of concepts through problem-solving. A learning style that allows creative responses can be nurtured by the teacher who can arrange the classroom for exploratory experiences and encourage occasional nonconformity as an indicator of creative thinking. The enculturation process, in which learning occurs through everyday experiences, quite naturally fosters creative hunches and educated guesses; on the other hand, discovery learning within the parameters of a school day or single class requires an ingenious teacher who can structure creative explorations within a restricted time frame.

An opponent of discovery learning was Ausubel (1968). He proposed instead reception learning in which the material to be learned is presented in final form to the student. Reception learning recommends that teachers pass information to students who relate new ideas to relevant ideas already established in their cognitive structure. While this method consists of oral presentations by the teacher, meaningful reception is not necessarily rote learning. The student must listen intently and seek actively to reorganize his existing knowledge with the teacher's ideas in order to formulate new ideas. Ausubel's theory offers important implications for the judicious use of aural learning in music. Teacher demonstrations of performance techniques, style interpretation, or problematic rhythms can be quickly absorbed by students who listen and then apply such models to their current skills and understanding. Meaningful reception does not oppose the development of creativity; rather, it suggests that new ideas be presented efficiently by the teacher for implementation and further development by the student.

Creative Musicianship: Improvisation and Composition

An early conceptual approach to creativity was offered by Wallas (1926). He suggested a four-stage theory of creative thinking that included preparation (initial ideas and sketches), incubation (informal thinking), illumination (energy applied to an idea to complete the creative work), and verification (evaluation by self and others). As applied to the creative process of music composition, the preparation phase may usher in the first thoughts on melody, harmonic progression, and the overall formal structure of the work. During incubation, which may last weeks or even months, the composer exercises his potential for divergent thinking and for problem solving the possibilities for the composition—whether it will develop through repetition, sequence, augmentation, or modulation, for example. The composer chooses from an array of possible developments during the illumination stage, and then completes the last drafts of the composition to be revealed to colleagues for evaluation during the final verification stage (Webster, 1988b).

The Wallas stage theory and Guilford's Structure-of-Intellect model have formed the basis of theoretical and experimental work on creative thinking in music by Webster (1988a). According to his model, enabling skills (aptitudes, conceptual understanding, craftsmanship, and aesthetic sensitivity) as well as enabling conditions (motivation, subconscious imagery, environment, and personality) influence the process of creative thinking in music, which is demonstrated through the individual's composition (and improvisation), performance, and analysis of music (figure 5–2). Webster's "Model of Creative Thinking in Music" (1989) examines divergent thinking in a game-like series of activities designed to measure children's exploration of instruments and musical parameters of melody, rhythm, and dynamics, their application of instruments in musical question/answer dialogue, and their synthesis of musical ideas in a complete composition for instruments. Along with his conceptual model, Webster's assessment has guided much of the more recent thought on creative thinking in music.

Interest in the musical creativity of children was strong much

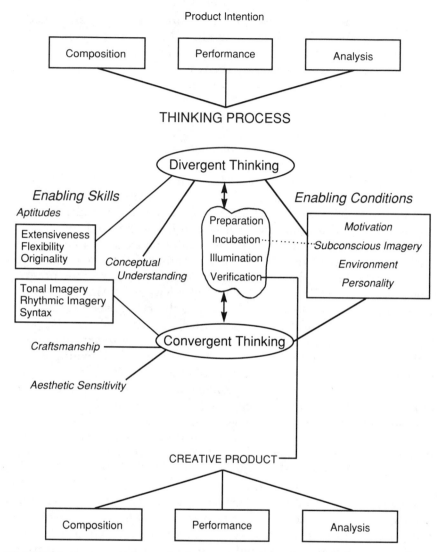

FIGURE 5–2   Webster's "Model of Creative Thinking in Music."

Courtesy of Peter Webster, Northwestern University.

earlier in the century. One of the most comprehensive examinations of children's musical creativity occurred through the work of Moorhead and Pond (1978) in the Pillsbury Studies. Their observations of self-initiated chants, songs, and experimentation with pitched and nonpitched percussion instruments were documented in an attempt to determine the emergent musical ideas of children ages three to six. Along with a discussion of specific features of children's creative improvisations and compositions, Pond offered these conclusions:

> First, that young children have an innate apprehension of the function of formal procedures when sounds are being structured. Second: that the practice of improvisation (vocal as well as instrumental) is at the heart of the matter in the development of the innate musicality they evidently possess. Third: that their constructional predilections are protopolyphonic; that the free use of polyphony is the end that is most consonant with their musical instincts; and that the conception of sound-structures based on organized harmonic procedures is completely alien to them. (1981, 11)

The Pillsbury Studies sought to discover the principles governing children's relationship to music; the results of the studies highlighted the interest and ability for creative musical expression that children display relatively early in life.

Children's ability to think in musically creative ways may be present from birth, to be developed as they mature. Spontaneous singing may be the first clear sign of creativity in music; beginning when a child is about eighteen months old. Dowling (1982) observed that for a two-year-old child, songs will consist of brief repeated phrases, set within a steady beat but with a wandering key scheme so that the melody repeats at various pitch levels. Still, such spontaneous songs have "a systematic form and display two essential features of adult singing: they use discrete pitch levels, and they use repetition of rhythms and melodic contours as a formal device" (1982, 416). Syllables, words, and babbling are often intermixed in the improvised songs of children through the third year. Imitation of songs sung by family members or heard from recordings, television, and radio gradually replaces spontaneous singing before the child enters school. Only through specialized instruction and reinforcement do children continue to improvise as they mature.

Children's creative experiences as composers and improvisors tend to reflect the musical laws of their environment. When six-year-olds were observed while creating songs from familiar rhymes they had previously learned as rhythmic chants, most tended to improvise melodies that resembled songs they had learned in preschool (Kalmar and Balasko, 1987). The "new" music that children invent may thus be the product of a creative transformation of the familiar music which the teacher transmits to them, and which comes to them from the culture at large.

The extent to which children use exploration, development, and repetition in their creative compositions was studied by Kratus (1989). He found that creative thinking in music appears to be affected by maturation, and as children grow from age seven to eleven, development and repetition replace exploration as the more prevalent compositional processes. Younger children are inclined to explore the possibilities of the instrumental medium, with few specific references to music played earlier. By the time children reach fifth and sixth grade, however, they are capable of using exploration, development, and repetition in a manner consistent with that of adult composers.

Children possess the potential for creative musical behaviors although these abilities may often be held in reserve. School music instruction seldom encourages divergent or critical thinking; instead it emphasizes the convergent thinking needed for performance and knowledge *about* music. In tracing the development of creative thinking, Torrance (1967) noted that while such ability increases in the primary grades, there is a "fourth-grade slump" through which nine-year-olds pass. This decrease in verbal and figural fluency and originality corresponds with unfavorable attitudes toward school. Creative ability is seen to manifest itself again by early adolescence in art, music, and mathematics, reaching a peak in early adulthood. When divergent thinking is encouraged through independent self-discovery, or with intermittent guidance often from outside the formal schooling process, there may be no "slump" or static period. While basic research is still needed to refine the construct of musical creativity for children and adolescents, pioneering efforts have already begun to shape an understanding of the relationship of creative expression to music knowledge and skills. Creative music-making through improvisation and composition is well within the capability of elementary and middle school children, as it can also be nurtured in secondary school students.

SUMMARY

The aural acquisition of music and the processes of thinking and behaving in musically creative ways are partly explained through theories of learning and child development. The scope of teaching and transmission behaviors and the learning strategies which students employ in developing skills as performers and creators of music have been examined in various schools of thought. Substantial contributions in formal and informal music instruction have come from efforts of music educators, psychologists, and sociologists.

The matter of enculturation, proposed by Merriam, and later defined as Learning I by Bateson, is acknowledged as an important avenue for acquiring and understanding one's culture, including music. Bruner, Lewin, Bandura, Skinner, and other behaviorists refer to the significance of the environment in shaping the child through enculturation and through the more formal processes of training and schooling. Experiential learning, including exposure to musical sounds before their symbols are introduced, is advocated by Piaget and encouraged through Bruner's modes of representation. To an extent, these theories can also be identified with enculturation, in that musical experiences may be a part of informal social learning or may be intentionally organized by a teacher in an instructional setting. In any case, the appropriate pedagogical sequence is sound before symbol so that notation can take on meaning as a result of prior experience with the musical sound.

The importance of the listening sense in the accumulation of information is affirmed by several theories. Ausubel's meaningful reception suggests that music learned aurally in part may efficiently add to the student's prior base of knowledge, to be subsumed, interpreted, and reapplied. Modality based instruction is of tremendous importance in transmitting information through the students' preferred sensory avenues. Particularly for those students who are aural learners, demonstration by the teacher of musical passages, performance techniques, and style followed by their imitation by the student can maximize the learning potential of these children. For visual and kinesthetic learners, listening experiences strengthen their weaker modality.

The various parameters of creativity have been addressed by psychologists and educators, including the concept's definition, components, process, and measurement. Theories of creativity suggest that creative musical behavior is an inherent trait that is further nurtured through training. The veil of mystery is removed from creativity as the construct is clarified and behaviors are targeted for observation and analysis. Like performance skills, conceptual understanding, and the formation of values, creative thinking in music is becoming solidly based in theory as a quality that is responsive to training.

While learning theories have been aptly applied in various music settings, the transfer of theories by Western psychologists to the learning styles and processes of children in other cultures remains mostly speculative at this time. The combined efforts of educators, sociologists, psychologists, anthropologists, and ethnomusicologists will contribute to a broader understanding of music teaching and learning as a human phenomenon.

PART II

---◆---

Music Learning in
the World

CHAPTER

6

◆

Music Learning in Cross-Cultural Perspective

Popular literature praises music for communicating love and friendship, promoting peace, and restoring hope in the future. The concept of music as a universal language is a romantic notion, embodying the belief that while spoken languages are closed systems that distinguish a culture, music is the unspoken communication of ideas and feelings that transcends all cultures. Although it is true that music traditions of the world share common elements, the treatment of those elements varies widely. Music in many cultures is organized around fixed pitches, but it is the *choice* of pitches and their relationship to other pitches that contribute to the definition of a style. In a similar way, while a rhythmic pulse is found in nearly all music, the duration and simultaneous or sequential organization of these beats characterize the music from a particular world region. Despite the universality of music—no culture exists without it—music is *not* a universal language: it communicates fully only to those who know the unique treatment of its components.

There do appear to be certain features in music that a number of cultures hold in common. Dowling and Harwood suggest that there are "cross-cultural universals" of pitch, rhythm, and timbre, and that it is "the design of our mammalian auditory systems" (1986, 239) that causes people from different cultures to organize their music in much the same ways. Also, certain similar treatments of pitch in different cultures and the widespread Gestalt mechanisms of organizing aural stimuli are discussed by Sloboda as evidence of a "universal cognitive basis for music" found in all cultures (1985, 253). These features might be more guardedly referred to as cross-cultural commonalities appearing in some traditions rather than as "universals," however, since their presence in all human societies has not been verified. At any rate, analysis of music traditions for their shared elements should proceed cautiously, with consideration given to differences in the definition and function of music as perceived by people in various cultures.

As to music teaching and learning, the development of cognitive and creative processes may progress naturally through common stages of human growth throughout the world, although there may be culture-specific aspects of transmission to consider as well. At present, we may want to accept with full confidence only those teacher and student behaviors—as opposed to mental processes—that are clearly observable, considering with caution statements regarding transcultural features of thinking and creating music. As various performance behaviors are seen and heard, they can be discussed as they appear in particular cultures. The frequency of their presence may suggest a cross-cultural need for certain teaching techniques and learning strategies; that certain principles are commonly employed in a diversity of cultural settings may suggest that they are commonsense, practical, and human approaches to music learning.

When considering the development of the young musician in various world cultures, the following principles warrant discussion: aural learning, (including imitation); improvisation (as a manifestation of creative thinking in music) and the presence, partial use of, or complete absence of notation; and rehearsal strategies such as vocalization, solmization, and mnemonics. All these principles, commonly found in a variety of world traditions today—as they were also practiced throughout history—are relevant to teaching and learning in contemporary classrooms and studios.

AURAL LEARNING AND IMITATION

In nearly every society, people recognize the uniqueness of music as the aural form of their potential for artistic expression. The evolution of European art music is tied closely to its beginnings in the oral tradition of ecclesiastical chant, its notational experiments, and the eventual balance of notation and creative expression so carefully controlled by the musician's aural sensitivity. Music is a listening art, and performers must listen most intently to themselves in order to improve their own performance. In the traditional and popular music of the East and West and in many classical traditions of the world, aural and oral strategies are one means of transmitting music (and one that is natural to this aural art form).

An understanding of music requires an awareness of the aural elements, in particular, the characteristics of melody and rhythm. Conservatory training in the West has historically included courses in solfége and ear-training in an effort to enhance the student's aural capacity. For musicians who advance kinesthetically on their instruments, and are capable of a variety of pyrotechnic feats, the ear must keep pace. A number of approaches for teaching music to children encourage ear-training among their goals; these include Dalcroze eurhythmics and various techniques employed by advocates of Kodály and Orff. Such practices suggest that a repertoire of tonal and rhythm patterns be presented to students, so that eventually they can identify a functional vocabulary of isolated musical phrases in the context of a musical work and later use these in the process of improvisation. The aural acquisition of musical phrases is considered by at least some Western educators to be a necessary phase in the development of the musician and to facilitate music literacy and understanding.

In some traditions, aural learning is the principal—and sometimes the only—way music is learned. Learning by listening to master musicians and teachers is common among Ghanian drummers, Indian *sitarists*, European fiddlers and pipers, African-American gospel singers, performers of the Lao kaen (mouth organ), Japanese *shamisen* players, Andean harpists, rock guitarists, members of the Javanese *gamelan* orchestra, Caribbean steel drummers, and jazz musicians. Even where there is a system of music notation, as in much of the world's art music, aural learning may frequently still take precedence.

In a description of learning to play the instruments of the Javanese gamelan through the traditional process, Harwood named observation, imitation, and experimentation as the chief techniques (Dowling and Harwood, 1986). He intimated that notation cannot replace the tacitly implied knowledge that is gained through experience, and suggested that "what is true of Indonesian music is equally true of the western European music more familiar to most readers: that much of our knowledge is also tacit—not bounded by the explicitly verbalized or by textbooks on music theory" (p. 2). Music learning can hardly avoid the obvious channel of knowledge: it is primarily the ear that relays information vital to the performer's acquisition of music and performance technique.

If aural learning is inherent in the acquisition of music, so too is imitation a natural outgrowth of aural learning. Learning to eat, to walk, and to talk is usually a result of a child's observation of a model and his subsequent striving to mirror the model. Imitation is a cognitive process in which the child develops a mental image, models behavior, and practices emulating the model.

A number of theories have been posed on the nature of imitation. Yando, Seitz and Zigler defined imitation as "motoric or verbal performance of specific acts or sounds that are like those previously performed by a model" (1978). Freudian thought interprets imitation as a childhood behavior that occurs when a child has not yet developed a true self and thus seeks someone whom he admires and can be like. Imitation may be a natural part of social learning in which the learner must form an internalized representation or mental image of the modeled acts until acquisition occurs. Bandura (1972) suggested that rehearsal may be key to the acquisition and long-term retention of a behavior in an imitative situation. The conditions necessary for the occurrence of imitation as a learning device include the ability of the observer-listener to discriminate and attend to the model and the importance of seeking behaviors that are visible and thus observable. Bandura illustrates the futility of attempting to imitate behaviors that are not easily observed: "An aspiring operatic singer may benefit considerably from observing an accomplished voice instructor; nevertheless, skilled vocal reproduction is hampered by the fact that the model's laryngeal and respiratory muscular responses are neither readily observable nor easily described verbally" (p. 47).

Imitation is an innate ability that surfaces in infancy as walking and talking skills are developed. The imitation of songs is frequent after the age of two and one-half to three years. Words and small melodic fragments are sung in imitation of songs heard in the environment (Davidson, McKernon, and Gardner, 1981). The child's increasing tendency to repeat syllables and words is succeeded by the imitation of partial phrases of melody, rhythmic passages, and finally, entire songs. The speed at which a five-year-old child learns a song is the result of a sharp and uncluttered mind and a strict adherence to the details of the song in the imitative process. The capacity for imitation remains as the child grows to adolescence and adulthood, although in some societies divergent and critical thinking replace imitation as the more acceptable way of learning. The acquisition through imitation of musical phrases at an earlier age provides the young musician with a musical vocabulary from which to choose should he determine to improvise.

In many musical traditions, the performance of music as it has been earlier performed is a desirable goal. Whether in reference to a single phrase or a complete work, imitation demands an exact duplication of the music. Both visual and aural senses come into play in the lesson, class, or rehearsal as students observe the sound, performance position, and techniques of the fingers, hands, wrists, and embouchure. The student models the teacher immediately following the performance of a single musical passage and over a period of time, using a trial-and-error system.

The effective use of imitation in musical learning is based on an accurate perception of mental image of the musical sound, an ample amount of repetition, and the appropriate kinesthetic adjustments until the correct sound is produced. The various sensory organs serve as monitors of a performance and are used to assess the quality of the music. The bodily senses of hearing and sight as well as the kinesthetic complex send to the mind the feedback that leads to correction during practice. In this way, imitation becomes precise and error is eliminated.

Just as a picture is worth a thousand words, so the teacher's performance is a meaningful device in teaching students the appropriate musical sound, technique, and performance behavior. The actual demonstration of how to perform a given passage appears to be far better than explaining how to do it. Suzuki (1982) recognized imitation of the teacher's performance as a natural part of the learning process, noting that children learn by doing, constantly repeating an activity until they "get it right."

Whether he or she is aware of it, the teacher is serving as a model in music classes and lessons. Performance skills and aspects of cognitive, affective, and social behaviors are learned by students who imitate or are otherwise influenced by the behavior and comments of their teacher. Modeling has been found to influence children's choice of movement to music (Flohr and Brown, 1979); it has helped beginning brass students decrease pitch errors, reduce mistakes in weekly lesson assignments, and improve pitch matching skills (Zurcher, 1975); and modeling has improved the musicianship and accuracy of instrumental performances by college students (Rosenthal, 1986). The use of modeling is more effective than verbal explanation alone, or even the combination of modeling and words.

Two extensive studies on the competencies of instrumental music teachers noted that students in teacher preparation programs perceived or identified as critical teaching strategies the teacher's ability to demonstrate and perform music for students (Parr; 1976; Raiman, 1975). Sang (1987) observed that first-year instrumental teachers spent 40 percent of class time talking, however, leaving only 26 percent for modeling appropriate performance technique and 34 percent for the performance of students. The theory and practice of the teacher as model musician are not yet closely linked, indicating the need for an emphasis on the development of modeling skills in undergraduate teacher education programs. While modeling—and the subsequent imitation of students—may be recognized as an effective technique, teachers immersed in score preparation and behavior management may need to be reminded of the opportunities to serve as model musicians for their students.

In many societies, modeling and imitation are widespread as prominent means of music learning. Indeed, it may be a shared "first step" in the process. The developmental years of Balinese children are centered on imitation of their elders, and they reproduce in play certain aspects of music and dance that they have observed in performance (McPhee, 1938). In the Akan society of Ghana, Nketia (1954) observed that state drummers often picked up the art by watching others play. Among traditional Irish fiddlers, Koning (1980) noted that the tunes are learned by imitation: playing, or first whistling or singing nonsense syllables, a process called jigging. Among the Venda children of the Northern Transvaal, Blacking (1967) noted that the reason for their competent musicianship despite the lack of formal musical training was that they learn to sing, dance, and play music by imitating the performances of adults.

While it is true that a society provides the conditions for teaching and learning, aural learning and the technique of imitation appear to be widely employed. No culture would claim to adhere to an absolute form of mimicry, but in many traditions, the teacher's model musicianship is observed, absorbed, and reinterpreted by students in their own performance. In folk and popular music as well as many art music genres and styles, aural learning and imitation are integral to the acquisition of musical skills and repertoire.

NOTATION AND IMPROVISATION

It was over a period of several hundred years that European composers developed a system for capturing musical sound in symbols on a page. As acknowledged by those who originated and developed it, this system was an inadequate representation of what a composer such as Mozart could hear in his mind and which only he who knew the piece so intimately could accurately reproduce. No musical notation has yet been capable of expressing in a visual way precisely the way the music should sound.*

* There have been many elaborate attempts in the West to develop more accurate representations of musical sounds (see Read, Gardner. *Source Book of Proposed Music Notation Reforms*. New York: Greenwood Press, 1987).

A close approximation of sound is accepted by Western musicians, who express the printed notes in their vocal and instrumental performances. Aspects of timbre, dynamics, and tempo can be only partially conveyed through Western notation, and some systems indicate far less. A personal interpretation resulting from years of listening and study is thus unavoidable; therefore, when a performer translates signs to sounds, a margin of improvisation is evident even in composed music.

In folk traditions and oral cultures in which music is transmitted from person to person without the aid of notation, there may be considerable variation among performances. The music sounds fresh with each rendering, and indeed, it is re-created in a uniquely different manner each time. While the fundamental shape of the piece usually remains the same and certain key motifs are maintained, the details of each successive performance give a somewhat different flavor to the music. The performer carries a mental image of the music's function, its design, instrumentation, and fundamental aural characteristics, but he or she may personalize the music as directed by his or her feelings at the moment of performance.

In the art music of much of Asia, where the traditional lesson calls for teacher demonstration, notation serves as a minimal reminder to the student of what transpired during the lesson. Sheet music and notebooks are memory aids in the absence of the teacher, and the student's memory for passages and techniques is triggered by the symbols for them.

Whether music is learned completely by ear, through notation, or in some combination, a truly musical performance requires personalization by the performer that ranges from interpretation to free improvisation. Improvisation is the musical by-product of creativity and is attributed to the individual who can spontaneously generate a new sound within the framework of a given musical style. The range of improvised music stretches from the ornamentation of a Baroque keyboard work to the melodic filling-in of a harmonic structure in a jazz performance to the expression of an Indian *raga* from a thematic statement through its lengthy development. Improvisation requires that the performer know the rules of the musical tradition; it is seldom entirely free and unrestricted, nor is the process haphazard and makeshift.

The relationship between improvisation and composition is an interesting one, and while they are distinguished by the use or absence of notation in Western art music, this is not the criterion used by certain non-European cultures that employ largely oral processes in transmitting their art and folk music. Nettl cited the example of the Plains Indians who seek visions to learn songs. Once the song is worked out and rehearsed by the visionary, it is presented to the community and "takes on the trapping of establishment, like a composition in the Western sense. The composer is known, remembered, and named" (1974,5). It is composed music, even while it is an oral tradition. Nettl observed that improvisation, like composition, might be divided into two groups based on spontaneity of thought rather than the presence or absence of notation:

> One of these would be the music which is carefully thought out, perhaps even worked over with a conscious view to introducing innovation from piece to piece and even from phrase to phrase; the other, that which is spontaneous but model-bound, rapidly created, and simply conceived. The first gives up spontaneity for deliberation, while the second eschews a search for innovation in favor of giving way to sudden impulse. (p. 9)

As examples, Nettl placed in the first category the music of Beethoven, the songs of the Plains Indians, and the South Indian *niraval* (a vocal piece that retains the text while allowing for melodic variation) song form; he placed in the second group the rapidly composed and almost spontaneously conceived works of Schubert along with highly improvised genres such as the North Indian *alap* (an opening improvisation in a classical work that functions to introduce pitches of rāga to the listener) and certain Persian classical music. It is the suddenness of inspiration that characterizes the second group, and it is this element that is the creative genius of true improvisation.

Improvisation (including ornamentation and the personal reinterpretation and expression of music that came before) is an important cross-cultural feature. Certainly some music traditions permit greater freedom than others: the Baroque basso continuo style, the North Indian classical tradition, kaen music of Laos, the Persian *avaz*, and free jazz, to name a few. In those styles with restrictive notation, improvisation may be no more than an interpretation of tempo and dynamics; these are relative concepts that vary easily from performance to performance and from one performer to the next. In those traditions in which notation is not used in the training of musicians, there are still unwritten parameters to be observed. The culture determines certain aspects of melodic modes and patterns, rhythm and meter, and texture, all of which become the framework of the spontaneously created music. The learning and retention of tonal and rhythm phrases are at the heart of training for improvisation, and the immediacy and fluency of the recall as well as the creative placement of these phrases in a spontaneous performance are the marvels of the musical art.

Although very young children are prone toward spontaneous song, unstructured pitch and rhythm play, and free and improvisatory movement to music, by the age of three or four they replace this developmental stage with the desire to reproduce familiar songs heard in the environment. The music they hear in live performances and through the media of radio, television, and films is frequently the only music experienced by children in the West. The formal constraints of music are then supplied by the culture, which at a later time may become the blueprint for the expression of those individuals who seek out the performance of an improvisatory music as a profession or avocation.

Learning the art of improvisation, as it has been implied, requires a sophisticated and highly developed aural sense. Certain melodic and rhythmic formulas (and, in the case of vocal improvisation, textual formulas) become a part of the musician's vocabulary through training and exposure. Notation is an aid, but it may not be as vital as listening to the style. Jazz musicians and rock guitarists often read no music at all; similarly, pages of Sanskrit notation are more within the realm of the Indian theorist than the performer. The profile of an accomplished improviser would undoubtedly include extensive experience in the tradition both as a listener and as a performer, a keen aural and kinesthetic ability to hear and then play (or sing) standard formulas of the musical style, and a capacity for creativity in knowing which formulas to insert at what musical moments.

For performers of instrumental forms such as might be typical of jazz piano or Indian *sitar*, there are certain patterns that lie within easy reach of the hand (Sudnow, 1978). The fingers find these formulas quickly, sometimes in the first attempt to transfer an aural pattern to the instrument. The bank of formulas expands as the student listens to the master performers, and the facility for improvisation develops as he or she spends rigorous practice time selecting and executing these formulas. The art of improvisation rests in personalizing these rigid patterns with logical yet expressive transitions, dynamic nuances, and variations in tempo.

Vocal improvisation is more restrictive than the instrumental form as the text may control the extent of the singer's free musical play. Melodies might be embellished through *melisma*, or through the use of neutral and sometimes semantically meaningless syllables such as the English "fa la la" or the jazzy scat-song vocabulary of "doo dit doo bee." Passing tones, trills, and glides are decorative means of vocal performance, but care must be taken not to lose the meaning of the words by too many interpolations to the text.

Improvisation is a creative act that demands of the performer extensive knowledge of the music tradition. It is a technique that is acquired aurally, and the extent of its use depends on both the musical tradition of a particular culture and the talent of the individual performer. The more elaborate the improvisation, the less emphasis will be placed on the symbolic rendering of sounds on paper. The world's many music traditions are performed by those who have tuned their ears to the intricacies of melody and rhythm that distinguish the music of their culture, and who then use their performing skills and expressive abilities to create and re-create music within cultural parameters.

PRACTICE AND REHEARSAL STRATEGIES

There are several cross-culturally observable strategies teachers and students utilize for learning and retaining passages and complete works of music. In many cultures, teachers introduce music through vocalization techniques, singing a melody, or chanting a rhythm; their expectation is that students will imitate vocally or "join in" with the teacher through many repetitions of a phrase. The vocalized passages are often as essential for the instrumentalist as for the singer. Special strategies for learning and remembering, called mnemonics, are also practiced in many traditions; these may consist of personal cues devised by the student or systems of learning and remembering melodies and rhythms that are widely used within a culture. Solmization is a mnemonic system associated with the learning of notated melodies in the West; a variety of rhythm mnemonics exist in the West and throughout the world.

Educators generally agree that speaking and oral recitation aid students in remembering subject matter. Vocalization techniques have been shown in Western settings to increase short-term memory (Kellas, McCauley, and McFarland, 1979). The benefits of singing melodic patterns and chanting aloud rhythmic phrases may refine perceptual skills as well. Ramsey (1983) noted positive correlations between singing and conservation of intervals, melodic contour, and rhythm among preschool children. Grutzmacher (1987) found that the echo singing of tonal patterns using Movable Do improved the sight-reading skills of beginning band students, and it also increased their ability to identify major and minor tonalities. While these investigations relate the effects of vocalization practices in the West, similar strategies occur in other cultures that develop aural perception and retention of material.

The use of mnemonics as an aid to memorization appears to be a significant learning device in many cultures. Mnemonics helps to organize information through a transformation or recoding process. Rhythmic and melodic units are easily remembered when associated with vocal sounds that are arranged in logical groupings (Dickel, 1983). An acoustic code is present in mnemonics, and these vocalizations are easily rehearsed and likely to be set into memory storage. Mnemonics appears to be more helpful in rote-learning concrete facts and skills than in developing conceptual understanding, although conceptualization occurs as a result of assembling such pieces or chunks of information.

Mnemonic devices are consistently used in Western studios and classrooms. The solmization of a scale or melodic phrase assigns solfége syllables to pitches; these syllables then serve as associative tools. Singers or instrumentalists who are asked to sing a problematic segment of a composition in study may develop a·better melodic sense of the discrete pitches and their relationships by sounding Movable or Fixed Do syllables. In several improvisational styles of music, most notably the Indian classical tradition, tonal patterns are sung in practice using a solfége system that forms the foundation of later improvisatory performance. Frequently the solfége syllables are retained intact, particularly in the South Indian Karnatic style of vocal performances; sometime the syllables are dropped, and either words are supplied to the pitch patterns or the phrases are vocalized on a neutral syllable such as "ah."

The designation of syllables to rhythms is shared by many music traditions. From the studio instrumental teacher who demonstrates a phrase with a personal system like "dick-ah-dick-ah-dee" to the Kodaly-oriented teacher who chants "ti-ri-ti-ri-ta," rhythm mnemonics offers an important avenue for attaining an aural understanding of a rhythm without the laborious intellectual analysis. The chanting of mnemonic syllables have been found to improve perception and performance of particular rhythms (Palmer, 1976; Atterbury, 1983; Shehan, 1987; and Colley, 1988).

The vocalization of rhythm syllables aims for the transfer of vocalized rhythms to the instrumental or vocal part and gets to the heart of the performance in a more expedient manner than counting out the durations. Drumming practices, in particular, utilize a diversity of syllable schemes in their practice mnemonics. The Japanese theater and ceremonial drums, Indonesian dance drums, the Indian *tabla* and *mṛidaṅga*, drums of the classical court ensembles of Thailand,the darabukka and tombak of certain Arabic traditions, the ceremonial dance drums of Native Americans, and the drumming traditions of West Africa and the Caribbean—all feature unique mnemonic systems that assist the musician in learning and memorizing characteristic rhythms.

Certain common practice and rehearsal behaviors appear to be found among musicians in various cultures. As music is learned and committed to memory, a variety of syllable systems are offered by the teacher or created by the student. Singing and chanting, regarded by some as musical activities to be reserved for the young child, have apparent pedagogical implications at all levels and in many cultures.

MUSICAL STYLE AND ORAL TRADITION

A study of transcultural processes of music transmission must take into account musical style and function. The approach used to learn music for ensemble performance may be somewhat different from that used for solo repertoire, and there may be elements unique to the teaching and learning of vocal and instrumental genres. The function of music may well influence the transmission processes; thus, music performed for aesthetic purposes may employ teaching and learning strategies distinguishable to some degree from those used with music for entertainment or communication. In this way, a culture may determine that art music requires a set of procedures different from those used in folk or popular genres—procedures that may be more formal than informal and rich in social and religious ritual rather than left to chance. The style and function of the music may determine whether learning is formal or informal, intentional or incidental, and associated with enculturation, training, or schooling.

The oral tradition is frequently associated with folk music genres; in fact, folk music is often referred to as "traditional music" or music in the oral tradition. The oral transmission of folk music depends on the memory of the singer and the mnemonics he or she may use to learn a song (Bohlman, 1988, 15). The text may help to recall the music, just as the music may serve the memory as the student learns a song text. A folk musician typically learns standard musical and textual conventions orally, choosing to perform a song in exact repetition of the way he or she first experienced it or improvising new musical or textual phrases. A convention, known also as a formula, may serve simultaneously as a mnemonic device and a catalyst for creativity (Bohlman, 1988, 17).

With the growing use of broadsheets in Europe, and then songbooks that have preserved songs in print since at least the nineteenth century, folk music came to be transmitted through written tradition. Literate transmission is not always complete, however; even today, it is not unusual to find folk song stanzas published without staff notation or with incomplete texts so that the entire story is not conveyed. While intimately related to the oral tradition, aural learning and improvisation are important features of folk music in the incomplete literate tradition as well.

The oral tradition is an important component in a number of the world's art music genres. Their complex musical structures, including highly evolved systems of pitch and rhythm and the brilliant performance techniques that define them, are often learned aurally (entirely or partly) and then improvised. The Chinese *qin* (zither), Egyptian *'ud* (lute), and instruments used in American jazz are played for aesthetic reasons, are enjoyed by small and select groups, and yet are recognized by the greater population of the culture as instruments on which complex, serious, and virtuosic music is played. Their repertory is party preserved in notated form, but the essence of the music is locked in the oral tradition and linked closely to the performer's creative ability.

Art music may be performed for ceremonies, rituals, and worship, but its greatest function is to reflect life in artistic and deeply expressive ways. Experiences with art music—performing, creating, responding—allow an individual opportunities to be inspired, to develop feeling, and to broaden his or her thinking. It is no wonder that the preservation and transmission of art music is taken seriously by people within a culture, and that instruction is often treated as a formal procedure. In many societies, only the most talented are offered training in the performance of art music. It is a specialized training for the few who will benefit most from it, a serious endeavor whose ultimate achievement is the rare but profoundly moving rendering of a classical work.

The value of folk music as entertainment, as an energizer and a socializer, and as accompaniment to dances and games allows it to be transmitted more casually. Folk music is intended to please and to satisfy a broad audience, and it is easily accessible to them. Folk music genres are often less complex than classical styles; usually they embrace repetition and variation on a theme rather than continuous development of thematic material. Commonly regarded as "music of the people," folk music is quickly learned and requires little training. It is therefore less likely to be passed on in organized and institutional settings than is art music.

The style and purpose of music in a society greatly affects its manner of acquisition, teaching techniques, and learning strategies. Folk music is learned through informal avenues, frequently through an enculturation process; the instrumental traditions are often picked up by new players through association with competent musicians. Alternatively, art music in oral or literate traditions is more likely to be tied to the formal training in lessons and classes that schools can provide. Despite the diversity of functions and styles present in the world's art and folk music genres, however, components of the oral transmission process are identified with both.

CULTURAL SAMPLES OF MUSIC LEARNING AND TEACHING

Classroom teachers, ensemble conductors, and studio instructors may find themselves intrigued with the styles of music teaching and learning found in various cultures, and rightly so. Large ensembles without conductors, and performers without scores, sheet music, or even "fake books" are fascinating to many classically trained musicians in the West. The extent to which music repertoire and techniques are informally acquired, in particular the traditional and popular genres, is often a startling revelation. The relationship of student musicians to their teachers is still another wonder; students in certain world cultures bestow gifts and perform rituals of respect in tribute to the ultimate wisdom and talents of their teachers. These are curious practices to Westerners, and yet a knowledge of the context that inspires them provides a fuller understanding of music of a particular culture.

More important to teachers of music, however, is the suggestion that aural learning plays a significant role in the making of a young musician in many of the world's cultures, and that creativity as demonstrated through improvisation follows naturally from the emphasis given by certain traditions to ear-training and the development of aural perception. The oral presentation of musical passages, the use of vocalization or solmization by the teacher and the student, and the imitation of the teacher by the student are behavioral patterns that have been observed in numerous settings around the world. While such practices may appear culture-specific in many art, folk, and popular styles, in that they are generated by a particular culture's needs and values, they are cross-cultural phenomena as well. Furthermore, these behaviors are relevant to the performance of Western music and to the instructional settings in which Western performers are trained. Western art music is a notated tradition, and yet some of the principles of aural learning and improvisation can be successfully adapted to classrooms and lessons in an attempt to develop students' musical sensitivity.

The fieldwork of ethnomusicologists and anthropologists provides many views of music as it is learned and taught. In the next three chapters, a series of cultural samples will present various teach-

ing strategies and learning processes that have been observed in parts
of Asia, Africa, Europe, and in the jazz world. Traditional processes
will be discussed, and changing practices due partly to the Western-
ization of societies will be noted. Some aspects have been gleaned
from the author's own observations in India, China, Japan, Bulgaria,
the British Isles, among Southeast Asian refugee groups, and in jazz
sessions, but most are derived from the comments and analyses of
those with specialized training in the study of people and their music.
These chapters do not attempt to describe all the world's traditions of
music and music transmission nor to give an account of every music
genre within the selected cultures. Rather, the samples are compila-
tions of observations that offer cross-cultural perspectives on music
learning and teaching.

The cultural samples present the processes of music instruction
and performance in a diversity of cultural settings. Some illustrate
music learning through enculturation while others discuss training
and schooling. Some define the role of teachers; others describe
teacher-student relationships. Some present the use of solmization
and vocalization practices to train singers and others illustrate their
use with instrumentalists. Some discuss specific memory and rehearsal strategies while others describe the routine of practice behaviors required by performers. Some show oral traditions of
learning music; others present the use of oral strategies to enhance
the learning and performance of notated music.

Taken separately, the samples are cultural vignettes. Viewed
collectively, they illustrate the preponderance of aural learning and
improvisation in the world's music traditions. The importance of
ear-training cannot be underestimated in the training of young musicians in the West, as it is the most distinguishing mark of the art
form. Moreover, music is a living and creative art form in the world,
sometimes re-created but often spontaneously improvised—or at
least reinterpreted—by the performer. The cultural samples tell the
tales of music as it is traditionally learned and performed, linking
music's aural and creative qualities in the world at large to music
education practices in the West.

SUMMARY

As chapter 5 discussed theories proposed by Western psychologists, anthropologists, and educators in support of learning and creativity, this chapter examined principles of music learning,
improvisation, and teaching/learning strategies that are present in a

number of world cultures. Aspects of aural learning and imitation are evident in Western conservatory practices as well as in many folk and art music traditions; they can be traced developmentally to the natural tendency of children to observe and then mirror the model. The presence of improvisation in many traditions suggests the secondary role that notation may play as a memory aid and a means for providing only the outline for a personally expressive performance. Similarly, the oral recitation and singing of syllables are common practices for learning the basic patterns of rhythm and melody from which improvisation derives. As theories propose ways in which we learn music, and specific principles further explain features of our teaching and learning, we cannot help considering that music and its processes of transmission and performance may indeed consist of features that are cross-cultural in nature.

CHAPTER
7

♦

Traditional Music Learning 1: Japan, India, and Thailand

The traditional training of performing musicians in Japan, India, and Thailand involves an assortment of techniques, some of which are familiar to Western musicians. It is the degree of their use, rather than their mere presence, that distinguishes these teaching and learning approaches from the West. Except for the Lao folk music of northeast Thailand, the genres and instruments of these samples fit the description of art music.

JAPAN

Philosophical Foundations

The education of a Japanese musician was historically attached to and influenced by the religious principles and practices of Buddhism, Confucianism, and Shinto. The followers of Zen perceived music as unexplainable by words and communicable only through souls (Komiya, 1956). Students were "guided toward enlightenment" rather than taught. The discovery of self through a variety of approaches including music developed under the Shogun-supported religion. Individuals were led to learning subject matter in ways that emphasized intuition and introspection. The tenet that "what one learns is not the truth . . . but that one cannot find the truth without it" was strong in the ancient Buddhist view of music learning (Malm, 1986) and remains so in contemporary Japanese thought. Students of music selected by the priests of Zen were traditionally taught in an oral manner, and their "secret pieces" were kept away from the students who could not attain a certain state of grace (May, 1963). The practice continues today by musicians who adhere to the teachings and rituals of specific guilds.

Despite the limited use of written notation, a theory and notational system of Buddhist chant, or *shomyo*, was codified as early as the eighth century.* The establishment of chant schools perpetuated the ritual music of Japanese Buddhism, and the compilation of chant repertoires in schools and monasteries necessitated the development of a fixed notation system to record them. Hill (1982) suggested that with Japanese Esoteric Buddhism, "the teachings of the religious sect may have been secret, but the musical repertoire was codified and written down" to be preserved for posterity.

Confucianism places great importance in filial piety, a respect for the elders; it therefore may be responsible for the widespread use of student imitation of teacher behavior in the music lesson in much of East Asia. Since common people and the young were not thought to possess great wisdom, they were instructed by precept and example. The relationship between teacher and student derives from the beliefs of Confucianism (Harich-Schneider, 1973). The student emulates the teacher, calls him *sensei* (a title of reverence and honor), and measures his own success by the completeness of his imitation of the teacher. The high regard in which teachers are held is notable even among contemporary court musicians of the *gagaku* orchestra, who proudly trace their teacher-to-pupil lineage as far back as the eighth century. These musicians strive for a purely preserved performance tradition, learned aurally from the masters. Still, gagaku has changed significantly over many generations although it retains the essence of its ancient roots (Garfias, 1985).

Ceremony and ritual are the essence of Shinto, the indigenous Japanese religion. Social behaviors with a ritualistic structure are evident in the personal greetings—the bows and the verbal expressions—and are personified in the performing arts of music,

---

* Several other Asian religious chant practices, including the ancient Indian vedas and the most ancient Babylonian traditions, were also known in theory and notated. The technique of vocalization, however, has been widely employed by Asian Buddhists in large-ensemble choral singing as a means of the storage and retrieval of information on the Buddhist canon and its associated literature (Ellingson, 1986).

dance, and theater. Festival music, folk music and dance, and gagaku, the oldest form of Japanese art music, are integral parts of ceremonies at the great imperial Shinto shrines. Shinto has traditionally emphasized cleanliness and order; it may also be related to the manner in which music is performed as a concept equivalent, if not superior to, the musical sound itself. Stage presence, posture, position, and the execution of movement are thought to be indications of refined musicianship. The performance of music is a means to a greater end rather than an end in itself. The issue is not so much *whether* a musical behavior occurs as *how* that behavior unfolds as a refined choreography. While the American teacher facilitates the learning of music, the traditional Japanese teacher guides the student into the ritual of musical behaviors and spiritual communication.

Aural Learning

In the traditional music lesson that might typically be offered for the *koto* (thirteen-string plucked zither), *shamisen* (three-string plucked lute), *shakuhachi* (large bamboo flute), or theater drums found in *Noh* and *Kabuki* performances, a Japanese teacher transmits melodic and rhythmic patterns orally by sounding them to the student who immediately repeats the phrase. Instrumental pieces are initially learned through mnemonics—semantically meaningless aural cues that use pitched or rhythmic syllables to represent the music. The use of mnemonics is a primary and preferred learning strategy although notation is available as a reminder. Each instrument has its own mnemonics structure, and each individual guild keeps the secrets of its style within its own unique system. The student then learns the syllables that indicate strokes, strums, tonguings, pitches, and rhythms, chanting the phrase and sometimes the complete work before the instrument is even approached.

Researchers have investigated the relevance of mnemonics in the memorization of large amounts of information and have found that the neutral syllables are especially useful in the retention of material learned by rote and do not require conceptual understanding (Bower, 1972). In a traditional Japanese lesson the student absorbs aural and kinesthetic elements, an activity that demands absolute attention and focus. The intellectual nature of this learning is initially overshadowed by the requisite imitating and repeating behaviors, and yet the sound and the spirit of the music are channeled into the ear and mind of the student through diligent and directed mental activity. The performer eventually develops a conceptual understanding of the music as the mnemonics are internalized and the musical fragments are combined into a whole.

Following the teacher's demonstration of a melodic or rhythmic phrase, the student is encouraged to play the mnemonically learned vocables. The student imitates the instructor's hand positions and sounds. Seated opposite the teacher, the student must do all movements in reverse—an additional challenge. Through repeated attempts at approximating the teacher's playing position, movement, and sound, the student commits the phrase to both auditory and motor memory.

Master Musician, Master Teacher

Verbal explanations are rare in traditional Japanese music instruction. Instead, demonstration and the physical interaction of teacher and student in the clarification of finger and arm positions are common learning strategies. Instruction in theory, history, and style is incidental and usually not intentional in the lesson. Because notation detracts from the observation of correct performance position, reading and writing are not permitted during instruction. In the music lesson the student's eye absorbs the subtleties of performance etiquette and execution while his or her ear attends to the sound.

Lessons are seldom private, although they are individual. As students await their own lesson, the sound and sight of correct tones and positions are reinforced through their observations of other lessons in progress. If the waiting period is at all extensive, there may be ample opportunity for learning through the merits and mistakes of other students. The teacher may occasionally request that a waiting student perform a piece that another has just finished in order to provide the first student with a listening and observing experience before attempting the piece again. While the private lesson is available on request, especially for foreigners, the results of "group lessons" include the stimulation of a competitive spirit among students—an external manner of motivation—as well as the benefit of considerable time spent listening, a vital element in a largely oral tradition.

In training for the performance art of the Kabuki theater, the young actor proceeds through a similar course of nonverbal and nondirected steps. For hours on end, the student watches and is immersed in the best of Kabuki acting but is never given explicit explanation. The absence of reprimands for inappropriate stage techniques was noted by one actress, who recalled the response of a master-actor when she questioned him on the matter:

> The young person growing up to become a Kabuki actor must find his own way to the part; given time and opportunity for

observation, the young actor will correct errors or deficiencies. We are sincere in our desire not to tamper with or to attempt to influence, or to interfere with the individual expression of the developing actor. (Pronko, 1967, 190)

Instead of extensive verbal analysis of appropriate performance techniques, teachers often employ the Skinnerian method of shaping. Students are reinforced by gesture or brief exclamatory remark for successive approximations of correct sounds and playing positions. In approaching the teaching of Japanese instruments in the Japanese style of instruction, Malm (1986) observed that "the less I said about how to play something, the better progress the student made." Both negative and positive examplars are employed nonverbally in teaching so that students are encouraged to hear and feel the difference between appropriate and inappropriate sounds. Teacher response to student performance is demonstrated also by lingering on a specific musical phrase until it is correctly sounded; only after mastery of that phrase does the session proceed to the next challenge.

The few verbal analogies and examples of imagery that do occur suggest the beauty of the body form: the "beautiful performer" ideal is a key aesthetic component in Japanese music. The specific rituals of picking up drum sticks for the *taiko* (large floor used in the noh and folk ensembles) or the striking noncontinuous poses in the preparation for lifting a small shoulder drum from the floor to the knee to the shoulder are important preludes to the musical sound. Students often use mirrors to study and check their body positions. Performers on theater drums (including the *taiko, o-tzusumi,* and *ko-tzusumi*) and shamisen learn to fix their gaze on the audience and are carefully schooled from the initial lessons to focus on hearing and feeling without looking at the instrument.

Notation

In the *noh hayashi*, an ensemble of flute and drums that accompanies classical noh drama, a repertoire of aurally perceivable stereotyped patterns is the standard goal of the student musician. The performer on the *nokan* (seven-holed wooden flute of the noh ensemble) learns a series of melodic patterns for each section of the drama, singing a specific mnemonic based upon "hya" and "hyo" syllables. The extant notation for medieval Japan indicates a system of symbols that outline the contour of the melody rather than individual pitches or rhythms; precise learning of the melody could occur only in the lesson. Instrumental parts are learned largely through listening, and books of notation serve as cue sheets rather than detailed sources. Often the names of the drum patterns (rather than individual strokes or rhythms) are placed alongside the text of the play, and for the trained musician, the name is a sufficient cue for playing the entire pattern.

Continued audience interest in the medieval noh theater is sustained partially by the audience members' study of the noh songs and singing style. Professional noh performers support themselves in Japan by giving lessons to the million or so affluent adult devotees of noh. In group sessions or privately, the amateurs learn the songs by repeatedly singing the chorus parts of an actual play. The printed pages of the libretto tell very little, so students commit themselves to the teacher as a guide to the subtleties of performance. An annual recital similar to a master class is often planned by the teacher for the students; the principal goal of the performance is "to teach [students] certain specifics while at the same time demonstrating the polished manner in which professionals perform together" (Johnson, 1982). Any deviations by student performers from the master's style are clearly evident and quickly noted by attentive students in their study books to be clarified by the teacher following the recital.

For the student of the *koto*, both the oral method of rote teaching and note-reading are presently employed. In rote teaching, the teacher plays the koto while singing a special series of mnemonics. The student imitates both the singing of the solfége and the playing technique. Seldom are exercises presented; even at the beginning, students are introduced to standard works in the repertoire such as "Rokudan no Shirabe." Lesson books until the nineteenth century gave only poems of the songs with a few private and undecipherable symbols that served as reminders of the course of the melody. Contemporary notation is far more complete, however. A cipher system is used in which vertically placed numbers, read from top to bottom and from right to left, are matched to the thirteen strings. Rhythm is indicated spatially in the placement of numbers in whole and half boxes (see figure 7–1). Students often begin note-reading after a number of lessons in which tonal patterns are presented aurally by the teacher. Once the student's playing positions and techniques are assured through practice, he or she is given notated music consisting of tonal patterns learned aurally.

In "A Portrait of Shunkin," a statement attests to the difficulty of playing the three-stringed shamisen: "People said that with a good teacher it takes three months to learn to play the koto and three years for the shamisen" (Tanizaki, 1963, 22). The time required was due partly to the extensive apprenticeship that existed prior to World War II. The absolute reliance on aural learning, both indirectly

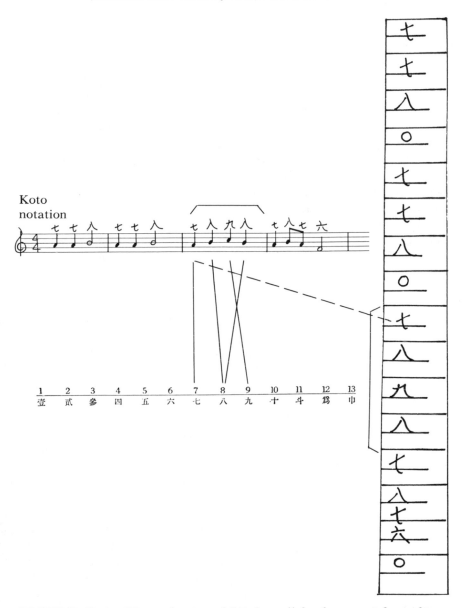

FIGURE 7–1   First phrase of "Sakura" for koto, with realization on staff, and symbols for 13-stringed koto.

through exposure as a live-in member of the teacher's household and through the music lessons, was all-encompassing for those who chose to study shamisen of the *gidayu-bushi*, music of the *bunraku* puppet theatre. Traditionally, no written materials were available to the student; he or she learned to develop a sensitive ear that could absorb not only the gestalt but eventually the nuances of the music.

A student of gidayu-bushi shamisen would later reflect on the libretto of the puppet play, searching for a few sketchy pitch symbols scattered throughout the chanter's text. Although not encouraged by teachers, the use of notation beyond the lesson became increasingly common in the modern Meiji era which began its ascent in the mid-nineteenth century:* "Pupils use the symbols in tablature form as an aid to memorization, scribbling them next to the lines of the text, but beginners are never formally taught how to use them and are criticized for being arrogant if they ask. They eventually learn by copying from other pupils" (Kiyoko 1984, 102). But since each pedagogical school held highly individual interpretations of a character, scene, or plot, the shamisen apprentice learned through experience that the ear was the finest avenue toward the continuity of a musical tradition.

Traditional Music in Postmodern Japan

As Japan became modernized, certain music traditions faded, often requiring state intervention for their preservation. Western classical and popular music, standardized Western teaching methods, and the written score have been adapted, in some cases, in their entirety. The performance of traditional music, along with the processes of oral transmission, is relatively rare today.† Still, for some traditional Japanese genres that have lasted many eras, the aural sense is held in great esteem as an important channel of learning.

The musical training of a performer of traditional Japanese music remains a multisensory approach encompassing aural, visual, and kinesthetic elements. Exact imitation of the teacher is the goal, and "self expression" or improvisation is not typically permitted (Johnson, 1982). Although notational cues are available as reminders following the lesson, literacy is not required. Pitch and rhythm vocables are chanted prior to actual performance on the instrument, and in this way, phrases are committed to memory. It is the student's imitation of sounds and choreographed movements that

---

* The notations in gidayu chantbooks are for the singer, not the shamisen player. Only in the last 150 years has there been much shamisen music because many earlier gidayu shamenists were blind. Thus, they played by knowing the complete text of the chanters. (Communication from W. P. Malm, October, 1988).

† At least, Japanese art music is as rare as Western art music in the United States— although a shamisen concert is more frequent in Tokyo than a string quartet in New York.

gives the music-making immediacy and the possibility of being accomplished without the constraints of notated symbols for music.

INDIA

Oral Transmission

Indian musicians have long understood that notation is only a memory aid and not a meaningful part of the music process or product. One of the chief aims of the first All-India Music Conference in 1916 was to debate the institution of notation as introduced by Europeans in South Indian academies. There was condemnation by some: "Our music is not intended for notation. . . . Even as the Vedas have been preserved without notation, music must be preserved" (Ramanathan, 1961, 85). As notation is a means of transmitting fixed and unchanging musical materials, its place in the performance of Indian classical music has been unnecessary. Written transmission restricts the heart of classical Indian music, improvisation, and its generative patterns that have always been orally transmitted.

The Gharana

The talent of the student, his inclination for disciplined practice, and his teacher's guidance, are key to the making of a musician in India. An important principle associated with Indian music is *sadhana*, a dedication to music through intensive practice and self-discipline (Shankar, 1968). Various schools of performance called *gharanas*, sometimes conceived of as "families by association," have traditionally assured a devotion to long hours of arduous training under the guidance of the master teacher, or *guru*.* Even at the elementary stage, which may last five years for the talented, students are expected to spend about eight hours daily in conscientious and purposeful practice. Ravi Shankar recalled a story about his guru, Ustad Allaudin Khan, which illustrates the commitment of the student to arduous practice:

> Sometimes when he practiced, he tied up his long hair with a
> heavy cord and attached an end of the cord to a ring in the

* *Guru* is a Sanskrit word for learned men who are teachers; *ustad* is a Persian-derived Urdu word meaning master, a title of reverence given many North Indian teachers; *pandit* is a respectful title for a learned man. A Muslim musician may add ustad as a preface to his name, similar to Dr., while a Hindu musician may add pandit.

> ceiling. Then, if he happened to doze while he practiced, as
> soon as his head nodded a jerk on the cord would pull his hair
> and awaken him. (Shankar, 1968, 51)

Some contemporary teachers consider shorter practice periods to be as productive as the marathons if they are done with the utmost concentration.

A high degree of technical proficiency is demanded by the guru; he searches out qualified students who possess the creative imaginations so vital to the process of improvisation. The guru is viewed as representative of the divine, charged with the power to stimulate in his students high standards in performance and creativity. Students become disciples of their guru, developing love, adoration, and complete respect for him.

In India, master teachers are as dedicated to teaching as their students are to them. The most serious students, whose self-discipline and devotion to practice are all-consuming, receive the master's dedication. Cormack and Skagen described the relationship between one teacher and student: "The ustad gives his pupil the maximum personal attention possible. He spends from five to ten hours a day with him, until the disciple understands the mind as well as the movements of the teacher. The teaching of music is the creation of a complete understanding between the two" (1972, 181).

The master teacher is frequently associated with a gharana, a setting still prominent in the training of Indian musicians. Gharanas are recognized when at least three generations of performers following a distinctive style can be attributed to the founding guru (Neuman, 1980, 200–201). Beyond the stylistic similarities in performance, including articulation, ornamentation, and phrasing, a distinctive mode of instruction is also found within each gharana. Teaching exercises are similar from one student to the next. Also, the phrases presented by the teacher in a lesson are used later in improvisations by students; therefore, the improvisations of students from the same gharana bear striking resemblances (Silver, 1976, 47–48).

The guru transmits to his students several elements that cannot be derived from written sources: a body of musical knowledge (melodic and rhythmic ideas and a unique performance style) and the life-style of the musician. A guru's musical style, imitated by his students, may be reflected in an emphasis on or absence of strong rhythmic stresses, or in a particular playing technique—for example, whether to press a string with the fingertip or the fingernail. As a model for his disciples, the master demonstrates appropriate moral behavior and a social demeanor that will likely exclude excessive talking, smoking, and drinking alcohol (Neuman, 1980, 46). Music forms the basis of the musician's life, his thinking, and his relationships; extramusical events are viewed as an interruption in the enveloping process of becoming a musician. The Indian guru operates in a framework much wider than most available to teachers in other cultures and traditions.

The changing contemporary Indian life-style has somewhat reduced the importance of gharanas and has brought about the development of class lessons in schools and universities. At one time, young students customarily lived with their teachers, to be totally consumed by the music. With the growing difficulty of making a comfortable living by performing and teaching, some tradition masters have abandoned musical careers, encouraging young aspiring musicians to do the same. Instrumental lessons are now offered more often as sidelines to professional education in engineering, the sciences, and business. Still, for those who seek performance skills—even in class settings—an attempt is made by the teachers to respond to individual students in the manner of the gharana lessons, with the realization that the direct method of personal attention is proportionate to the student's progress toward becoming a musician (Neuman, 1980).

Teacher as Model

In both North Indian Hindustani and South Indian Karnatic traditions, exercises and compositions are learned through imitation of the teacher and are played entirely from memory. Ramanchandra, a performer of the *vina* lute, describes the learning process as "the thousand times method. Once you learn something in this way, you can never forget it. . . . the 'book' is in your head and in your hands" (Reck, 1984, 218). Every pitch, ornament, and phrase is introduced in the traditional manner: the teacher plays; the student watches, listens, and then imitates.

The didactic approach is largely absent in the training of the Indian musician, and the lesson is generally devoid of theoretical and historical discussion. The emphasis is instead on performance. Ali Akbar Khan, a master performer of the *sarod* lute, commented on the futility of teacher talk in the music lesson: "Talk? Nothing to do with talk. Just like, when you sleep, you sleep. When you eat, you eat. When you learn music, you learn music. Why talk?" (Booth, 1983, 4).

Imitation is viewed as a higher-order aural perception skill. For this reason elementary training features scalelike figures and sequential melodic patterns intended primarily to develop the hearing capacity. Imitation implies listening skills and frequently demands repetition of a phrase to be wholly effective. The internalization of these patterns occurs through singing and rhythmic recitation. This emphasis on vocal practice reinforces the reception of melodies and rhythms by the student, establishing the sound firmly through the association of the physical process of vocalization and the mental art of aural discrimination. Such patterns are later recalled as material for improvisation segments within a performance.

The Vocal Foundation

Instruction in Indian music begins with exercises. For singers and instrumentalists alike, *sargam,* or solfége drills that employ syllables, are the foundation of classical style. Vocalists will utilize the syllable patterns in improvisatory sequences, instrumentalists will transfer syllables to fingerings on their lutes and flutes, and percussionists will develop a sensitivity to melody that remains even as they perform rhythmic formulas to complement the *ragas.* All students perform within the structure of the *tala* cycle, clapping and counting on fingers the number of beats as they vocalize sargam and rhythmic passages prior to instrumental performance.*

In the Karnatic tradition of South India, a typical voice class at the intermediate level is confined to three or four students who sit cross-legged on mats. The teacher faces the class, seated in a similar position, with a low desk in front of him for beating out the tala or word rhythms. A *tambura* sounds a continuous drone throughout the lesson, and a mṛidaṅga drum often provides a rhythmic framework. After the voices have been tuned to the first and fifth pitches of a raga, a scale is sung in solfége at three tempos—slow, double and quadruple speed. Ascending and descending sequences of thirds are sung through two octaves, followed by tetrachord exercises that mix the order of pitches at various levels. The exercises are sung in as many as five different ragas and talas, mostly as a group although occasionally by the individual student.

A new song is taught in small phrases consisting of one or two words of text, with the student imitating the teacher. The song is repeated as the students and teachers sing together while keeping the tala. The quick recall of words and music is the result of extensive lessons, although the performance is not flawless and occasional pauses and uncertainty occur. A third review is followed by the teach-

* Ragas are scalelike melodies that prescribe pitches, ornaments, and other melodic nuances that form the basis of a vocal or instrumental performance; talas are cycles of beats that provide a rhythmic framework for a performance.

er's dictation of words which students write in notebooks. Sargam or solfége syllables are sung by the teacher so that the student can record the more melismatic phrases. Singing is the predominant activity throughout the lesson, with little time devoted to lecture or questions. The teacher maintains eye contact and dispenses frequent approval through stylized responses, such as head shaking, tongue clicking, or brief verbal comments.

The procedure for instrumental lessons is similar to that of vocal music. Instruction in sitar, sarod, sarangi (lutes), shenai (double-reed), and flute is offered following the requisite training in vocal music. Posture and position, fingering technique, and various styles of striking the strings and "half-holing" are demonstrated in the initial lessons. All compositions are learned aurally as the students echo on their instrument the passages sung in sargam by the teacher. Variations of this approach include direct student imitation of the teacher's instrumental performance and student vocalization in sargam before playing, imitating the teacher's vocal or instrumental performance.

For students of tabla or mṛidaṅga drums, an oral language system of mnemonics facilitates the learning of rhythmic patterns. Drum strokes produced by the fingers, palms, and heels of the hands are named by onomatopoeic syllables (figure 7–2). Students imitate both the rhythmic recitation and drumming techniques of their teachers. These are first sounded in separate succession and then together; they are internalized in the final stage. The vocalization of the rhythmic patterns is crucial to student learning, allowing for greater concen-

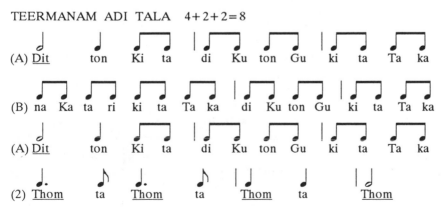

TEERMANAM ADI TALA   4+2+2=8

(A) Dit   ton   Ki ta   di   Ku ton   Gu   ki ta   Ta   ka

(B) na Ka ta ri   ki ta   Ta ka   di   Ku ton Gu   ki ta   Ta   ka

(A) Dit   ton   Ki ta   di   Ku ton   Gu   ki ta   Ta   ka

(2) Thom   ta   Thom   ta   Thom   ta   Thom

FIGURE 7–2   Mnemonic chant for mṛidaṅga drum of South India.

tration and a subsequent strengthening of the memory (Booth, 1983; Bennett, 1981).

The Heart of Indian Music

Learning Hindustani and Karnatic music has been compared to learning a verbal language in that it is learned best through an oral tradition. Once the basic vocubulary of the musical system is mastered, the musician learns to combine the phrases into meaningful musical ideas. As language involves extemporaneous communication, so does Indian music lend itself to improvisation. Booth related an incident that illustrates the ease by which even a young six-year-old might improvise after he has learned the fundamental musical "alphabet":

> We had been talking about the improvisation of gaidas and Suresh, by way of example, began reciting a theme to his son, who had certainly heard and recited it before. Satyajit began to recite along with his father and then went on to improvise, by himself, for five or six minutes. As he kept strict time with his hand claps, he continued to combine the elements of the gaida into new, grammatical "sentences." (1987, 8)

Fixed compositions are taught to instrumentalists and singers following a preparatory phase that often exceeds five years. Traditional melodies of several rhythmic cycles in length are taught, along with improvised passages, in the traditional imitative manner. The South Indian Karnatic style adheres more rigidly to the transmitted version of the composition so that an exact reproduction by the student is often highly valued, while the North Indian Hindustani teacher prefers performance in which the student intersperses improvised phrases in a creative and original manner.

The ability to incorporate musical passages in an improvised fashion is the mark of an intelligent musician. The many years of tonal exercises and rhythmic chanting are spontaneously recalled in the act of improvisation. Although improvisation is not isolated as a separate skill within the lesson, the re-creation of small memorized units of pitches and rhythms developed through earlier exercises becomes the basis for musical expression. The realization of the Indian musician demands a strong educational foundation based on rigorous exercise, extended periods of practice, a remarkable memory, and a capacity for creativity within the limits of raga and tala.

According to Wade, the most memorable performances of Indian music are those featuring "the delicate combination of continuity and creativity" (1986, 4). Both qualities are developed over time and under the tutelage of a master teacher.

THAILAND

Genres of Thai Classical Music

Southeast Asian music cultures share a number of features, not the least of which is the emphasis on oral transmission. On the mainland—in Thailand, Laos, and Cambodia—the presence of gongs, xylophones, lutes, and zithers shows a mixture of indigenous and borrowed elements. Cultural exchanges with India and China for several millennia were influential in shaping the Southeast Asian countries' performance genres, their adoption of certain instruments and their performance techniques, and perhaps somewhat indirectly, their music transmission processes as well.

Thai classical court traditions of the *pi phat, mahori,* and *khru-ang sai* ensembles were historically taught entirely by rote. The instrumental melodies that converge in a form of polyphonic stratification were learned by students on *ranat* (wooden xylophone), *kong wong* (circle of horizontal bronze gongs), *pi nai* (quadruple-reed oboe), two- and three-stringed fiddles, flute, and various zithers through private instruction. The different melodies are not independent; each instrument has its own *tang,* or idiomatic version of a composed melody. Rhythmic patterns on barrel-shaped drums, tubular drums, and goblet and flat drums were acquired through a mnemonics system of chanting the onomatopoeic drum stroke words. Thai musicians developed sophisticated aural skills and memories for a vast repertory of music.

The process of rhythmic and melodic elaboration of an orally learned fixed melody was characteristic of pi phat music. However, contrary to the perception of the music as strictly improvisatory, the idiomatic melodies were learned by ear through the student's precise imitation of the teacher. The melodic sections between important structural points were not spontaneous "filler melodies" but were fixed and intentional, demonstrating a minimal accommodation for improvisation in Thai classical music (Hood, 1975). The master teacher would convey an instrumental part to a single student or to a group of students as it had earlier been transmitted to him, guaranteeing the preservation of traditional court music with little variance throughout the eighteenth and nineteenth centuries.

Cipher and Staff Notation

Until the overthrow of the absolute monarchy in 1932, the patronage of musicians by the royal court nurtured classical Thai music. When the traditional music began to show signs of disappearing, the government funded a project to notate nearly 500 extant court music compositions (Morton, 1976). A cipher system was employed in which pitches were numbered and ordered horizontally from left to right, and bar lines were organized into two-bar beat units (Duriyanga, 1973). Western staff notation was also utilized in some transcriptions, with the understanding that while the conventional symbols designated pitch frequency and duration, Thai and western tunings were quite different from one another. For the double-headed drums that have a repertoire of eleven different sounds, special symbols were invented.

Notation of court music for the pi phat ensemble was carried on by a commission of Thai music specialists for almost twenty years. Some pieces are fully notated, preserved to be played in much the same way they were heard until the early twentieth century. Although twenty-nine orchestral suites are preserved in full orchestra scores, many of the remaining notations consist of only the main melody. Players of stringed instruments in the mahori commonly learn their parts from notated scores, but the teacher, trained in the Thai classical tradition, must transmit orally the stylistically appropriate melodies for the ranat, kong wong, drums, and wind instruments.

The preservation of a genre in frozen form through notation may tend to transform Thai classical music into a museum piece today rather than the live musical expression that was once spontaneously generated. Traditional music of the Thai courts no longer plays a significant part in the musical activities of most Thai people; the absence of personal expression, so inherent in a thoroughly improvised style, may be partially responsible for this indifference. Morton offers another but related rationale for the public apathy toward Thai music:

> Musically, traditional Thai music seems to have reached a stage of development in the golden age of the courts beyond which it probably cannot advance without fresh musical stimulus. . . . For within the system as it stands today, little more seems likely to be accomplished beyond continual restatement of well-tried and overworked musical material. (1966, 105)

Still, Morton later concedes that Thai court music has always offered the *potential* for creative expression within its structural framework, as long as the variation does not destroy the identity of the principal pitches of the melody (1976, 182). The xylophones, gongs, strings, and wind instruments of the various Thai ensembles can combine to produce many simultaneous variations of the principal melody; this heterophonic texture has traditionally been one of the leading characteristics of Thai classical music. As performers today allow for the creative expression that was the practice of past performers, the image of the "frozen form" of Thai music as preserved in notation may be dismissed by listeners who experience the subtleties of spontaneous improvisation.

Traditions of Improvisation

Considerable differences are found between the cultural patterns of the central Thai or Siamese and the Lao ethnic people native to northeast Thailand and Laos. The Lao are distinguished from the Siamese by related but different forms of language and script. The literary and musical heritage are not the same in the two regions. The most widespread form of traditional Lao music is *mawlum*, a style marked by alternating male and female singers accompanied by a raft-shaped, free-reed bamboo mouth organ called a kaen. The sung poetry is memorized from written texts or learned orally by younger performers from their elders. Mawlum is a folk tradition rather than an art genre, and yet its complexity and virtuosity parallel that of the most sophisticated classical music.

Career singers of mawlum improvise, adapt, and add to the original texts and melodies. The oral and written traditions are not separate but supplement each other. As a singing master trains and transmits songs to the student, any new creative impulses by the teacher are added by the students to the copied texts. These become further embellished as students learn to express their own musical and textual ideas through improvisation in performance (Miller, 1985).

Because Lao children grow up hearing mawlum, they come to their first formal lessons already familiar with an assortment of melodies and texts. Singers are not led through vocal exercises, nor do they have vocal coaching as it is known in the West. One report of mawlum training demonstrates the initial emphasis on learning poem texts, followed by learning the music:

> Mawlum Tawng-yoon (born 1919), who began study at the age of twenty in 1939, first learned to repeat her texts without music but soon added the melody. She said she memorized by

first learning the general outlines, then the details, and must
still practice periodically when the material becomes unfamiliar. (Miller, 1985, 45–46).

The mawlum singer's memory is legendary, especially since
some story-songs require several nights for complete performances.
The poetry is fairly invariant once learned, but the melody is mostly
improvised. Veteran performers may even spontaneously create passages of poetry but will insist they are inferior to the memorized
verses.

Miller cited traits of the mawlum singer as enumerated by one
informant, including the ability to "be well-read and able to memorize numerous poems"; to be "able to maintain good rhythm and
coordination with his accompanist," the kaen player; and to be "intelligent, able to choose apt texts, and able to make quick and appropriate replies to questions, riddles and challenges" (pp. 53–54).
Clearly, the singer requires talent and training to perform mawlum.

Lao kaen players appear initially to be self-taught. Closer study,
however, reveals that informal instruction through the careful observation of master performers is the key to learning. There is no musical notation for this instrument nor is there any articulation of the
music theory in northeast Thailand. Kaen music is conceived of in
modal fashion, so that improvisatory passages are based on characteristic melodic figures and harmonic combinations that result from
unsystematic imitation of other players. Kaen playing derives from
exposure to master performers and actual performance experience.

Roles and Relationships

Returning to Thailand at large, the teacher-student relationship, *wai kru,* is an important element in the pedagogy of music. Wai
kru literally means to "honor the teacher." Through a wai kru ceremony one becomes a student of that teacher for life. After a period of
paid lessons, the teacher recommends that a ritual be arranged, complete with offerings from the student that include pig heads, boiled
chicken, rice, cigarettes, eggs, candles, and money. The wai kru ceremony solidifies the teacher-student relationship, so that the teacher
then opens the riches of his knowledge to the student. Before a performance, the student recalls the memory of his teacher. This lifetime
arrangement leads to schools of style that stem from an individual
teacher (communication from T. M. Miller, November 1988).

Duriyanga described the balance between the teacher's instruction and the student's need for independent practice in the making of

a musician during the golden years of classical court music in nineteenth-century Thailand:

> All Siamese musicians received their training in playing and singing orally from their teachers, through constant playing and singing in their presence. They had nothing else to rely upon except their own memory which they perhaps possessed in a very remarkable degree, and if they happened to forget any passage, they could fall back on their teachers. It was only through much labourious grinding that they gained their technical experience and practical knowledge in the arts of playing and singing. (1982, 57)

The music traditions in Thailand require students to be able to learn musical patterns and sung textual passages aurally. In the time-honored process for learning classical court music and various folk instruments and forms, demonstration and imitation are paramount. Despite the notation of court music compositions and mawlum verses, aspiring Thai and Lao musicians learn largely by listening and then by doing as the teacher has done.

SUMMARY

Teachers and students of art music in Japan, India, and Thailand commonly employ imitation and modeling techniques not unlike those of the master teachers of Western conservatories. The practice of listening, looking, and then following the performance behavior of the musician-teacher is common in the training of classical musicians in these Asian countries. While notation is available in these traditions, it is used in Japan and Thailand mostly as a reminder to students of what they learned aurally (and orally) in the lesson; performing musicians of India rarely employ notation at all. Although minimal variation is permitted in the performance of standard classical works by Japanese and Thai musicians, improvisation is the ultimate musical act for performers of Indian classical music as well as for Lao folk musicians of northeast Thailand. In the traditional courts, private homes, and temples of Japan, India, and Thailand, students acquire musical ideas through observation and imitation. This practice, although leading to different performance styles in different countries, has over the years sustained some of the world's most sophisticated musical traditions.

CHAPTER

8

◆

Traditional Music Learning 2: China, Indonesia, and the Middle East

As in the West, the training of classical musicians in traditional China and in parts of the Middle East occurs through formalized private and small-group lessons. The instrumental techniques and repertoire of the Indonesian gamelan are acquired through a process that combines enculturation and formal instruction, with students learning every instrument in order to understand the ensemble and its works in their entirety. Some practices are similar to those in the West; other techniques and procedures are specific to the indigenous culture.

CHINA

Music and the Extramusical

Music and learning have a long and continuous tradition in China. Although performance was occasionally accepted as entertainment, the principal purpose of music was to lead people toward more virtuous living. The ancient phrase "yu jiao yu yue," meaning that music in education should be emphasized, implied that music learning might serve also as moral education. That goal of moral cultivation is adhered to even today. Although the essence of the musical sound is a meaningful part of a performance, the ideology of music—its philosophical, cosmological, and educational meaning—is a far more critical rationale for music's inclusion in the individual's life.

The theory is different from the practice of music in traditional China (and elsewhere in the world); in fact, the two appear to have had almost separate existences throughout history. During the Han Dynasty (202 B.C.–220 A.D.) theory was seldom based on observations of performance, nor did it summarize the general consensus of scholars and performers toward the practice of music. Instead, government authorities articulated the meaning and value of music to reinforce their own ideology. In the writings of the later Ming (1368–1644) and Qing (1644–1911) dynasties, music is interpreted subjectively with little attention to the objectivity of its form and structure. Extramusical symbolism forms the foundation of Chinese music theory; sometimes the aural qualities of its practice go unheeded by theorists. Except as they apply to Confucian ceremonial music, the theoretical writings have rarely been put into practice (Picken, 1957).

Notation and Instructional Handbooks

The notation of Chinese music is a complex system that began to develop approximately 2,000 years ago. An art catalogue dated 92 A.D. gives evidence of notated music as it describes "tone movements" of sung poems (Kaufmann, 1967, 9). Music scrolls from the Tang period (618–907) have been uncovered and although their pitches have been deciphered, there was no indication of what the rhythms for these melodies might be.* Various systems of notation were developed through the ages in China, and all have served well to guide musicians in the realization of religious chant, instrumental music, and songs from the regional operas. Rather than performing directly from the notation, musicians have regarded the written music as a memory aid following study with a revered teacher.

An interesting issue is whether notation is read the same way by each user. In Tibetan Buddhist chant, where notation consists of horizontal curves and colored ink coded for various categories of syllables, there is controversy concerning its interpretation. While Tibetans claim that the notation prescribes invariant qualities in

---

* Recently, however, Chinese scholars have determined a system for assigning rhythms to these scores (communication from Han Kuo-Huang, October 1988).

performance, there is seldom agreement on the interpretation of the curves. Further, each individual singer chants the same text differently over several performances although the singer will claim the performances are alike. Whether these differences result from dialectal variances among singers or simply poor performing habits, the notation is nonetheless only a guide and not an absolute authority in performance (Kaufmann, 1975).

The ancient *qin* may serve as an example of the manner in which instrumental music is traditionally learned. One of the most highly regarded Chinese musical instruments, the qin is a long thin zither of seven silk or metal strings. Indigenous to the region, the qin was referred to often in literature and was associated with scholars who prized the instrument for its capacity to restrain human passions and thus restore man's original purity. As a symbol of scholarship, literary life, and a certain mysticism blending Confucianist principles with Daoism, the qin was viewed as a way to wisdom and the achievement of harmony with nature.

Handbooks were once common sources of information on performing on the qin. While notated melodies form the main part of most handbooks, there were other sections that provided the author's biography; a history of the qin; a discussion of how to build, store, and repair the instrument; a theory of modes and pitch; and a key to decoding the notation. The melodies are presented in a tablature notation called *gongchi* and are set in vertical columns to be read from right to left, with commentary between the columns in smaller characters (figure 8–1). Note symbols indicate the string number to be plucked by the right hand, the position along the string to be stopped by the left hand, and the particular manner of execution. There are occasional circles to show the end of a phrase, and also instructions on tempo ("slow down," "pause," "accelerate"), but there are no signs for the time values of individual notes.

Schematic drawings of the correct posture of the right and left hand are presented in the qin handbooks, with captions that suggest imagery such as a flying dragon grasping the clouds (plucking with the thumb or middle finger) or three clouds sailing together (plucking with the middle three fingers), or a wild goose carrying a reed stalk in its bill (two fingers plucking the same string). The finger notation for qin is in this way not unlike the numbering of pitches for appropriate fingers in editions of Western keyboard music. The finger and hand techniques are often quite specific; Van Gulik (1969, 2) reports no less than twenty-six kinds of vibrato alone. Some techniques may be more kinesthetic than aural, such as this example: "One should not move the finger at all, but let the timbre be influenced by the pulsations of the blood in the fingertip" (p. 132).

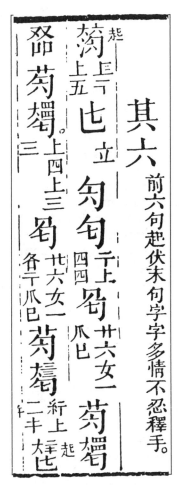

FIGURE 8–1   Chinese gongchi notation, from the Wu-chih-chai handbook for qin, circa 1300.

From R. H. Van Gulik, *The Lore of the Chinese Lute*, Charles E. Tuttle, 1969. Reprinted by permission.

In qin performance, the meaning of the signs can be understood according to the designated code, but an understanding of the spirit of the various touches is far more demanding. The great Ming dynasty master of qin, Wu Chen, advises that "one must understand the meaning of a tune. If one just plays the music as it is written, one will not be able to express the sentiments of the composer" (cited in Van Gulik, 1969, p. 75). To know the mood of the composer and the thoughts he wishes to express is to understand the spirit of the music.

For this, a teacher is vital to the development of true musical qualities that will allow the performer to communicate the ideology of the music and its tradition.

The Traditional Lesson

A student of the qin today becomes skilled through the combination of oral transmission and written notation. The performer who attempts to perform from manuscript alone is still somewhat hindered by the elusive nature of rhythm in qin notation, as Pian observes: "By reading the tablature alone a player who is familiar with the general style of chyn [qin] music can render an unfamiliar work into something plausible to our present-day ears . . . [although] there is still the question of the rhythm of a whole phrase" (1967, 81).

The music lesson provides answers to matters of rhythm, interpretation, and the spiritual essence of the music. Yung (1987) describes the oral transmission process the student undergoes:

> He learns a composition phrase by phrase by imitating his teacher's performance. A common form of learning is for the teacher and student to play the same composition together in unison, thereby insuring that the student inherits the nuances of the music, especially its rhythm and phrasing, from the teacher. The notation, which the student copies from his teacher and keeps, plays a secondary role in the learning process; it serves mainly as a memory aid for finger positions and plucking methods. When a student has achieved a certain level of proficiency—particularly if he is recognized as an accomplished performer in his own right—he may consciously modify the composition according to his own liking by changing the rhythm and phrase structures of the music, aspects not specified in the notation. (p. 85)

Master teachers of the qin provide the student with demonstrations of the appropriate rhythms, phrasing, posture and hand position, and kinesthetic elements that are not clearly indicated in the handbooks. The importance of a choreography is not expressed in words or symbols but can be observed and imitated by the student. The aesthetics of qin performance represent a combination of visual and aural elements, and the tradition adheres to an unwritten choreography of the hands. The movement of the body is a significant factor in tone production as well as in maintaining the performance ritual, whether alone or for a group (Yung, 1984). By observing the master, a student can learn aspects of the music and its performance not to be found on paper.

The Creative Process

Beyond the direct imitation of the teacher, a creative process known as *da pu* is practiced to reconstruct qin works preserved only in writing. The student who has been thoroughly trained in the performance of the qin reads the tablature, researches the literary content of the composition, and makes personal decisions regarding the expression of the mood and spirit of the composition (Yung, 1985). It is likely that two musicians may play from the same notation but arrive at different interpretations of rhythm and phrasing in their performance. Da pu is the privilege of the professional musician who, following years of training with a teacher, has reached the stage of independent musicianship. That achievement allows the musician the ultimate creative process of interpreting the score.

Study of other Chinese instruments follows a similar sequence, although the study of the qin, with its long association with Confucianism, court rites, and ceremonies, is perhaps more formal and fixed. The lighter entertainment pieces of the sixteen-string zither known as the *zheng* are learned orally, with notation serving as a mnemonic. Cipher or number notation replaced the older gongchi in the early twentieth century as the standard system for zheng music. In a similar manner, numerals have replaced the older notation of the virtuosic plucked lute called the *pipa*. The scarcity of instructors in the late twentieth century threatens the continuity of these instruments as their essentially oral tradition requires musical insight far beyond that which notation alone can ever convey.

Training for the Opera

Chinese opera offers a rich conglomerate of the arts, a *gesamt-kunstswerke* that displays song, speech, story, instrumental music, dance, acrobatics, pantomime, and costume design in a single performance. Music for most of the regional operas is learned orally and tends toward improvisation, as the texts and music are rarely written. Only the high art music drama of the elite or educated, of which Peking Opera is representative, is fully notated and based on written librettos.

Actors have always been trained for the Peking Opera by direct transmission. The student actor learns his art from professional actors, either in an academy or in private lessons. When there was a certain segregation of actors from the mainstream of society, fathers passed on their professions to their sons. A system was also established whereby young boys were selected for training at about seven years of age and were attached to one of the large opera troupes. Individual actors were assigned as guardians who were then responsible for the boy's welfare and training as an actor. Although stories of harsh training abound, the result was highly disciplined actors committed to upholding the art and tradition of a beloved Chinese entertainment form.

Among the schools for training in the opera was the Conservatory of Dramatic Art. Founded in 1930, it provided students with a six-year general and professional education. The school was selective, but the training was tuition-free, intensive, and interdisciplinary. Students began their school days with vocal exercises to develop their projection; to achieve this they spoke and sang their phrases against a stone sounding board. Teachers encouraged their students to increase their volume throughout a thirty-minute period. Next, students engaged in singing with instrumental accompaniment, dance, and then acrobatics. Body endurance was constantly promoted through a range of exercises—from those that demanded lengthy "frozen" postures of immobility to those that developed the flexibility necessary for handstands, flips, and the extreme bending of the torso backward from the waist (Scott, 1983). The process of vocal training for the sung portions of the opera found the instructor fully engaged: "Preliminary singing exercises were given without musical accompaniment, the instructor providing onomatopoeic guidance and beating out the time with his hand on a table, while students sang in a low voice following the changes in rhythm, striving to attain correct pitch and intonation" (p. 122).

In Beijing, the National School for Peking Opera trains about four hundred girls and boys who study intensively from the age of ten until twenty-one. Complicated stage actions, symbolic gestures, and the ornamental melodic phrases are reduced to a science by teachers who have perfected their art through an extensive performance career, and who teach through their own modeling of the ideal performance (Alley, 1984). Today, as in the past, mastery of various aspects of traditional opera requires great concentration, discipline, and practice. Mei Lanfang, the great twentieth-century actor-singer, underscored these vital qualities as he recalled his own struggles in becoming a master:

> I was not gifted. The need for diligent practice was all that I understood. All these decades, I have depended on my teachers and friends who have been outspoken enough to point out my shortcomings so that I could correct them in time (Zuguang, Zuolin, and Shaowu, 1981, 11).

Like that of the instrumentalists of traditional China, the commitment of Peking Opera performers to artistic perfection is legendary. Their teachers instill this perfection through the rigorous daily exercises they provide, and Chinese opera devoteés continue to expect the highly disciplined performances that long and arduous training with master performers allow.

The aesthetic principle that most clearly describes traditional Chinese opera (and opera in general) is stylization—of the singing and speaking voice and the body movements. There is a divergence between everyday natural behaviors and their nonrealistic presentation on the stage. The purpose of the physical and musical stylizations of traditional theater is to transcend realism and thus convey the spirit of life. Young actor-singers were led to the development of hand and eye movements, walking patterns, posture, and vocal styles that were fixed in the tradition. The performance was to appear effortless and without strain; this was the ultimate beauty for which actors strived. Their training time was spent in formal lessons and in the informal observations of their teachers as performers. In this way, their learning of much of the performance practices seemed largely unconscious; it was handed down from performers to aspirants through oral tradition. As in the case of instrumental study, learning the opera through listening and watching the masters, followed by imitation and practice, supercedes any other mode of instruction.

INDONESIA

The Gamelan

Among the musical splendors of the world, the sound of the Indonesian gamelan is one of the most spectacular. On the tropical islands of Java, Bali, and Sumatra, this ensemble of instruments can be heard in the royal courts, in urban centers, and in the many towns and villages. Xylophones, gongs, drums, and occasionally flutes and stringed instruments combine to offer an aural experience of tremendous beauty in a form that has remained fairly constant for at least nine hundred years.

Gamelan music is not solely for listening; it is a highly integrated form that is combined with the dance drama, the puppet theatre, and the literature from which their stories are derived. Still, the brilliant musical sound is remarkable for itself. The performers of melody and rhythm instruments center on a principle melody, and each instrument expresses that melody in its own idiomatic style. The resulting sound complex of the gamelan is a many-layered fabric of somewhat independent melodies with certain common structural pitches that relate to the principal melody. For the Westerner accustomed to harmonic textures, this stratification challenges the ear to follow the simultaneous variations in a strange new world of sound.

The Traditional Sociocultural Context

Few gamelan players are professional musicians; they are employed as merchants, farmers, and service workers for the steady flow of tourists through their islands. They consider gamelan performance to be an important community activity, a product of their village, town, or neighborhood. Music for traditional festivals, holidays, and ceremonies is performed by the people themselves, and thus their music rests solidly on its communal foundation. Nearly all the men can play the instruments; generally their sons listen and wait their turn at performance, and many of the young girls learn the traditional dances for which the gamelan plays. Mead observed the involvement of the Balinese in gamelan performance:

> Everyone participates, the distinction between child and adult—as performer, as actor, as musician—is lost. . . . Nor is there any gap between professional and amateur. There are virtually no amateurs in Bali, no folk dancing in which people do traditional things without responsibility to an artistic canon. . . . From the moment an orchestra begins to practice an old piece of music, there is a ring of spectators, aspiring players, substitute players, small boys and old men, all equally engrossed in the ever-fresh creation of a new way of playing an old piece of music. (1970, 145)

Most musicians in Bali belong to a club called a *seka*, which organizes the activities of the village or neighborhood (McPhee 1966). The seka attends to matters of agriculture or road maintenance as well as to public celebrations. Musicians, dancers, and actors rehearse nearly every evening under the auspices of the seka; indeed, they are members of the club. Those not engaged in performance are called upon to maintain and repair the instruments. Rehearsals are public, and since there is little distinction between rehearsal and performance, the community may often experience the rich and evolving sound of a new gamelan composition in preparation for an upcoming festival occasion.

Like the Western orchestra, the gamelan also requires a community of performers. However, while a violinist might make musical sense practicing his part alone without his comrades, one does not hear of a gamelan musician playing alone without singing or chanting another interlocking and complementary part. The integration of individual instruments is key to forming the whole of the gamelan style—thus, the communal basis for the music.

The Learning Progression

The traditional music learning process in Indonesia is best understood by viewing first the behavior patterns of children. McPhee noted that

> their early life is based upon imitation of the elders; their play is partly reproduction in miniature of various adult activities, carried out with a careful regard for detail. They are enthusiastic patrons of the arts, and never seem to miss a musical or dramatic performance.... They sit in the front rows in swarms, watching with intense interest every movement of the dancer or actor. (1938, 2)

Imitation is central to the traditional training of the Indonesian musician. Informal observations at performances and rehearsals lead gradually to instruction within the gamelan itself, more so than through schools or academies. Children absorb the music gradually and naturally; through listening they unconsciously take in the instrumental idioms and formal structure. Their first performance activities are sporadic attempts to imitate what they have heard, sometimes with coaching from the father. Rather than specializing in one instrument, the child learns each instrument from the simplest to the most complex in a gradual process that allows a broad understanding of the gamelan structure. Becker gives this account:

> A child begins his gamelan experiences as young as five or six, at rehearsals in his neighborhood gamelan, by playing the gong which marks the largest formal unit of the piece. He thus learns to experience a complete musical section. Later he may be entrusted to play a smaller gong, which subdivides the largest formal unit. (1980, 23)

Xylophones are added later, from those "fixed melody" instruments with medium density like the *saron* to the high density elaborating instruments such as the *bonang*. The child begins with a total view of the piece, followed by the pursuit of smaller sections of greater melodic and rhythmic detail. In this way, the complexity of gamelan music is learned in small steps that reinforce at once the idiomatic performance techniques of the instruments as well as the formal organization of the music.

Since gamelan playing is not suited for soloists, one does not learn a specific instrument. Rather, the musician learns all the instruments and thus experiences the interrelatedness of the style's structure. While there is some opportunity to specialize on one instrument, especially the more complex ones such as the bonang (a set of kettle-like gongs), the fiddle, and the flute, the player is still expected to be able to shift to other instruments in the course of a concert.

The Musician-Teacher

The teacher's techniques stem from his role as a transmitter of musical information. He demonstrates through his own repeated performances, and thus leads students to a discovery of the correct sound. Verbal exchange is minimal and sometimes entirely absent. One traditional Balinese teacher employed only demonstration, repetition, and imitation, proving these to be effective tools in shaping performance skills:

> The method of the teacher is strange. He says nothing, does not even look at the children. Dreamily he plays through the first movement. He plays it again. He then plays the first phrase alone, with more emphasis. He now indicates that the children are to commence. Two or three make a tentative attempt, following him, and watching every movement. The phrase is repeated, and they try again. Another joins in. Those instruments which do not play the melody are ignored for the moment, for the melody must be learned first; the players, however, tap the tune out to themselves, as they grow familiar with it. Bit by bit the children who are learning the melody go from phrase to phrase, forgetting, remembering, gaining assurance. The teacher remains silent, unless to point out a repeated mistake; generally he is gazing off into space. At the end of an hour, however, several can play through the whole melody. (McPhee, 1938, 7–8)

The Balinese concept of music teacher requires expert musicianship so that students might learn through example the necessary performance techniques and an expressiveness appropriate to the style. McPhee notes further the behavior of a teacher engaged in gamelan lessons with children:

> The teacher does not seem to teach, certainly not from our standpoint. He is merely the transmitter; he simply makes concrete the musical idea which is to be handed on, sets the example before the pupils and leaves the rest to them. It is as though, in teaching drawing, a complex design were hung on the wall and one said to the students, "Copy that." No allowance is made for the youth of the musicians; it never occurs to the teacher to employ any method other than the one he is accustomed to use when teaching adult groups. He explains nothing, since for him, there is nothing to explain. (p. 11)

Creative Improvisation within the Gamelan

In the aural learning of Indonesian gamelan music, the emphasis is on process rather than content. While the gong structure is set for designating unchangeable structural pitches of the rhythmic cycle, most of the remaining instruments are played with greater liberty. Melodic and rhythmic formulas are acquired and form the basis for variation, expansion, and rearrangement that will occur with each performance. Once the formulas are internalized, they are used freely and creatively by the best musicians who create new music while still conforming to certain parameters of melodic contour, phrase length, and general style. These formulas are capable of supporting innovative treatments with each performance. Thus, for the musicians, the process of creating these changes within certain style restrictions is much more in the tradition than repeating a fixed content with precision time after time.

The musician's initial exposure to a gamelan piece requires close attention, and there is little room for improvisation at that time. Traditionally, every part is played as demonstrated by the teacher in order to advance to the next melody, the next section, or the next instrument. After the piece is learned, however, each musician has the freedom to make modifications; in this way the same piece may exist in as many variants as there are gamelans. Hood (1966) refers to nine levels of reference governing improvisation; the final four (instrumental or vocal idiom, local style, group empathy, and personal style) are the factors that most frequently distinguish gamelan improvisation. Tempos and dynamic levels are group improvisatory behaviors, signaled by the drum and responded to by the full ensemble.

In the traditional practice of gamelan music, a deep familiarity with the style, acquired through a lifetime of exposure, serves the musician in the creative process of improvisation. Each gamelan performance is then unique, as each musician's memory of the past converges with the creative impulse of the present. The many hours of melodic dictation and the precise phrase-by-phrase imitation are committed to memory during the learning process. The feelings of the moment allow a personal abstraction and divergence from the original music, while the deeply internalized melodies provide a skeletal structure from which the musician is not likely to stray too far.

Notation of an Oral Tradition

Today, there is a disparity between the traditional oral transmission of gamelan music and the process that was established as a result of the more recent arrival and use of notation. Beginning with the second half of the nineteenth century, systems of musical notation began to appear in the Javanese courts. Because it was fashionable for Indonesians to emulate Dutch models at every level, European modes of thought coaxed musicians into believing that older gamelan pieces could be preserved for posterity through notation. Gamelan music was accepted as fixed music, with no thought given to the evolving nature of its creative and re-creative process. Experiments with notation were attempted from 1886 to 1942, and although the original intent was simply to preserve this music in the libraries of the courts, the pedagogical use of the notated form has had a major impact on the creativity inherent in the more traditional view of gamelan.

Several of the early notation systems resemble the tablature for guitar, with horizontal and vertical lines used to pinpoint pitches, especially for gongs and the melody of the saron xylophone. Another type of notation illustrates melodic ornamentation by wavy lines drawn between the structural pitches of the melody. The Kepatihan system, now well established throughout most of Java, uses a cipher technique of designating pitches by numbers and indicates rhythm through the spacing of the numbers (figure 8–2). The origin of Kepatihan notation is clearly in the French solfége system of Galin, Paris, and Chevé (Becker, 1980).

The emergence of a written tradition can be observed in Indonesian cities, in towns, and in a growing number of villages. Where there once were diverse interpretations of a single piece, there are now attempts to render gamelan music in a close approximation of its preserved form, with apologies offered when the performance is "too far afield." The version of the court is viewed as the ideal ren-

```
Buka: . . . 2   2 3 4 5   7 6 5 4   2 1 2 6
              2 3 2 1   6 5 3 5
              2 3 2 1   6 5 3 5
              2 2 . .   2 3 5 6
              7 6 5 4   2 1 2 6
```

FIGURE 8–2 Indonesian Kepatihan notation, circa 1890, and realization on staff.

From Judith Becker, *Traditional Music in Modern Java*, Honolulu: University of Hawaii Press, 1980.

dition, and the greater the conformity, the more excellent the gamelan is perceived to be.

Printed part-books feature the notated interpretations of gamelan pieces at the courts in Yogyakarta and Surakarta. The young musicians trained to play the published pieces at these courts are in demand as teachers. The formal education of these musician–teachers is requisite in securing positions at other conservatories throughout the country, so their printed versions are then transmitted to their students. In this way, the diverse local traditions of the gamelans are gradually being replaced by a monolithic version (Becker, 1980).

As the gamelan repertoire becomes fixed and standardized in the cities, there are still many rural areas where gamelan pieces are learned by listening. The coexistence of oral and written traditions of gamelan instruction illustrates the merging of the East and West in Indonesia. The West appears not to have influenced the sound of the gamelan itself; still, it will be interesting to note whether further developments in the transmission process (i.e., a greater dependence on printed part-books) may cause an ossified sound that is reproduced rather than created anew for each performance.

THE MIDDLE EAST

Mood and Mode

The ethos of Greek music about which Aristotle and Plato philosophized centuries before Christ was shared by many cultures through the ages, including Persia, Turkey, and other countries of the Arab Middle East.* Contact between the Greeks and Persians may have brought about their similar ideas regarding mood and mode, concepts that were later shared with other Middle Eastern cultures. The *Bahjat al Ruh* (Gladness of the Soul), written by an unknown Persian in the seventeenth century, contains passages that pertain to the suitability of music for certain classes of people, an observation probably made by musicians for many millennia before the writing. In addition to achieving technical mastery of the instrument and genre, the musician was also accountable for adapting his music to his wide variety of listeners (Zonis, 1973, 209–210). Specific modes were prescribed for people of particular physical characteristics, such as skin color, height, and weight, and for those of particular occupations, such as artisans and merchants, kings, scholars, needy men, musicians, poets, and intellectuals.[†]

The same *Bahjat al Ruh* defined rules of conduct thought to be indispensable to the musician. Among them were references to the manner in which learning and rehearsal should proceed:

> [8] Every day he should sing and memorize songs, both easy and difficult, teaching them also to novices so that they become part of his technique.

> [9] He should not sing a tune which he has not thoroughly memorized. (Zonis, 1973, 210)

Clearly, the memorization of songs occupied the musician's time, as did the sharing of these songs with other performers who wished to increase their repertoire of standard songs as well as learn others to use in melodic improvisation.

Oral Transmission

The oral medium was by far the most popular for transmitting music and poetry from the fifth through the tenth centuries in Persia,

* Theoretical writings were particularly influenced by the Greek ethos, although empirical accounts, such as narratives, show no evidence to that effect (communication from G.D. Sawa, November 1988).

[†] Such matters of mode may have been more speculative than they were clearly related to practice.

Arabia, Syria, and Iraq. Written transmission was known but not widely used; although pitches could be precisely designated in terms of lute fretting, there was no accurate system of rhythmic notation until the work of the Arab theorist, al-Farabi, in the tenth century. The oral transmission of music was dependent upon the accuracy of the transmitter, the receiver, and the phenomenon of memory erosion. Sawa (1989a) noted that the odds were against accurate oral transmission of a song, due to an assortment of factors which included

> performance creativity, musical capriciousness [of the performer/transmitter], musical dispositions (taste, style, performing and learning abilities [of the transmitter and receiver]), relative difficulty of songs, intoxication, economically motivated alterations [protection from theft through constant variation in performance], and, most seriously, memory erosion. (1989a, 12)

The receiver was often a future transmitter. Thus, if he learned a song inaccurately, he was likely to transmit it with greater inaccuracy. Consequently, the final product was often quite different from the original music. Music historian al-Isbahani informed his audience that music was compounded from teacher to student over many generations so that "after five generations, the final version of a song had so little in common with the original that the musicians who caused changes had virtually become the composers of the final music product" (Sawa, 1981, 238).

A contemporary practice among urban musicians in Egypt allows for the assistance of a *hafiz*, one who transmits compositions as he has learned them from the composer, other performers, or from recordings to active solo and ensemble performers. His personal interpretaion of a musical work enters into the oral transmission process, and while the conductor (*ka'id*) retains the skeletal melody, the hafiz may alter a piece through

> ornaments, cadential formulae, pitch order, rhythmic values, phrasing, repetitions of phrases and sections, and lexical items. Some of the changes . . . include (1) assigning specific rhythmic values to ad libitum sections; (2) the simplication, standardization, or elimination of ornaments and cadential formulae; and (3) assigning definite pitches to sections previously performed with indefinite pitches. (El-Shawan, 1982, 60)

The custom of using the hafiz as a receiver and transmitter of music provides a more efficient means of oral transmission as it assigns the function to those few with the gift for listening, remembering, and preserving intact a musical composition. The use of the hafiz appears to be an Egyptian alternative to the practice of preserving and re-producing music through notation (although in Egypt both are used today).

The Source of Music

The art music of ancient Persia, which is still heard in the mod-ern nation of Iran, is derived partly from sacred verse and Persian poetry. As in many music traditions in the Middle East and through-out the world, the performance of vocal music preceded that of in-strumental music historically and thus pedagogically. Knowledge of the metrical schemes of poetry provides a fundamental rhythmic framework for the student musician, who may begin with the vocal performance and later transfer melodic, rhythmic, and expressive aspects to an instrument. The guidance of the teacher, combined with active listening to live performances, recordings, and the radio, pro-vides the student with the aural experience necessary for singing and playing in the appropriate style. The occasional use of books and manuscripts, especially for some of the religious songs, provides the musician with the poetry for which he or she improvises melodies (Blum, 1978).

The education of the *naqqal* poet-singer in Iran illustrates the balance between literacy and illiteracy that is prevalent in the learn-ing of art and traditional music genres throughout much of the Mid-dle East (Blum, 1978). The naqqal is a singer whose principal functions are the use of the Persian language for the propagation of the Shi'ite Islamic faith and the cultivation of classical Persian liter-ature. He is usually distinguished from the population by his literacy, which, according to one informant, is critical to learning the written literature of the profession: "You have to sing those [verses] from books. You've got to have books, baby" (Blum, 1978, 44).

The master, or *ustad*, is important to the musical development of some of these poet-musicians, although much of the learning is dependent on books that contain the poems for eventual vocal per-formance. One singer commented that "only a long process of study-ing 'the history of Iran' in books, together with instruction from an ustad," had given him the capacity to recite the "Shah-Nameh" (a religious poem) in a suitable manner (Blum, 1972, 256).

Naqqal generally regard their books and manuscripts as neces-sary for learning the trade, while those who do not read often rely on the mediation of others who read the poems to them. In many cases, the printed poems serve only as mnemonic devices to singers to safe-guard against memory slips and permanent losses of previously learned musical material. There is no reliance on notation for the melody, however; it is learned and retained through the aural/oral process. Subtle variations of text and music occur in the naqqal's performance, and

> the manner in which a performer transfers a particular text through several rhythmic and melodic frameworks, and the extent to which consistent features of his frameworks accommodate a number of texts, demonstrate his degree of proficiency. . . . Competence extends to other levels, as he isolates and reorders particular relationships among words, lines, tristichs or quatrains, and various temporal orderings of attacks, pitches, and timbres. (Blum, 1978, 86)

Occasionally, singers of religious poems create new verses or change the somewhat traditional melodies in drastic ways, but this appears to be rather uncommon. Nevertheless, some degree of variation is expected as the singer maintains the traditional religious poetry while using melodies he has heard to sustain the verse.

Notation as Documentation

Throughout the Middle East, notation gradually appeared as a means of documenting the performer's practice or of illustrating a theoretical point. Notation of pitch existed in the eighth century and notation of rhythm by the tenth century. Although Western staff notation was introduced four hundred years ago, its use as the primary means of learning music in such countries as Turkey and Iran is a twentieth-century phenomenon. In particular, the prevalence of notation in Turkey may have broadened the *makam* (also spelled *maqam*—modes from which improvisations are derived) repertoire, but the freedom of melodic improvisation in this art music tradition is at least one generation removed (Signell, 1977, 31). The contemporary art music of Turkey consists of a greater proportion of melodic phrases standardized through notation than it did just twenty-five years ago.

The learning of urban music since mid-century has increasingly combined oral and written techniques. At the Conservatoire in Egypt, instruction in music theory, solfeggio, *'ud*, and *qānūn* was achieved through written exercises that emphasize Western notation. Sawa described a typical lesson on a traditional instrument:

> The notated pieces were given in skeletal form; it was thus the
> duty of the instructor to teach ornamentation techniques idio-
> syncratic to each instrument. This was achieved orally, and in
> the absence of tape recorders, which many teachers would not
> allow in class, it was a case of "catch as catch can." Students
> with quicker learning ability caught more ornamentation tech-
> niques than those with slower learning ability. (1989b, 14–15)

Vocal music at the Conservatoire, on the other hand, was often transmitted orally since teachers frequently do not read music. Instead,
after presenting the song's text, the voice teacher sings while accom-
panying himself on lute. Students repeat as a chorus until the framework of the melody is learned.

Expressive-Creative Music

The great Middle Eastern traditions of art music for the voice
include composed pieces that are fixed and unchanging from one
performance to the next, but the greater portion of instrumental music is improvised. Music for the *santour* (hammered zither), the *tar*
(four-stringed plucked lute), and the *nay* (flute), among other classical instruments, is never quite the same from performer to performer
nor from one musician's performance to his next. The concept of
improvisation is viewed differently in the West and in Iran; in fact,
many Persian musicians are unaware that they improvise. Nettl and
Foltin (1972) describe the confusion of one young violinist who was
told that his performance of the "same music" differed each time:
"He maintained that this was not so, but rather that he played chahargah [improvised music on one of the classical modes] the same
way on every occasion. When confronted with objective evidence of
the differences in performances, he retreated, saying that they resulted from changes in his mood" (1972, 12). Sometimes the intent of
melodic improvisation of a precomposed piece is to serve as a pro-
tection against the confiscation of one's personal music by another.*
In the Arab Middle East, when musicians are asked to repeat a piece
for the purpose of teaching, some give distorted versions, altering the
melody and its ornamentation to prevent its proper transmission
(Sawa, 1981). The virtuosic flourishes for which the performer may
be known are often removed, and only the structure and contour of
the melody remain.

---

* There are two fundamental types of improvisations throughout most of the Middle
East: (1) alterations to precomposed pieces by means of ornaments, and (2) improvi-
sations in free rhythm that are never duplicated (communication from G. D. Sawa,
November 1988).

According to theorists such as al-Kindi, mood is important to the performance (Sawa, 1989a). The selection of a mode and even individual sets of tones upon which an improvisation is based is thought to be dependent upon the hour of the day, in a way similar to the Indian raga. The series of pitches were thought to create an ambience and to influence dispositions for a particular time. In reality, however, al-Kindi may have copied the Greek theorists rather than reporting practical evidence. In the ten-thousand-page narrative of al-Isbahani's *Book of Songs*, there is no evidence that performers used modes and tones to set mood; like many theorists, al-Kindi may have had little experience with actual practice (Sawa, 1989a).

The performer's *personal* mood might cause unpredictable inconsistencies in the standard form of a musical work. In an "inspiration of the moment," the performer might not begin an improvised piece with the typical introductory tetrachord nor proceed as customary to the next of a set of selected tetrachords. At times, there may appear to be "nothing constant except change" in the performance of much music of the Middle East.

Transmission and Improvisation in Iran

The system of Iranian classical music is traditionally learned through the study of the *radif*, a body of music that serves as the principal teaching material. Within the radif is a tonal vocabulary of about three hundred short melodies known as *goushehs*, which are organized into twelve scalar units called *dastgahs*. These modes are viewed as the foundation for the creation of music through improvisation. Once the dastgahs are learned and memorized, the student is primed for the creation of his own version. The radif is learned from one of several printed versions or from oral transmission by the teacher.

The influence of Western musical culture on the region began to be felt in the early twentieth century. The radif then came to be notated, and teaching pieces were composed and presented as instructional materials to students at the University of Tehran (Nettl, 1985, 65). Before the 1950s, the individual learner's personal radif was delivered to the student. Today there is generally a single accepted radif that is learned through its notation. For students whose schedules are filled with academic courses in music history and theory, general university courses, and part-time employment, the notation of the radif is welcomed as an efficient means for learning to perform.

Still, for those who elect to study with an ustad, the emphasis is on aural learning rather than reading from notation. Older musicians in particular find quick learning through visual means less desirable because it is less encompassing. Contemplation and the association of music with philosophy and mystical experiences cannot be internalized through memorization of the printed page. Teachers have traditionally directed their students in learning small amounts of material by listening, reflecting, and then performing. These expectations may fade further as the pace of the modern world necessitates expedient approaches to learning, including notation.

According to some observers, traditional teaching techniques are still adhered to rather uniformly by the some of the great masters. Nettl described the use of the aural and oral techniques of imitation and repetition as practiced by the highly regarded teacher, Dr. Nour-Ali Boroumand:

> He would play only a short bit in each class or lesson, repeat, ask students to repeat, requiring precise reproduction of ornaments, and of rhythm despite the lack of metric cycle, and then tell the students quickly to go home and practice it. He discouraged their tendency to transcribe the music on the spot, but wanted them to learn from the sound. (1984, 103)

The standard curriculum of Persian classical music at the university includes two radif classes a week for a period of four years. The classes are usually small, with about eight students performing on Persian instruments such as santour, tar, nay, and even the western violin. In addition to the eventual mastery of the radif, students learn composed pieces of the Persian tradition (Nettl, 1985).

In building the capacity for improvisation, the student may learn the master's version of a dastgah mode—or several of its many micromelodies called gousheh—intact, and then be encouraged to play a variant of it. Another approach is for the student to learn several versions through active listening and performance, and thus to experience four or five potential variations. With the former, improvisation may be limited to ornamentation and brief developments, while the latter method provides a more discriminating sense of the similarities and differences inherent in two or more performances by the same musician. By learning multiple teaching versions of a dastgah, the student develops the flexibility so necessary in the creative process of improvisation (Nettl and Foltin, 1972).

The musician is confronted with numerous decisions as he performs in an improvisatory fashion; the foundations of this style are best learned through training with an ustad and from listening to other performers. The performer decides the dastgah, and from that selects the number of gousheh and the order in which to perform them. The variables of a performance include also the transitions between the micromelodies and the manner in which such elaborating techniques as repetition, sequence, and ornamentation may occur (Zonis, 1973, 99–113). The learning of the radif provides the fundamental structure of the music, and while there are commonly used gousheh performed in a somewhat standard order as prescribed by tradition—and by the student's teacher—the performance becomes both personal and creative through the elaboration techniques. The ultimate Persian classical music maintains the traditional form, yet demonstrates the performer's yielding to his own inspiration and musical ability.

The practices of improvisation and ornamentation are important in music throughout the Middle East. The teaching process may be gradually shifting from rote to note, but the development of aural skills and the ability to improvise are still at the heart of music learning, whether it be classical, folk, or popular. The infusion of Western culture has presented the region with new instruments, performance techniques, and the practice of notation. Whether the new written transmission will be accepted, and to what extent, remains to be decided.

SUMMARY

Students in three important regions of Asia continue in varying degrees the practice of learning music from their observations of the teacher's own performance. Throughout much of China, Indonesia, and the Middle East, the long-standing role of the teacher as preserver and primary transmitter of music still prevails. Notation is available for some traditional genres, but the ear is considered the principal means by which students catch the stylistic nuances of the music. Formal instruction frequently resembles Western-style studio lessons and master classes, in which the teacher is regarded as the source of musical knowledge, and imitation, repetition, and vocalization are prominent learning strategies. As for the creative process of improvisation, the outlets for personal expression in the traditional music of China, Indonesia, and the Middle East continue to be many and varied.

CHAPTER

9

◆

Traditional Music Learning 3: Africa, Europe, and the Jazz World

The transmission of traditional music in much of Europe and throughout sub-Saharan Africa has been historically embedded in the oral tradition. Likewise, American jazz evolved from orally transmitted genres, and its improvisatory style is now learned through a combination of reading and listening skills. A sampling of practices in countries from two continents, as well as a description of the transcontinental style of jazz, is featured to illustrate the exceptionally broad-based use of aural learning strategies and improvised performance. Through enculturation and training, the traditional approaches to teaching and learning parallel techniques found in Western classrooms and studios.

AFRICA

The Continent

Geographers and anthropologists frequently divide the massive African continent into two regions: Islamic North Africa and sub-Saharan Africa. Broadly stated, the first region carries Middle Eastern characteristics from Egypt through Morocco, and through the deserts of Chad and the Sudan to the borders of West and East African countries. Sub-Saharan Africa is the non-Islamic and non-Arabic region that lies west and south of the deserts, consisting of a myriad of societies with separate religions, languages, economic systems and artistic traditions. Nigeria is far removed from Malawi, both in distance and in cultural traits, and yet they are more similar in social structure and cultural traits than either are to the Mediterranean North African countries of Algeria or Tunisia. In the following discussion, "Africa" and "African" are used to designate cultures south and west of the Sahara Desert.

Music as Life Experience

Music is integrated into every aspect of African life. While African cultures have words to express distinctive forms and genres of music, few have separate words for the art of music. It is so pervasive and so much a part of the environment that it is seldom viewed as a separate entity. Like religion, music and the dance penetrate every level of existence; they serve as reinforcement not only of religious beliefs but of societal attitudes and values as well. Music is interwoven throughout a culture, providing unity among its members. Performers are not usually viewed as separate and isolated individuals, but as a part of the larger societal unit.* Blacking offered this assessment of the importance of music among the Venda people of South Africa: "Music and dancing permeate every social activity from youth to old age, and no one is excluded from performances: people with hunchbacks or other deformities are expected to sing and dance with everyone else, and they are often exceptionally keen and efficient musicians." (1967, 32)

That music is life and that music learning occurs through life experiences seems to be a perspective shared by Africans. A mother's lullaby, children's game songs, songs of passage through life stages (birth, puberty, marriage, death), and occupational songs are examples of the integral part music plays in African life. Much music is a communal activity, and the acquisition of musical sounds and genres occurs through social experience. In some cases, social position is a strong determinant of who will become a musician. People learn quite naturally through their considerable exposure to music within the environment and the frequent opportunities they have for partic-

---

* An exception is the West African professional musician known as the *griot* (see Cutter, "Politics of Music in Mali." *African Arts* 1 (1968): 85).

ipation. The arts of music and dance are deliberately cultivated in African communities for their social benefits and for their impact on daily and occasional events.

Europeans once boldly and blindly referred to Africans and their cultures as "primitive." Their music, it was thought, was elementary in its pitch relationships and harmonic development. Their rhythms were thought to be corporeal and fundamental—the sort that were found in the earliest stages of Western music before its evolution to more sophisticated forms. That misconception has largely disappeared today. In its place is a high regard for African polyrhythms that layer pattern over unique pattern, with different meters and accents creating an intricate webbing of sounds.

Moreover, music in sub-Saharan Africa consists of more than mere rhythms: the choral traditions are some of the finest in the world. The different scales and tunings that exist from one community to the next are not accidental; each region has its own interpretation of pitch that is intended and purposeful. These tunings create fine pitch gradations that differentiate the music of one group of people or village from that of the next. It is from these tunings that melodic phrases arise, often short and repeating, played in a seemingly endless variety of rhythms on stringed and wind instruments, xylophones, drums, and other percussive instruments. This is but a beginning attempt to describe African music, a style that challenges the non-African not only to perform but even to perceive fully.

Learning as Enculturation

Songs, instrumental techniques and repertoire, and dance are learned largely through informal processes. The distinction between teaching and learning is rare in traditional African societies. Music learning occurs largely through observation, followed by imitation. Jones commented on the informal and unstructured learning behaviors of Ewe drummers:

> There is no direct teaching or school of instruction: it all happens spontaneously. You start as a boy and if you are seen to be musical, your father or musical relations will unostentatiously encourage you. In fact the art is acquired to start with through play, during which one graduates through mastery of two play-drums. (1959, 70)

Music learning begins at the earliest age. In the Tshokwe society, expectant mothers move their bodies rhythmically as they participate in communal dancing in an attempt to expose their unborn infants to music and dance. Mothers move their infants and toddlers to music in swaying, rocking, and shaking motions, developing a sense of rhythm and dance patterns in their children (Schmidt-Wrenger, 1985, 79). Among the Igbo, after a baby is washed it is bounced on the mother's lap to the rhythm of the song she sings. When the baby begins to walk, the mother often dances it along, so that the child develops no clear distinction between the movements of walking and dancing (New, 1983, 45).

Lullabies are frequently sung by mothers to their babies, and even as the babies sleep, there is music sounding around them. Blacking suggested that if "sleep learning" really does occur, then the musical memories of the Venda children are advanced as they fall asleep listening to the music of the adults. He described the relationship of infants to their mothers:

> For the first eighteen months of their lives, infants spent much time on their mothers' backs, and then on the backs of siblings and other children. They therefore heard songs and felt rhythmical movements as their mothers and minders sang and danced or played singing games in many different social contexts. After feeding, most mothers held their babies in front of them in face-to-face interaction, singing to them and "dancing" them up and down. (1985, 46)

As children mature, they begin to look to their peers or older siblings for music-making activities. Children learn, adapt, and create musical games that make up a unique repertoire. They also spend many hours imitating the social behaviors of adults, much of it with the accompaniment of music that is sung, played on toy instruments, and danced. As they sing, they acquire the vocabulary of language and musical style. Since most African languages are tonal, the pitches of song melodies are sometimes closely related to the words and phrases of ordinary conversation. In so many shared musical experiences, children offer each other opportunities to learn music.

The child learns instrumental music as he or she develops the motor capacity to grasp, strike, shake, or pluck the instrument. A young boy may become interested in the xylophone because his father plays; he will sit and observe his father's physical activity, which he promptly imitates even in the air and away from the instrument. In some societies, the child of a particular caste is expected to learn musical skills and is considered a failure if he does not acquire them. Tracey tells of the initial stages of xylophone-playing among the Chopi:

> A father will take his seven- or eight-year-old boy and sit him between his knees while he plays. The boy will hold the two beaters with his arms well-flexed and pliant while the father

claps his hands over his son's and continues to play in the
usual way. (1970, 148)

In this way, the child develops a physical feeling for the instrument;
this eventually leads to the performance of short melodies, rhythms,
accompaniment, and transition figures. The movement of the body is
not reserved for the dance alone but is closely linked to all types of
African performance. Thus, kinesthetic involvement is critical to even
the initial learning stages on the instruments. The union of mind and
body is both cause and consequence of performance of African music.

The Apprentice Musician

Although most learning is informal, there comes a time when
affiliation with an instructor may be necessary. To progress to the
more advanced stages of performance, the young musician must seek
a competent teacher to follow. In the past, the apprenticeship often
entailed subservience to a strict master who punished slow learning
and mistakes harshly. Today the practice is far more lenient but is
nevertheless directed toward developing the student's musicianship.
Knight describes the learning style for students of the *balo* (wooden
xylophone) and the *kora* (harp-lute):

> The actual instruction on an instrument is done by observation
> and imitation, although if it is the balo, the teacher may reach
> over the student's shoulder to guide his hands on the keys.
> Structured lessons, exercises, and practice are largely foreign
> to the tradition. Instead the student is encouraged to partici-
> pate in actual performances in any way he can. At first it may
> be only singing or tapping a rhythm pattern on the back of his
> teacher's kora, but later will include performance on the in-
> strument as well. Instruction is usually limited to the kum-
> bengo, or basic ostinato, but through participation, the student
> quickly learns the basic birimintingo [variations and ornamen-
> tations of the basic ostinato] technique. In an advanced stu-
> dent, this skill leads to the eventual composition of new pieces,
> something again that is not formally taught but grows out of
> the creative element of performance. (1984, 76)

Mastering the Drum

Drumming is an art widely practiced throughout Africa. Those
who acquire the skills for the complex rhythms of a drum orchestra
are likely to be male, the sons of master drummers, and former apprentices, having worked with a master drummer as young adoles-

cents. The hereditary nature of drumming is particularly evident in the Akan communities along the Gold Coast, where there is a belief that the son follows the father's path (Nketia, 1954, 39). For a son to hear his father's drumming constantly as the boy matures is undoubtedly a strong environmental influence on him.

For those Akan who aspired to become members of state drum ensembles, the training in the past was intensive. Secondary drummers learned through observation, but the development of master drummers required more rigorous lessons. Techniques for learning drums are described by Nketia:

> Instruction was not always on drums: sometimes it was on boards, bamboo or short branches of rafia palm. Instructors spoke rhythms—sometimes in intelligible utterances, sometimes in nonsense syllables, especially if there happened to be some unwanted person about. Sometimes rhythms were tapped behind the shoulder blades of a pupil to give him some idea of the distribution of the sequences of drum beats to the hands. This training sometimes extended over years for boys, during which rhythms were memorized and technique mastered. (1953, 40)

Drum lessons among the Ewe of Ghana featured techniques of demonstration and imitation as well as a kinesthetic approach for slower learners that was more extreme than the shoulder tapping of the Akan:

> Less talented persons are made to lie on the ground barebacked and face-downwards, while the master sits astride them and beats the rhythms into their body and soul. There is a less drastic method which consists of imitating the rhythms orally. A third method consists in allowing the pupil to repeat on his own drum what the master plays. (Cudjoe, 1953, 284)

The transmission of drum music in Africa entails the use of mnemonic syllables or phrases. Duration, timbre, accents, and strokes are learned and retained through a system of "oral notation." Kubik described the mnemonic system of drumming in Malawi, noting that "syllables containing the affricate sound *ch*, for example, usually indicate where the beat is, the basic reference line; plosives, such as *k*, *p* or *t*, indicate accents or accentuated strokes, while nasal sounds such as *m*, *n* or, especially *ñ* often show mute or 'empty' pulses" (1987, 78). Other instruments are learned through the use of mnemonics as well; rural and urban, traditional and Western-style popular music employ this oral notation in transmitting songs, melodies, and rhythms.

The African "talking drum" is a phenomenon that translates

poetry into rhythm.* Words of a tonal language are beaten out on a drum, their pitches produced by squeezing and releasing the cords that run from one drumhead to the other. The drummer breaks down the elaborate and repetitive language of poetry into rhythmic groups, each of which is followed by a brief pause to separate the poem's lines and stanzas. An illustration of the close music-language relationship of the talking drum is the incident told by one linguist who asked the drummer to recite a poem without playing the drum, as it was interfering with the linguistic sounds which the researcher hoped to hear more clearly. The drummer reluctantly obliged, yet continued to tap his fingers on the table in the same rhythm of his oral performance (Bird, 1976, 90). The association of rhythms and words in drum performance is not easily dismissed, nor can the kinesthetics be neatly removed from the oral (and aural) entity. The drummer learns rhythms through mnemonics or nonwritten aural pieces and recalls these strategies with each performance.

In certain African societies, drums are usually learned in a sequence progressing from simple to more complex techniques. Training for the Mandinka drum troupe in West Africa offers an illustration of the hierarchy of drum ranks through which one progresses in order to attain the position of lead drummer. There are three drum types within the ensemble, each with its distinctive performance technique and rhythm vocabulary. Beginners learn the drum that starts the ensemble and is associated with less variation. Then a second drum and its repertoire of rhythms is learned. Because this drum is related to the first, the performance technique is familiar and the apprentice can begin to improvise more freely, developing a personal style of performance that was not possible earlier. He learns the lead drum only after he has acquired considerable performance experience on the first two drums. Playing the lead drum requires a large vocabulary of rhythms and strokes and an ability to respond in an improvisatory manner to singers, dancers, and athletes also engaged in performance. Improvisation is key to drumming among the Mandinka; it is a highly regarded skill that is developed most efficiently in the learning sequence of the three drums (Knight, 1984, 83–84).

Vocal Traditions

In African vocal practices, the voices are not trained in the Western sense. Singers use no warm-up exercises or scales to prepare

---

* To a person outside the culture, the talking drum appears to be a musical instrument, but for those who speak the language, the drum rhythms may be more a transformation of the poetry than music in the Western sense.

them for public performance. And yet the voice is viewed as a principal vehicle of musical expression in every African society. Since voices are used to echo speech and to convey thoughts, a command of the language and a mind for improvisation are essential factors for singers. Vocal technique is not as important as it is in the West; rather, the aim of vocal music is to communicate intelligently and expressively to an audience.

In the Mandingo culture, a professional poet called a *jaliya* learns to express a refined style of verse in song through an apprenticeship. While boys may learn an instrument over a period of seven to ten years, young girls learn singing as a part of their development toward womanhood.* Singing is embedded quite naturally in their daily activities. One woman poet comments, "You can learn singing by sitting near a singer. The voice is not controlled by any teacher. It is natural. Some voices are good, others are not" (Bai Konteh, in Knight, 1984, 75). The observation of other poet-singers and then a gradual immersion in the performance experience nurtures the student's necessary skills. Although the art of singing requires no formal instruction in vocal production techniques—that is, through lessons or schooling—an informal apprenticeship appears to be a common practice.

Improvisation plays a significant part in vocal performance, and so through listening and singing experiences, spontaneous musical expression evolves. In the African Apostolic Church, a syncretic religious sect in Zimbabwe and five Central African nations, improvisatory singing is the ideal. The religion merges Christian and indigenous African beliefs and practices, using song as a didactic means of offering ethical messages and biblical passages. Songs are not written down, and both the text and music are highly improvised. Outside the religious ceremonies, free-floating verses are taught in special song sessions that form the basis for the improvisation that will develop in the service. By using these taught songs as models, singers can then develop their own personal styles of improvisation as their religion inspires them (Jules-Rossette, 1985, 122).

Composed Music in an Oral Tradition

In experiencing the performance of an African ensemble of voices, instruments, and dancers, the observer is convinced that a mastermind must have designed such a sophisticated event. Chopi villages each have their own *ngodo* (a large ensemble), led by a mu-

---

* Some African societies also permit women to learn instruments.

sical director who also serves as composer. Every two years, a new piece is composed and performed, although none of the poem's words, the music, or the dance's instructions are written down. Tracey (1970, 2–7) describes the composer's creative composition and the production of a ngodo work, noting that first a poem is worked out, then a musical setting, and then a dance choreography. Once the verse and a melody or motive is aurally in mind, the composer develops the work by playing by himself at the xylophone. Eventually the orchestra is called together and the composer presents the theme and its potential variations. The composition process becomes communal as the individual musicians improvise on the central melody but utilize the musical variations of the composer's suggestions. An introduction and coda are devised, and the dance leader then develops a movement sequence by working closely with the composer and his ensemble.

Listening and Creating

The development of a performance akin to a symphony and its ballet illustrates not only the composer's fine imagination but also the ensemble players' incredible capacity for aural learning and retention. That the Chopi compose a ngodo piece and then discard it within two years is illustrative of the greater significance Africans place on the process of creation than on the performance itself.

The transmission of music in traditional African societies continues to utilize an aural approach based on informal and directed observation, demonstration by accomplished musicians and teachers, and imitation. Cudjoe's (1953) assessment of qualities for fulfilling the musical potential among the Ewe might be applied to all Africans: "an exceedingly sensitive ear, a good memory and sense of timing as well as considerable powers of observation" (p. 284). Since music is so deeply embedded in the social matrix and life patterns of a community, music learning occurs as part of the social development of the individual within the culture. As part of the enculturation process, which extends through life, music is a device for self-image and for understanding the world.

All young children learn the songs of their culture through an osmotic process; for those who seek instrumental techniques or even a profession as a chief instrumentalist or poet-singer, directed learning is available through apprenticeships. Players' rich use of improvisation in African music is a result of their long-term exposure to the sound patterns of the style and a belief that music should provide the outlet for personal expression. As music is a meaningful part of African life, music learning is considered vital to the full flowering of the individual.

EUROPE

Features of Traditional Music

The traditional folk music of Europe is distinguished from other music traditions of the world in a number of ways. The strophic form, in which a melody is repeated with different words each time, is far more prevalent in the music of Europe than elsewhere in the world. Stanzas consisting of three to six lines are sung to the same melody verse after verse. Melodies vary from those in children's songs and chants that use two and three pitches to the melodies that incorporate five, six, and seven pitches, but all have a tendency to fit within the diatonic structure. European music is generally isometric, consisting of the same number of pulses "per measure," in that the rhythms are ordered cyclically into sets of strong and weak beats that then constitute meter.

Until the 1960s, there was some adherence among scholars to a "seepage theory," which suggested that folk music may be a corruption of art music from an earlier generation (Bartok, 1931). This theory questioned the ability of peasant people to compose their own songs, as if only the more civilized members of the high culture could be musically expressive in an original way, while peasants were relegated to re-creative tasks. A more widely held belief today is that exchanges occur between folk and art music, so that a culture's traditional music is an amalgam of multiple layers within that society. Current thought is that the two styles are integrated, and Blacking's observation may reflect this view: "I no longer understand the history and structures of European 'art' music as clearly as I did; and I can see no useful distinction between the terms 'folk' and 'art' music, except as commercial labels" (1974, x).

European folk music has been traditionally preserved in an oral manner, passed on by word of mouth. An individual listens and observes the musical performance and then imitates what he has perceived. The memory is critical in grasping the song's melodic shape and rhythmic features and the substance of the text. For music to be preserved intact and unchanged is rare; alterations are always likely to occur in an oral tradition as the individual modifies the music to fit his or her vocal range, instrumental skills, aural ability, kinesthetic techniques, and capacity for remembering. Personal expres-

sion and interpretation are also factors affecting a song's continuity
and change. On occasion, even a musical pastiche may arise as the
individual fills in memory gaps with original material, or when several songs are interwoven, sometimes entirely by accident. Mistakes
in learning the song may change a tune considerably, resulting in a
uniquely new song. The absence of notation in the oral tradition of
folk music nearly guarantees that no two versions will be precisely
the same. Musical change over time and distance is thus inevitable.

Literate segments of Western society sometimes consider unprinted music, poetry, and stories as inferior to those in print. Yet,
oral literature can express sophisticated thoughts that can be structured in complex ways and presented with a virtuosity that parallels
the presentations of any printed forms. European communities un-
schooled in the ways of writing their music, or more rarely, their
literature, resort to word-of-mouth processes. Music in the oral
tradition—which may sometimes enhance the preservation of a culture's literature, as in the case of the narrative song—holds aesthetic
properties for those who perform and for those who listen, and the
issue of literacy is rarely significant to the power of the performance.
Genres and styles from various European countries illustrate the
transmission process more completely, including the preponderant
use of observation, imitation, and improvisation techniques.

Ireland: Ornamental and Improvised Music

Among traditional Irish musicians, there is a complex and
highly ornamented style of singing in Gaelic called *sean-nos*. The old
Gaelic style is melismatic and thus far removed from the English and
modern Irish lyrical style of one syllable per sound. The ornamentation is largely improvised, taking place in the form of spontaneous
melodic variation in successive verses. Within the sean-nos tradition,
there is a certain freedom of the performer to alter the melismatic
melody for expressive purposes. As O'Canainn explains,

> To someone who is not a part of it, the tradition may seem to
> be a narrow and restrictive set of rules, but the traditional
> performer does not view it in this light. He finds a personal
> challenge in refashioning the basic material, putting his own
> seal on it and expressing his musicality through it. (1978, 4)

The singer's personal style is then concerned with the spontaneous
choice of musical formulas that reshape the music as it is performed.
Sometimes music in the Irish tradition is varied with the change

of performance medium. When an instrumental dance piece is transformed into a vocal piece, the rhythm and melody may be altered to fit the words. If a fiddle piece is given to a bagpipe player for performance, there may be changes in the melody to simplify the fingering for the piper on the chanter pipe. Likewise, certain pitch patterns of a piper's tune may lie well beyond the fiddler's finger range, and so alterations will occur. The freedom to vary the music even as it is transmitted appears important in the Irish tradition.

On occasion, however, a more precise imitation technique is practiced. Koning recounts the learning of traditional Irish fiddling during informal jam sessions and in the homes of fiddlers:

> The players often would teach me a particular tune in which I had shown interest. Such an exchange of tunes is very common between players who rarely meet. The tune is copied aurally and bit by bit, but in the correct tempo. The one who learns the tune imitates either by playing or by whistling or saying nonsense syllables (jigging). The other player continues until his tune has been copied exactly. Ornamentation, variation in melody, and phrasing are left out by both. Once a musician has learned the basic tune, he will add his own ornamentations, variations and phrasing during the next few days. (1980, 423)

The fiddlers may meet again, at which time each listens to the other's version, and attempt to copy the ornamentation that they have developed independently of one another. Still, the improvisations and embellishmentes on the original melody will pay tribute to the individuality of the performer. In a session of Irish musicians, the sound of melodies that vary slightly through individual ornamentation from one to the other presents a heterophonic texture. For traditional Irish musicians, the transmission process is an aural one in which notation is seldom used. Irish music is thus clearly nonliterate, improvisatory, soloistic, and personal.

The Balkans: Mastering Aural and Kinesthetic Skills

Diagonally across the continent, the Balkans have a musical style that shares with the Irish tradition a penchant for melodic ornamentation. The Greeks decorate their melodies with grace notes, elisions, and complex passages of tones that lead to and from the skeletal structure. Rhythmic elements may include the use of anticipation, syncopation, and triplet figures. Instrumentalists and singers may exert a flexibility in pitches, bending them slightly to sound sharper or flatter than the pitches of the more customary European tuning.

The training of instrumental musicians in Greece follows the oral process of learning by imitation. Chianis distinguishes between the village performer and the professional folk musician in ability to ornament the melody, based on the musician's function and training:

> Largely "self-taught" and equipped with a repertoire limited to his immediate locality, the village performer plays for such local events as weddings, engagements, baptisms, name-days, and ecclesiastical celebrations. His interpretation of the instrumental line strays little from the vocal version and his instrumental and improvisatory abilities are rather limited. The training of the professional folk instrumentalist is completely different. He receives instrumental training (oral, or course) from the master teacher (performer): the bulk of the instruction consists not of repertoire development, but primarily of learning methods of ornamenting often skeletal melodic structure with its inherent basic melodic units and cadential points by means of ornamental formulae characteristic of the stylistic traditions of his particular region. (1966, 91)

Although the musical outcomes are varied, with the village performer on call for the community's musical occasions and the professional musician providing commercial entertainment, the aural/oral mode of preservation is the same for both.

In Bulgaria, there are amateur folk ensembles in rural and urban settings as well as professional "folk" musicians whose training in special institutes and later performances are supported by the state. As in Russia and other East European countries, the professional musicians of Bulgaria perform a folk-art music cultivated by the government to express ideological thoughts and to convey a homogeneous national image. Still, traditional music continues to be performed in scattered communities as an expression of local activities and sentiments that have been carried through many generations. The songs and instrumental music for *gaida* (bagpipe), *kaval* (flute), plucked lutes and bowed fiddles, and accordion belong to a people whose roots are in farming, animal husbandry, weaving, and rug making. Despite their incessant work, they had occasions for singing, along with seasonal celebrations, village festivals, and extensive wedding feasts.

Traditional music in Bulgaria is learned by listening. There is no formal process nor are there designated teachers. No one deliberately demonstrates or simplifies complex musical phrases for aspiring musicians. The peer groups of children who are together at play and at work assigned to them learn from each other, and through the imitation of the elders with whom they have contact. They recreate games, dances, and songs of adults, and so assimilate the musical culture of the village or collective. Children learn Bulgarian songs as complete entities: words, melody, dance steps, and the customary accompaniment. Through direct imitation, antiphonal singing that employs immediate repetition of the leader's melody, and recreation from memory, children become familiar with the traditional music that is their Bulgarian birthright (Aleksandrova, 1983).

Instrumental musicians are self-taught. A gaida player, for example, will watch the fingers of a player as he intently listens. He will imitate short musical gestures he has observed and gradually extend their length within the parameters of the tradition. Rice described his own discovery of learning to play the virtuosic music of the *gaida* (bagpipe):

> The breakthrough came when I finally figured out how to move my hands. In effect, I learned that my hands were the repository of musical ideas. . . . My ideas about this music had been represented in musical notation as melody notes plus various rather complex grace notes, but now they were encapsulated in hand motions that were much simpler and more efficient than musical notes. Five or six notes would now emerge out of one "idea" of hand movement. (1985, 119)

Only a few of those who attempt to learn the musical tradition in Bulgaria excel as composers, with the ability to generate new music on instruments spontaneously, or to ornament in new ways the traditional tunes they sing and play. Their capacity to absorb the substance of their music and their inherent creative talent are key to the making of master musicians in Bulgaria.

Norway: Apprenticing with Master Musicians

The *spelemenn*, or traditional fiddlers of Norway, recognize creativity as the mark of an outstanding musician. Improvisation and composition is, however, preceded by the aural learning of fixed pieces: "One must first learn many slåttar (traditional fiddle tunes) as they were made up by others and passed from person to person in the tradition. Only when one has mastered all this music, is one able to compose new compositions" (Hopkins, 1986, 75).

These fiddlers are aware of the necessity of laying a firm foundation for music early in life. The presence of music in the home, or at least within the community, makes a valuable contribution to the learning process. The learning potential is thus in the cultural milieu, and as the child listens, he acquires patterns that he will later incorporate within his performance. One spelemann described the circumstances of his son's learning process:

> When he was a little boy, he would come in to me at bedtime and ask me to play so he could go to sleep. He takes things I play—things he's heard around, since he was this high . . . If he comes to me and says "I want to play Myllarguten's 'Siste Slåatt.' " I play, slowly, and then we start together. (Hopkins, 1986, 221)

Mastery of the Norwegian *hardingfele* is developed over a long period of apprenticeship in which the student associates himself with a renowned player. The student observes and repeats phrases played by the master fiddler and will also listen and attempt to play on his own the music from tapes provided or recommended by the fiddler. The atmosphere of group instruction within a community center or sponsored by a civic organization has become increasingly popular, and the teaching techniques include "the memorization of a body of set pieces, note for note, ornament for ornament, and bowing for bowing" (Hopkins, 1978, 223). Unlike the process described for Irish fiddlers, ornamentation is learned by Norwegians as the melody is learned rather than by playing first the skeletal melody and then adding the embellishments later. Only after many pieces are learned, from folk songs and dance tunes to song cycles, is the student spelemann free to compose his own music. The spelemann's improvisation will then proceed more smoothly as the melodic and rhythmic patterns are in the ear and in the fingers.

Italy: Oral and Notated Music

On the Italian island of Sardinia, there are several traditional avenues for the development of a village musician, and all of them were at one time oral in nature: the father-to-son process of handing down tunes and performance techniques; learning from uncles or other relatives, followed by association with community musicians; and transmission from older to younger members of the nonfamilial community. One musician commented on his own "training": "When I was younger, I listened, liked and played" (Lartat-Jacob, 1981, 187). In recent years, young musicians have begun to abandon the oral tradition, choosing instead to study accordion and voice at an academy. They are becoming musically literate through learning to read notes, observing that "with that, music is precise" (Lartat-Jacob,

1981, 187). These village musicians recognize that notation can remedy the gaps left by a failing memory and bestow the power to perform a variety of pieces when oral conventions are lacking.

Folk music in Europe is not always in the oral tradition. In Italy and elsewhere, folk music is sometimes borrowed by literate musicians, rearranged and performed, and then sometimes reintroduced into the oral tradition. Members of amateur folk choirs in Italy relearn a song as it has been notated, complete with its fixed melodic version, harmonic arrangements, and reduced text. They may copy the text of the song into a copybook, using the words as a mnemonic device for their later solo performances. From oral folk to written art to oral folk again, the music of the song is learned and given individual expression (Keller, 1984, 82). These performances can be passed from one individual to another, for the written words alone serve to remind the singer of the salient features of the song as it was taught in the amateur choir, although they do not convey the details of melody or rhythm.

Narrative Song: The European Ballad

Among the song genres found throughout Europe is the narrative song. Since the Middle Ages, songs that tell a story, share a legend, or preserve historical events have been performed solo from the British Isles to the Balkans. Ballads and epics are sung, occasionally to the accompaniment of a stringed instrument. They are distinguished from one another mostly by length and attention to one or several events, for example, the epic is a longer account of multiple events of a heroic nature. Ballads tend to fall into a strophic organization of four- or five-line stanzas while epics are long poems broken with a repeated phrase that may give the singer time to think of the story's upcoming set of circumstances for telling through song. Although narrative song is found in many of the world's cultures it has been most thoroughly studied as it exists among European peoples.

The British ballads are probably best known, due to their extensive collection by Francis Child in the late nineteenth century. Examples are "The Cherry Tree Carol," "The House Carpenter," "The Two Sisters," and "Robin Hood," which recount the legend and lore of England and Scotland. Their counterparts are found among the Germanic and Scandinavian peoples, and to a lesser extent in Spain, France and Italy.* In Eastern Europe, the epic is more likely to be

---

* Cecil Sharp documented the vast incidence of British ballads and songs preserved intact among people in isolated mountain communities of the Southern Appalachians

heard than the ballad, although Russia and the Ukraine continue to preserve their folklore through balladry.

A comparison of ballad tunes indicates that they tend to maintain their melodic shape over time and across borders, but that divergences are natural and necessary to the form. The concept of the tune family across Europe and the United States shows a relationship between the ballads of Great Britain and their variants in other countries. There may be as many variants as there are singers, but certainly every region has its own versions of tunes that are traceable to British sources. For ballads, change is key to the tradition, and any note-for-note rendition suggests a fixed tune that may not be a part of the true oral tradition. Bronson (1967) noted that the folk memory does not recall a tune with accuracy but rather "preserves a melodic idea as an imprecise entity, which it condenses into a fresh particularization with each rendition" (pp. 150–151). Ballads exemplify the creative processes that can occur in oral transmission.

Broadside ballads were a break from the oral tradition. Popular in England in the seventeenth and eighteenth centuries, their texts were printed on large posters called broadsides. Notation was limited to the outline of the melody so that the purchaser might recall which tune, familiar through the oral tradition, was meant to accompany the text. Even when the poetic verses came to be read, the melody was still largely a part of the oral tradition.

The melody is the ballad's memory aid for communicating the message of the text. Many stories might have been lost and forgotten were it not for the tune. As Bronson explained,

> A tune is essential. Obviously, the tune has the best chance of being remembered, because it is repeated, as a near-constant, throughout the ballad; and if composed of recurrent phrases, has an even better chance of enduring in the memory. And some words will in all likelihood cling to the notes. (1976, xxv)

Narrative Song: The European Epic Poem

Where writing is rare or unknown, epic poems and songs flourish. The less industrialized the society, the less likely is it that the audience will seek its knowledge of historical and contemporary events through the printed page. Much of Eastern Europe remained agrarian until World War II; consequently, the remains of significant

---

in 1915–1916. Similar accounts of preserved songs were reported in the Ozarks, northern New England, along the Great Lakes, and in Canada.

epic traditions can still be found in parts of eastern and southeastern Europe. Nonliterate societies convey ideas orally in the living songs of the people. In this way, oral literature serves the same function as writing: to preserve and to communicate ideas.

Epic texts are long, and performances of them may last for several days. Improvisation of both verse and melody is important to the genre, with formulas and standard phrases recurring throughout. Eastern Europeans are particularly fond of epics; these may be referred to as men's songs, heroic songs, *bilini* (Russia) and *duma* (Ukraine). In the Baltic area, Finnish people are proud of their singing tradition of poems from the "Kalevala." Throughout Europe, the epic is nearly always performed by men—in cafés and in private homes.

An account of the Yugoslav epic singer and his art, given by Lord (1960), may provide the most complete known description of the traditional process of composition and performance of epics, one that transcends national boundaries.* The distinction between composing *during* a performance and *for* a performance, is underscored as characteristic of the performer's art. The singer learns, composes, and transmits his songs within the context of a performance. Rather than merely carrying the tradition, the epic singer is a creative artist remaking the tradition as he performs.

Lord distinguishes three stages in the learning of the art of the epic singer: an initial period of listening, observing and absorbing; a second period of practice and application; and a final stage of singing before a critical audience. He relates an account given by Seco Kolic on becoming a "singer of tales," drawn from the fieldwork of Milman Parry:

> When I was a shepherd boy, they [men of the village] used to come for an evening to my house, or sometimes we would go to someone else's for the evening, somewhere in the village. Then a singer would pick up the gusle [one-stringed fiddle], and I would listen to the song. The next day when I was with the flock, I would put the song together, word for word, without the gusle, but I would sing it from memory, word for word, just as the singer had sung it. . . . Then I learned gradually to finger the instrument, and to fit the fingering to the words, and my fingers obeyed better and better. . . . I didn't sing among the men until I had perfected the song, but only among the young fellows in my circle not in front of my elders and betters. (Lord, 1960, 21)

---

* The process is changing, however. Due to the availability of printed texts, story themes are now less diverse and the formulaic structure is rapidly disintegrating.

The foundation may be unconsciously laid in the first phase when the boy initially begins to attend performances of the epic, around the age of fourteen. He learns more than the expressed morals and historical events; he also becomes familiar with the structure of the poetry and of the music. He absorbs formulas, which are the frequently repeated melodic phrases that carry the poem.

When the boy begins to sing, he has entered the second phase. He has observed rhythmic and poetic patterns, including the ten-syllable line with a break after the fourth syllable, and he attempts to express his thoughts within the parameter of these fixed patterns. It may be that no one has told him about this form; he has simply learned it from listening. His composition of a story in song begins slowly, and he may insert musical interludes on a one-stringed *gusle* or a two-stringed *tambura*. He may also introduce a pause in the story by inserting formulaic phrases while he recalls his next set of ideas. "Now you should have seen it, my falcons" is one such phrase, which must nevertheless be used sparingly (Lord, 1960, 21–22).

The teacher is the singer whom the boy has chosen to emulate. His model may be a relative, or a well-known singer in the community. He learns melodic and textual formulas through repeated performance with the informal guidance of his favorite singer. His goal is to learn enough formulas to perform a complete song and to connect one formula to the next in a poetic and musically logical way. Learning music is an imitative process in the second stage as he copies the techniques of composition and improvisation rather than particular songs. The student assimilates phrases and formulas by listening to the master, imitating and practicing.

The young singer graduates to the final stage in the learning process when he has successfully performed an epic song for a listening audience. His songs will improve, and the length of individual songs will increase as he employs ornamentation in skillful ways. His repertoire increases as well, and he progresses toward his goal of performing for a full evening or even for several nights in a row. Lord describes the true mark of an epic singer:

> When he has a sufficient command of the formula technique to sing any song that he hears, and enough thematic material at hand to lengthen or shorten a song according to his own desires and to create a new song if he sees fit, then he is an accomplished singer and worthy of his art. (1960, 27)

The tales of a culture's history and folklore may be told by the poet-singers still living in mostly rural parts of Europe. While these bards may be nonliterate, they have sophisticated aural and cognitive skills with which they can creatively convey thoughts within a framework found acceptable by the culture. The epic tradition, like that of the ballad, has depended upon acute listening for its survival through the centuries. This is the oral tradition in its finest realization.

THE JAZZ WORLD

An American Musical Expression

Jazz and improvisation are often regarded as synonymous. Since the key to the fresh and innovative quality of jazz music is its spontaneity, the two words are frequently spoken in the same breath. African-American genres such as the spiritual, the work song, and the blues were important in the evolution of jazz in the early years of the twentieth century. These orally transmitted music genres were influential in the development of an all-American musical product whose performance practice lies jointly in the realm of the oral and the notated. Improvisation is generally regarded as an aural process; while ideas for jazz improvisation are derived from sketches or skeletal frames of notation, aural inspiration frequently takes precedence over the written note, giving jazz its characteristic quality of free expression.

Unlike earlier African-American forms, jazz is not folk music. Its performance can be extremely complex, requiring techniques that can occur only through long preparation. When performed by talented musicians, jazz improvisation sounds as if it were "meant to be," planned and so well constructed as to be indistinguishable from the best written compositions. Jazz rhythms are often syncopated and polyrhythmic, its harmonies ranging from blues progressions to modal and even mixed tonalities, and its melodies replete with slides and slurs, suspensions, and every type of passing tone configuration imaginable (figure 9–1). Some universities have recognized the complexities of jazz as equivalent to Western classical music and have established programs in jazz performance, theory, and history.

Some of the great jazz musicians think of their music as an extension of their lives and personalities. Sidney Bechet, a performer of the New Orleans tradition, commented: "I play what I live" (Berendt, 1981, 47). Charlie Parker similarly remarked, "Music is your own experience, your thoughts, your wisdom. If you don't live it, it won't come out of your horn." (Berendt, 1981, 47). Historically, jazz was an expression of life itself, and the spirit of life—its victories and defeats—was thus reflected in the music.

FIGURE 9–1 "Giant Steps." Composition and solo by John Coltrane (1926–1967). Atlantic Records SD-1311.

Transcription by Michael Brockman, University of Washington.

As jazz was beginning in the first two decades of this century, African-American musicians were organizing into orchestras that played ragtime, light classics, and even funeral and parade music. Despite the fact that jazz is "ear" music, evolving from the oral traditions, many of these early musicians were musically literate. James Reese Europe, a forerunner of swing giants Duke Ellington and Fletcher Henderson, conducted a "Negro band" that spread some of the earliest forms of jazz throughout the East Coast and abroad in Europe. His comments on its sound are addressed in an article entitled "A Negro Explains Jazz," published in 1919:

> To us it [jazz] is not discordant, as we play the music as it is written, only that we accent strongly in this manner the notes which originally would be without accent. It is natural for us to do this; it is, indeed, a racial musical characteristic. I have to call a daily rehearsal of my band to prevent the musicians from adding to their music more than I wish them to. Whenever possible they all embroider their parts in order to produce new, peculiar sounds. (Southern, 1983, 239)

Even while they were playing composed music, then, black musicians of the early Jazz Age had a tendency to syncopate, to swing, and to improvise. These elements continued through the various styles, from the 1920s swing to the 1940s bebop style, to cool and progressive jazz of the 1950s and 1960s, to the contemporary developments in free-form jazz and the jazz/rock fusion. Even though jazz is composed music, its unique offering has always been its freedom of expression within a given structure.

Learning to Listen, Listening to Learn

Jazz musicians throughout the century have been in agreement on several central issues regarding their own preparation and training and have advised aspiring musicians to follow a similar course. Fraser (1983) enumerated five stages through which jazz musicians progress: (1) attraction to the music for its rhythmic, emotive, and intellectual-analytical components; (2) ear-training and observation of jazz musicians in the acquisition of skills for performance; (3) development of technical and artistic skills in the manipulation of the voice or instrument; (4) emulation of master musicians for the refinement of jazz improvisation skills; and (5) self-actualization and individual stylistic development that derives from experience in observation, practice, and public performance.

The importance of observation and listening in the development of a jazz musician cannot be overestimated. At every level, from novice to master, the ear is trained to listen closely to the course a musician follows vocally or with his instrument. Shaw (1979) surveyed the methods of study followed by well-known jazz artists in the acquisition of jazz improvisation skills. Making transcriptions of solos played by exemplary performers contributed to their growth as musicians, but more critical to their own success as performers was the extent to which they listened to and imitated a skilled player's sound, articulation, and phrasing techniques.

Jazz pianist Mary Lou Williams received no formal instruction and recalled that while she never had a teacher, she was raised in a musical environment with professional musicians paying frequent visits to her home. She advised aspiring performers to recognize that musical ideas and inspiration come through listening: "That's the only way. . . . Jazz does not come from books. . . . It's all done by ear" (Handy, 1980, 196). Williams' style of teaching reflected her own experience as a developing musician when she commented, "I can't teach jazz, but I can show you how to teach yourself." Although she eventually learned to read notation, that was not the emphasis of her lessons. Her method unfolded neatly, from the student's experimenting at the piano to the use of notation as a memory aid to the transfer of learning to new musical settings. She explained the sequence:

> With my students, I first try to get a swinging left hand. Then I'll write out a tune that they like . . . such as "Over the Rainbow" or "Night in Tunisia." I'll give them eight bars each time they come to me. After four weeks I make them apply all the chords that I've given them to other tunes—in that way guiding them, teaching them to become their own teacher. (Handy, 1980, 196)

The great jazz bassist Charles Mingus began his musical career learning cello from an unskilled itinerant music teacher named Arson, who taught him through example and by ear. Mingus found that reading notes and then applying the notes to the instrument was a lengthy method of learning a piece. He advocated listening and observing as a shortcut to performance, and one that was "great for jazz improvisation where the musician listens to the sounds he's producing" (Mingus, 1972, 18)

Trumpeter Dizzy Gillespie remembered the influence of his teacher Alice Wilson, who provided him with an aural foundation in his early stages of development. Since she did not read notation, Gillespie learned through observation to play and to improvise. She remarked, "All I had to do was just show him . . . and he could imitate whatever I played on the piano on his horn" (Gillespie and Fraser, 1979, 29).

Like many jazz musicians, Eddie Condon taught himself to play the banjo through listening and imitating those he heard. His father criticized his music, saying his style was the result of young Condon's inability to read music. Condon's reply echoed the attitude of some of the greatest jazz performers: "What's that got to do with being a musician?" (Fraser 1983, 96).

The inordinate number of blind jazz musicians gives further support to the importance of the ear in learning and mastering the style. The advent of audio technology, including radio, the phonograph, and the sophisticated stereo systems of tape recordings and compact discs, provides aspiring musicians with convenient aids for training the ear in the jazz style. Once learning could occur only in the presence of other jazz performers—in jam sessions or during the rehearsal breaks of the early swing bands; now beginners and masters alike gather ideas for improvisation in their homes via recordings and even television and video. Although jazz is generally perceived as an art requiring both a heightened aural sense and the knowledge of notation, the absence of sight—resulting in the inability to read notation—does not preclude mastery.

Vocalization

A brief examination of some of the great jazz musicians and their individual views on listening, observation, and the training of the ear may underscore the importance of these techniques. Louis Armstrong, one of the most influential figures of all time, was a singer before he was a jazz musician. He learned by ear to play the trumpet, and only later studied notation so that he could join the emerging swing bands of the 1920s. He believed in the adage, "If you can't sing it, you can't play it," and his early experience as a singer in church and Sunday school gave him the informal vocal training that grounded him in his later instrumental work and in his improvisation (Armstrong, 1954).

Singing played a significant role in the musical development of jazz violinist Joe Venuti as well. He maintained that his ear was trained—before he began his study of violin—through the practice of solfeggio,

> "The Italian system under which you don't bother much about any special instrument until you know all the fundamentals of music. It's the only way to learn music right" (Shapiro and Henthoff, 1955, 272–273).

Jazz Instruction

The acceptance of jazz as a sophisticated musical style spawned an interest in the training of jazz musicians in American conservatories and college music programs. Techniques for the sequential development of improvisation were addressed in methods books, and master classes were offered for the development of aural and improvisation skills. As early as the 1960s, pioneer jazz educators such as Coker (1964) and Baker (1969) authored instruction books in jazz improvisation. These were followed by Aebersold's unique book and play-along records (1979). Soon after this came the methods of Dunbar (1976) and Lawn (1981). As Witmar and Robbins (1988) observed in their survey of instructional approaches to teaching and learning jazz, there developed since mid-century "a boggling array of published pedagogical materials" (p. 7) that offer tonal principles, rhythm and "swing," typical harmonic (often blues) progressions, transcribed examples of solos, ear training, and call-response exercises. Jazz began to be taught as a serious art form, and in some schools it has become an important branch of music, equal to the performance of any instrument in any style of the Western classical tradition.

While the methods book authors communicate through the notation of chordal progressions, melodic themes, and potential ideas for development, they emphasize imitation. Lawn noted that "learning by imitation is a basic principle throughout life. One learns to walk, to talk, and to master many daily functions through imitation. The beginning improvisor may also learn many skills through imitation. A student can learn a great deal through listening and imitating recordings" (1981, 69).

Listening, followed by imitation, was advised by Aebersold as well: "I can think of no better way to learn to improvise melodically than listening to the masters and trying to emulate their playing concepts. How can we expect anyone to listen to us if we don't earnestly listen to those already doing it?" (1979, 30).

The history of jazz education can be divided into two periods: the early years in which musicians utilized their listening skills, and the more contemporary use of transcribed solos and other printed materials to supplement listening in the study of improvisation. Baker, in recalling his own early development, lamented the fact that "we teachers, authors, educators and performers from the period B.J.M.B. [before jazz method books] have forgotten that we learned our craft by playing along with and studying the solos of our jazz heroes" (1979, 23).

The aural environment for learning jazz continues to be significant for the development of the improviser. The advice of Baker to jazz students suggests that certain aspects of the style cannot be learned in any other way:

> Unless the budding jazz player is in an aural environment where the language of jazz is spoken [played], he will not learn that language. Subtlety, correct use of inflection, a feeling of swing, interpretation, style, etc., are all things that are most effectively learned through the repeated hearing of those players who first defined the music. (1984, 26)

The establishment of the master class as a means of developing techniques in jazz improvisation began in the 1950s, and the use of guest artists continues to be an effective instructional approach in collegiate jazz programs. The big band once provided the setting for refining techniques, with the younger musicians learning from the seasoned ones; now the master class performs that function. A jazz artist or well-known jazz educator may be invited to serve a short-term residency as a visiting artist-teacher. He or she may perform in concert as well, but the principal purpose of having this individual on campus is to provide students with instruction, practice, and a critique of their performance by a master jazz improviser.

Fraser (1983) gives an account of a master class led by pianist John Lewis at the Philadelphia Kool Jazz Festival in 1982. Following introductory remarks on jazz improvisation, Lewis played for the students a melody that became the basis for improvisation. He addressed the possible avenues of variation and transformation of a tune, and then requested the students to improvise a two-measure phrase based on the original melody. Students played their inventions simultaneously so that they might hear how the "more definite musical statements stood out over less clearly stated ideas" (p. 177). Lewis presented further building blocks for jazz improvisation by encouraging the students to invent ways of departure from the original melody. Through exploration, performance, and feedback from the guest artist, they developed ideas on the nature of improvisation that were more immediate than could be conveyed in any manual.

Sudnow (1978) provided an articulate chronicle of the process of deciphering the mysteries of improvisation. In a stream-of-consciousness style of writing similar to a series of entries in a journal, he described the gradual development of improvisation skills germaine to the performance of jazz piano. He explained that lesson by lesson, an understanding of the cognitive nature of improvisation evolves as physical skills are acquired. As the teacher presents scales and chord progressions, he or she is perceived as offering a pathway for the fingers and hand to follow. From scalar passages to intervallic transposition, the student develops melodic ideas for later recall during performance. Various manipulations of set patterns are explored and practiced on the piano and are thought through as mathematical maneuvers. A significant breakthrough occurred for Sudnow when he first understood the manner in which the hand, and not the individual fingers, thinks and performs a musical idea:

> When I first learned the scales, attention was given to each note and that finger whose use with each note produced the most fluent production, but once this course was mastered, it became a way of my scale-playing hand . . . a finger-to-finger orientation was supplanted by a whole-handed entry. (pp. 21–22)

Sudnow surveyed his accomplishments after just six months of instruction in jazz piano, all of which help to define the essence of improvisation:

> I had: a stockpile of places to go, melodic resources of named notes . . . hosts of licks, written down, told by teachers to students . . . elaborate ranges of possibilities for "lending organization" to manipulations they themselves [teachers] told me nothing about, visually detected and then tactilely found fields and criss-crossing vectors for practicing maneuverability with, instantly available potential courses to be seen at a glance while trying to keep play as the "changes" went by. (p. 28)

In recognition of the relationship between the mental and physical capacities, Sudnow compared the learning of chord progressions and melodies for jazz improvisation to the procedure of a typist:

> The beginning typist may find himself spelling every word as he types, thinking the spelling of the words as a step-by-step search of the looking fingers for correct places. The advanced typist may make it through an unaccustomed passage by conceiving the fingers doing the spelling, not so as to "remember" where the proper characters lie through an image of the terrain, but so as to make it through an unfamiliar sight in the text being copied. (p. 92)

Sudnow remarks that the hands reach the level of "behaving spellingly," of producing musical units through a single gesture, and of unconsciously communicating complete musical ideas on keys that have become familiar territory through extensive practice.

What then is the art of jazz and the creative genius of its improvisation? Jazz is at once the creation of new compositions on the spur of the moment and an expression that is anchored in many long hours of listening and practice. It is an involvement of the ear and the body, a result of a refined aural perception and proficient kinesthetic skill. It is the unexpected (even to the performer) that produces the excitement for which jazz is known, and yet it is also modification and adaptation of a previously learned stock of melodic and rhythmic ideas. Once past the beginning period of an improvisation session, when the performer "blows himself out," thereby ridding himself of ideas close to the surface of his memory, the real expression begins. It is at that moment when the truly personal statements of jazz are communicated. This is improvisation at its best, the key to jazz.

SUMMARY

The diversity of music on two continents, along with the jazz style that evolved from African-American genres on yet a third continent, illustrate the extent to which careful listening can lead eventually to creative musical expression. Unlike most music of the Asian cultures sampled in chapters 7 and 8, many of the sophisticated African and European traditions are likely to be introduced through the process of socialization. Beyond enculturation, however, exceptional musicians learn techniques and repertoire from the master performers. Oral recitation of mnemonics and the initial singing of instrumental passages are important to the development of musicians in traditional Africa and Europe, and they are critical also to the training of jazz musicians. While jazz education has formalized the teaching-learning process of that style in recent decades, the common features it shares with earlier jazz styles and African and European traditional music are undeniable. Learning to listen and listening to learn prepare performers of diverse musical cultures and styles for improvisations as the ultimate level of musical performance.

CHAPTER
10

◆

Tradition and Change: Cross-Cultural Comparisons of Music Instruction in World Cultures

The brilliant art and folk traditions of the world are transmitted in various ways: from teacher to student, from master to apprentice, from father to son, and through formal and informal experiences. Musicians develop techniques and repertoires through avenues that are long established by the culture—through enculturation, training, and schooling. As classical musicians in the West have benefited from pedagogical approaches over the centuries, musicians throughout the world have become proficient through time-tested instructional techniques. Specific cultural needs have shaped traditional teaching and learning processes, and yet the phenomenon of music guarantees that the development of aural skills and creative talents is central to the training of the performing musician in every society.

In many parts of the world, music traditions are rapidly fading, and with them, their traditional methods of instruction. In these cultures, the Western concept of formalized schooling has arrived to provide musical training for serious performers and music education for the broad masses of children in elementary and secondary schools. The talented are frequently channeled toward conservatories where they are provided with intensive study on particular instruments, or to universities for study in the theory and history of the tradition. Teacher education programs have also been designed to prepare music teachers for positions in state-operated and private schools, where they practice the instructional strategies that were first developed in the West. Elementary and secondary school music curricula are frequently modeled on successful programs in the West. European and Euro-American ideals of music education have been adapted in many of the world's cultures.

The traditional and changing features of music teaching and learning merit further consideration. A summary of traditional approaches and techniques found among the cultures previously sampled (chapters 7, 8, 9) will provide the basis for reviewing contemporary practices. Cross-cultural comparisons of music learning —formal and informal, indigenous and Western-oriented—can offer a more complete understanding of music instruction in the historical past and as it presently exists in the world. The extent to which aural skills, improvisation, and learning strategies—including vocalization, solmization, and mnemonics—have been combined with the use of notation is discussed, and their occurrences in school settings and in the private lessons are noted. Performing musicians in the world today may well be the product of both tradition and change, reaping the balance of the old with the new in the training they receive.

TRADITIONAL MUSIC TEACHING AND LEARNING

In the training of musicians in many traditional societies, the music teacher is a highly respected musician—an active performer who guides students through his or her own performance. As a model of the ultimate musician, the teacher demonstrates performance techniques and etiquette that are observed and imitated by the student. Modeling may occur in weekly lessons, on occasions for informal learning, or through the intensive experience of an apprenticeship, as in the training of an Indian gharana. The reverence in which students hold their teachers is legendary in some cultures: Thai students honor their teachers through special ceremonies, traditional Japanese offer expensive gifts for their sensei, and Indian students play tamboura for the duration of their teacher's performances (which may last several hours). Honorific titles such as ustad and pandit are bestowed by Muslim and Hindu musicians.

The training of musicians in African societies and European folk communities has traditionally occurred through informal processes in which the teacher may be the father, uncle, distant relative, or neighbor. Where music is valued as an important community activity—as it is in these and many of the world's traditional and folk cultures—children observe their elders and wait eagerly for opportunities to become more fully engaged in performing music themselves.

Aural Learning

A number of sensory avenues for aspiring musicians are exercised through training; these include their aural, visual, and kinesthetic capacities. Students listen, observe, and imitate the teacher or master musician in lessons for Japanese koto, Indian sitar, Thai ranat and kong wong, Lao kaen, Persian santour, West African kora, Chinese qin, and instruments of the Indonesian gamelan. In a similar way the ear is presented with tremendous challenges in jazz performance, as aural skills are critical to the ability to improvise. As they listen to their teacher's performance, students also watch, and finally become active themselves in the kinesthetic process of performance. Musicians throughout the world carefully exercise their aural capacity as they build their technical skills to their maximum potential.

Whether in formal or informal settings, imitation is a critical device in learning music. Indian and Iranian masters play and then ask students to repeat the passages precisely as they were sounded, sometimes vocally and sometimes on their instruments. Indonesian children attend rehearsals and performances, and then imitate the songs, melodies, instrumental techniques, and dance gestures of their elders while at play during the "waiting period" prior to training. In the increasingly rare peasant communities of Europe, an aspiring musician listens, learns, and retains certain characteristics of a folk song, narrative song, or instrumental tune. Replication may vary from a modification or personal interpretation of an earlier performance to absolute precision, depending on the genre and tradition.

In most traditions, verbal explanation does not play a large part in the training of musicians. In fact, it appears to be entirely absent in some settings. The excessive use of words is often perceived as an inefficient means of training musicians by those who view demonstration, observation, and imitation as being at the core of learning. Performance, rather than discussion, is viewed as a far more direct and expedient means of instruction in many traditions.

Notation

Notational systems have been developed for many of the world's art music traditions, and yet they are used less frequently during the lesson than they are later to trigger the memory following the lesson. In a traditional Japanese lesson, reading notation is thought to distract the student from the observation of the teacher's positions and gestures that are integral to a performance. Some notation, such as that for Japanese Noh music, Chinese qin, or jazz charts, may only partly outline the melody or harmony. The music is thus best learned under the tutelage of an experienced musician who can supply the missing pieces.

Notation systems were developed about 2,000 years ago in China and from the eighth through tenth centuries in cultural centers of the Middle East. In India, Sanskrit notation has been important to theorists for many centuries but is unknown to most performers; this disparity between performers and theorists appears in many cultures. European notational systems were adopted or modified by some cultures during colonization, as were various instruments, genres, and instructional practices. Numerical systems are common today, including the Kepatihan system in Indonesia, the Chevé numerical system in Thailand, and other variants of cipher notation throughout Asia and Africa. Tablature is occasionally found for stringed instruments such as the Chinese qin or *zheng*.

Notation is used in many art music traditions today, as musicians recognize the efficiency of the device for preserving and transmitting music. Still, jazz and classical musicians of India and parts of the Arab Middle East use notation sparingly, as they perform music that is largely improvised. Similarly, the folk music of Europe and many traditional African genres are transmitted through the oral tradition, in which the use of notation is rare. The greater the reliance on notation, the more likely it is that even traditionally improvised music can become bound and regulated—as is the case of the twentieth-century changes in the Turkish *makam*—where it may have once been free and unrestricted.

Improvisation

Some music can be fully realized only when the musician applies his knowledge of melody, rhythm, and formal elements to the creative process of improvisation. In most classical music of the Middle East and India, in jazz, and in much African and African-American music, improvisation is a key characteristic of the style, a creative display of melodic and rhythmic phrases. The raga in India and the Persian dastgah or Middle–Eastern makam (or maqam) provide solid foundations for improvisation, so that students derive melodic ideas from their scalelike structures. The performer in these traditions works within a specific melodic and rhythmic framework, making musical choices before and during performance. Such a process is especially evident in the Iranian musician's preliminary selection of the dastgah and number of gousheh he employs and in his spontaneous spinning out of melodies.

The improvisation process for vocal genres often requires the singer to learn words from printed sources and add music that has been aurally learned or improvised. Mawlum singers in Laos memorize poetic verses, and then improvise the melody. The stanzas of broadside ballads, and sometimes folk songs, are printed, learned through imitation, and then improvised upon by soloists. The naqqal poet-musicians of Iran learn their poems from books and their melodies through aural means. They then perform with subtle variations which might be seen either as their personal interpretation or a restricted improvisation of the oral or partly oral tradition.

For instrumentalists, improvisation often means playing characteristic phrases and figures that are set "in the hand" through extensive drills. Performance on the Lao kaen, the Bulgarian gaida, the Irish fiddle, and jazz piano share the process of recalling kinesthetic gestures the hand already knows and delivering musical patterns spontaneously in new configurations. Not only is there an aural repertoire of patterns but a kinesthetic one as well.

Ornamentation is commonly employed in genres of the world's art and folk music, as are such improvisational elements as rhythmic diminution and augmentation, cadential formulas, repetition, sequence, and rearrangement. In the Arab Middle East, the Balkans, and the Celtic regions of the British Isles, ornamentation is often profuse. Vocal jazz solos, like solos in gospel and blues, are also ornamented in as many different ways as there are performances.

In some traditions more than in others, improvisation conforms more closely to style restrictions. Musicians of the Thai ensembles and Indonesian orchestra are given some latitude for free expression within the ensemble but must still conform to pillar tones, melodic contour, and phrase length. The Chinese *da pu* process allows performers some freedom in interpreting the rhythm of a partially notated composition, but the melodic content is kept fairly constant. Consequently, improvisation in these traditions is far more confining then the improvisation of free jazz, the Persian *avaz*, or the Indian raga.

Teaching and Learning Strategies

Mnemonic devices are utilized by musicians in many cultures. Regardless of whether notation is available, aural and often oral cues serve the memory well as one stores and later recalls certain passages. Japanese instruments—including the koto, shamisen, nokan flute, and various drums—each have their own sets of syllables that designate pitches, playing positions, and rhythms. There is an elaborate mnemonic system for designating durations and drumstrokes for Indian drums as there is for other percussion instruments in India and the Middle East. Drumming in Malawi and throughout much of sub-Saharan Africa employs mnemonics that cue the duration, timbre, accents, and strokes of instruments. In some folk songs, the words may serve the singer as mnemonics for retaining the melody, rhythm, and form.

The use of vocalization is significant in many traditional music teaching and learning processes. In a Japanese lesson for shamisen, koto, or theater drums, the student imitates the teacher's singing of solfége or chanting of mnemonic syllables. The singing of Indian sargam is a type of solmization considered essential by traditional teachers in providing phrases for later transfer to instruments and as a foundation for improvised passages. Students of classical Indian music typically sing or chant phrases before performing them on pitched and nonpitched instruments. The same practice is used in training Iranian classical musicians. In Africa, vocalization is important in learning the kora and balo: students first sing the melody and later play it on these instruments. Many jazz musicians claim that singing must naturally precede performance on their instruments, and that ear-training is enhanced through vocalization.

In traditional approaches to learning music, art and folk styles are transmitted in logical ways suited to specific cultural values and behaviors. Learning through enculturation and learning through specialized training are more prevalent practices than learning in an established school of music or in a curriculum for music within a school. Notational systems are available in many cultures and are occasionally adapted by teachers or students to enhance or increase their rate of learning. The presence of aural learning practices in formal and informal training and the prominence of creative improvisation in practice and performance are notable throughout much of the world. The aural and creative essence of music is thus recognized and reinforced in the traditional instruction of many cultures.

CONTEMPORARY PRACTICES IN MUSIC INSTRUCTION

In recent history, political, economic, and social changes have shifted the course of many countries, and many cultural traditions have been abandoned as more modern ones are adapted to conserve time and energy. European domination, with its infusion of languages, technology, and values, was a catalyst for change in much of Asia, Africa, and Latin America. External influences in education and in the arts have led to widespread acceptance of Western educational institutions and practices.

In many cultures, traditional styles and genres of music have been transformed. Early ethnomusicologists distinguished Western music from non-Western music by its harmony, equal-tempered scale system, and notation (Nettl, 1985, 16).* These Western musical traits spread rapidly into colonized regions, largely due to the efforts of missionaries and the military. In the Americas, the Middle East, China, Japan, India, and Southeast Asia, missionaries converted souls through the hymns they taught, first by rote and later through notation. Military bands stirred patriotic spirit through their music, and soldiers were as likely to be trained in instrumental performance as they were in military maneuvers (Harich-Schneider, 1973; Mazrui, 1986; Nettl, 1985).

The world's music today includes classical and folk traditions that have been preserved intact as well as a rich mixture of hybrid forms that have resulted from the interaction of indigenous traditions with Western styles. Acculturation, the process by which aspects of one culture are subsumed into another, is a twentieth-century music phenomenon. Western pop music can be heard in Beijing, Bangkok, Nairobi, New Delhi, and other urban regions throughout the world. African-American genres, including gospel and jazz, are derived from a synthesis of African and European elements. Latin American music includes Native American as well as African- and European-derived styles of the Mexican *mariachi* bands, the Andean harp, lute, and panpipe ensembles, and the *salsa* and *soca* music of the Caribbean. Cultural exchanges work in both directions: West African elements influenced African-American forms and have been borrowed back in the popular Nigerian *juju* music (Waterman, 1990).

As musical styles converged, traditional practices by which music was taught and learned began a transformation. Whether indigenous music changed as a result of modifications in educational practices or whether changes in music and music training occurred simultaneously is not altogether clear (Nettl, 1985). Christian missionaries brought with them their musical preferences and established congregational singing, Western harmony, and choirs. They brought to Africa, Asia, the Americas, and remote Pacific Islands their portable organs, harmoniums, and pianos. Likewise, brass, wind, and

---

* While those criteria are not absolute and unequivocal, they at least appeared useful in early stages of analysis.

percussion instruments were imported for use in the military bands. With these instruments came Western-styled piano lessons, Tonic Solfa, and notation.

A new brand of education competed with, and in some cases, replaced, apprenticeship systems. Even music learning as part of socialization and enculturation was eventually affected as villages and urban areas alike welcomed—or at least accepted—visitors from abroad. The environment from which traditional music derived was thus changing, and even music that was informally learned through socialization took on characteristics of the foreign visitors. In some instances, the appeal of urban life and the drift of people to towns and to modern schools gave way to the near abandonment of music learning as a social process. As a result of Western influence, both formal and informal music learning processes changed.

For many who observed the European method of teaching in groups and the use of notation, solmization, techniques of vocal production, and eventually the phonograph, the old ways of teaching and learning seemed time consuming and inefficient. Unlike the traditions of certain societies—in West Africa, for example—the newly adopted Western process of learning music was divorced from daily living and completely removed from the context of the culture. On the other hand, the Western way of instruction was fast paced and successful in developing performance technique, and notation allowed countless musical works to be "saved," that is, preserved in print. Musicians could repeat successful performances by reading notation, and music that was especially pleasing could be heard again.

The adaptation of Western music instruction and the acculturation of Western and indigenous techniques for training musicians was clearly different from one culture to the next. There were differences, too, in the degree to which instructional practices were accepted. A system of music education for elementary school children in Japan was more readily accepted in 1872 than are Western techniques for the training of performing musicians in India today, despite extensive colonization by the British in the nineteenth and twentieth centuries. The extent of change in music instruction and the balance between tradition and change can be partly surveyed through a description of selected cultures and their musics, with a view toward understanding the impact of Western-style schools, conservatories, colleges, and universities, and the teaching and learning process.

China

The Chinese have long been supportive of music in education for its aesthetic and moral values, but major changes have occurred in the means by which students are musically educated. Where music was once a subject of study for the elite or scholarly, music instruction for the general public is presently under discussion on the mainland. The traditional Chinese methods of music teaching were embellished with those of the British colonists in the nineteenth century. The notated hymnbooks in four-part harmony of the British and their solmization practices were widely adopted in Hong Kong and throughout many of the larger Chinese cities. While the Republic of China in Taiwan continues the use of British- and American-styled techniques in teaching both Western and traditional music, the founding of the People's Republic of China in 1949 brought political policies that wavered between passive acceptance and hostile rejection of nearly all aspects of Western culture, including music and music education.

Today, traditional instrumental lessons and the training of singers and actors for regional opera, banned during the Cultural Revolution (1966–1976), have been reestablished in China, along with the age-old Chinese methods of teaching. Eight conservatories of music, a number of secondary and elementary "key schools" associated with the conservatories, and ten fine arts schools train professional musicians. While the conservatories are principally designed as places of tertiary education, key schools concentrate on physical education and the arts. Those who "major" in music study theory, score reading, and a given instrument. The exclusive fine arts schools are designed for training students in traditional opera, dance, music, and stage design.

Of the eight conservatories, the Central Conservatory of Music in Beijing and the Shanghai Conservatory are the most prominent. As there was traditionally a hierarchical ranking of students according to their scores on imperial exams, there follows today a professional ordering that places students graduating from these conservatories in line for the premiere positions in symphonies, opera and ballet ensembles, and schools. All students at the tertiary level register for basic music courses in aural training, harmony, individual piano instruction, history of Western music, and introduction to Chinese music. Students choose from majors in musicology, composition, conducting, voice, Western opera, Western instruments, Chinese instruments, and piano. A music education major is not offered in Chinese conservatories (or nearly any other conservatory in the world). Most music teachers, of whom there are very few even at the secondary level, receive their training in normal schools of education, e.g., Beijing Normal University.

The Chinese greatly value the arts and are concerned with preparing talented students to perform traditional and Western classical music, song, and dance at a high level of perfection. The philosophy for many millenia has been that art entails beauty and personifies morality; if one is moral, one is a performing artist. The master musician-teacher is revered for his or her role in the continuation of Chinese culture and of all that is beautiful and moral. Talented young musicians are led to greater musicianship in the traditional manner of "bazhe shou jiao"—"teaching by holding his hand," in which Skinnerian principles of modeling, imitation, and shaping are practiced. Skillful and highly technical performances are important goals to be achieved for the good of the Chinese culture, and musical creativity is viewed by performers "not as a massive dislocation or a radical reconceptualization but as a slight-to-modest alteration over time of existing schemes or practices" (Gardner, 1989, 280).

The music education of the masses is currently undergoing major reform in China. According to documents of the Education Ministry, the goal of music education is to develop "in students the mastery of independent music literacy, a sense of hearing and the faculty of memory" (Ministry of Education, 1985, 26). At the secondary level, curricular content is expected to include experiences that will serve "to develop progressively Chinese musical artistry, to understand the music of the national minorities, to be able to comprehend foreign music, to master basic knowledge and skills in music, and to possess definite ability to perform, experience and appreciate music" (p. 26).

Despite curriculum statements, however, music instruction in the public schools is often unavailable, especially in the countryside, due to a lack of trained teachers, instruments, books, or classroom materials. Yang Mu gives this account:

> In those schools where a music course is offered, it is usually limited simply to singing songs; apart from learning some popular songs by rote and in imitation of the teacher, the students have no other school based musical experiences. . . . Most Chinese school teachers engaged in aspects of music teaching have never heard names such as Kodaly, Carl Orff and Dalcroze. (1988, 26).

The standard notation system employed in the schools, if there is any at all, is the European-derived cipher notation, called *jianpu* or "simple notation," which is useful in recording and transmitting Chinese folk melodies. Plans for the introduction of Western staff notation and the development of music literacy through the elementary and secondary grades have been discussed, but neither has yet been implemented.

   Teachers of music in the public schools are prepared in teachers' colleges. Elementary music teachers are not likely to have obtained qualifications in music, but secondary school music specialists are often products of three years of teacher training. Courses are distributed equally between general studies and music subjects, which include piano, voice, solfeggio, theory, dance, and folk song. Piano improvisation and three song repertoires are emphasized in methods and student teaching experiences: Western songs, national Chinese songs, and popular songs (Lepherd, 1988, 63).

   Public school classes are teacher active and student passive, with students in rows of desks or chairs and the teacher directing lessons at the front of the room. Elementary and secondary classes in general music may employ solfége singing, conducting, and more rarely, the playing of instruments. Movement is rare, as classes generally have large numbers of students. The piano and the electric keyboard are frequently used—although the condition of these instruments is often questionable. Loud synthesized rhythms are provided to keep an ensemble of singing children together. Even at the secondary school level, choirs, orchestras, and bands are nearly unheard of in the public school (Lepherd, 1988, 52–55).

   Key schools associated with conservatories provide special training in music at the secondary—and sometimes the elementary—level. Musically gifted students are identified as early as the age of five or six and are placed in music programs that develop children's aural and solmization skills as well as their vocal and instrumental performance technique. Their solfége and ear-training drills are intensive, and as Reimer (1989) observed, it is there that the Chinese can " 'out-Kodály' us flat on our backs" (p. 29). These students are often channeled directly into the conservatory at the tertiary level. Their specialized training at an early age is likely to lead them to become outstanding performers and winners of international competitions.

   The role of music in general education has been important for the Chinese through the ages. While the official policy is that private instruction should be discouraged because it is a capitalist venture, there is an apparent elitism present through the channeling of the most talented children into conservatories, key schools, and fine arts schools. Today, the Western masterworks are studied by young violinists and pianists in conservatory lessons that use Western pedagogical techniques. Music literacy is heralded as an important goal, and for the chosen few in specialized schools, solmization experiences are intensive. The open-door policy toward the West and the world at large may be critical in shaping the future of music and music education in China, both for the serious performers and for the greater Chinese population.

India

India has adapted a number of Western elements into its music. The harmonium, a portable reed organ introduced by British missionaries, was modified by vocalists and instrumentalists for the rehearsal and performance of classical, folk, and popular forms. The Western violin became fully acculturated into South Indian classical genres, with adjustments made for tuning, timbre, and playing position. A lively film industry spawned the immense popularity of film music, a hybrid of Indian and Western instruments, textures, and forms. Yet despite India's awareness of Western cultural practices, its traditional music and approaches to learning remain strong.

Prestigious public schools (a misnomer, as they are actually private tuition schools) offer music appreciation classes, choirs, and occasional private instruction in Western and Indian instruments. Similar to experiences in secondary school general music classes, music appreciation includes the singing of folk songs from India and other parts of the world, listening lessons, and written assignments in the theory and history of Indian art music. Choirs may sing devotional hymns to the accompaniment of a harmonium or arrangements of folk songs featuring melody and dronelike vocal harmony. Tabla classes attract boys more than girls, and group instruction in brass and wind instruments carries on the tradition of the nineteenth-century British military bands. In most Indian schools in which academic subjects are viewed by parents and teachers as the primary purpose of schooling, however, music instruction is minimal.

The gharana tradition, which allows students of the Hindustani style access to music through living arrangements within a household of musicians, is less prominent than it was in the past; however, many teaching and learning devices of the gharana continue to be practiced. As before, vocal exercises precede instrumental instruction, with students performing age-old sargam drills in double- and triple-time. Classes before and after school, at universities, and at designated music institutes feature whole groups singing sequential melodic patterns as they keep the tala through clapping and finger counts.

For those students and their families who value classical music and can afford instruction, instrumental study is pursued through private or group lessons. It is not unusual in Bombay to find five or ten students chanting together the mnemonics of their tabla patterns, which they subsequently perform on their drums. In Madras, Saturday morning *vina* (a large plucked lute) lessons are delivered to groups of adolescent girls—sometimes twenty or more—who sing and play melodic phrases and fixed compositions in unison for two hours. Some students prefer to study privately, going to the home of a traditionally trained guru, where "every note, every ornament, every phrase is taught in the traditional way. . . . [The teacher] plays, the student watches his hands, listens, and then imitates" (Reck, 1984, 218). As in the past, the ear continues to be the principal channel of information for the student of Indian music. A sargam notation is used by the students to transcribe the pitches of vocal exercises or fixed compositions after they have been presented and practiced, but it is unusual to learn music directly from the notation itself before it has been aurally introduced. A remnant of the British colonial period, the written sargam resembles the Tonic Sol-fa, in which initial letters representing the solfége syllables are printed from left to right. Spaces, dashes, and dots convey the rhythmic values of the pitches.

Vocalization, solmization, and mnemonics remain important in the training of Indian musicians, whether done privately or in groups. Fixed compositions are learned through weekly lessons, but the art of improvisation requires time to develop. Frequent observations of master musicians, a close association with the musician-teacher, and a commitment to practice are vital to the making of classical musicians in India. Professional and amateur musicians alike become skilled through practices that are essentially unchanged even today.

Indonesia

As is the case in many other Asian countries, Indonesia has experienced great changes in music and education since colonization. The Dutch introduced Western values, including schooling. By the early twentieth century, public and private schools offered European-styled instruction in math, the sciences, humanities, and the arts. Western classical music and folk songs were gradually mixed into music classes, so that today there is concern for students' knowledge of traditional melodies, genres, and instruments, especially in urban areas: "In general, too many children today are facing the fact that the music of their fathers is becoming the music of the minority. There is a definite need for revision in education" (Suryabrata, 1976, 394).

For Indonesian children, learning to perform on instruments in the brilliant gamelan tradition was once an oral, aural, and informal learning process, one that unfolded gradually through demonstration and imitation. Becker commented on the more contemporary method of instruction as it reflects the changing Indonesian society:

> Today's urban gamelan teachers cannot spend infinite hours
> demonstrating for students. The teacher may have a job that

requires him to be in an office for most of the daytime hours and therefore he cannot teach long hours at night. Notation gives this teacher an easy answer to his problem. He need only write out the parts for the instruments and the student can practice them privately. It therefore becomes possible for the student to conceive of one part as separate from the total gamelan sound. (1980, 24)

Western attitudes prevail in the work world of Indonesians, as their schedules now require more expedient methods for doing what once was spread across hours and days. Notation allows students of the gamelan an independence in the learning process—a far cry from the communal and teacher-directed process of several decades ago. The use of notation may challenge the traditional nature of gamelan performance as partly improvisatory. In a changing society, music and its methods of transmission are adapting to the needs of the Indonesian people.

Japan

The centuries-old training of Japanese instrumentalists for solo performances and for court and theatre ensembles continues today. In traditional families, koto lessons are still regarded as an important skill to be acquired by young girls. Businessmen and women frequently study shamisen, shakuhachi, koto, and even noh-styled singing, as recreational activities. Like the traditional arts of *origami* (paper folding), calligraphy, and the tea ceremony, the study of music is regarded by many as an important cultural experience to be pursued if time and money allow it. Instruction in traditional music is generally embedded in traditional practices; these may include ceremonial greetings, demonstration and imitation, vocalization of mnemonic phrases, and limited use of notation in the lesson itself.

The move toward public school music education in Japan began through the efforts of Isawa Shuji and Luther Whiting Mason in 1872. As author of the National Music Course and one of the foremost authorities on vocal music education in the United States at the time, Mason was invited to Japan to assist in creating a curriculum for music. He taught singing classes in elementary schools for two years and collaborated with Isawa in building a repertoire of school songs known as *Gakko Shoka*. These three volumes contained songs in staff notation composed in a style that blended Western and Japanese elements (Berger, 1987).

American curricular content and methods in music are apparent in Japan's public schools today. Music is a required subject for all years in elementary school, for three years in junior high school, and for one of three years in high school. The goal of music instruction is music literacy, and on completion of elementary school, most students can read music and play recorder and keyboard instruments. It should be noted, however, that many become competent readers and performers through private instruction outside the school setting (Hara, 1970).

With general music classes that meet for forty-five minutes twice weekly during a ten and one-half month school year, proficiency in Fixed Do solfége and in the reading and writing of staff notation is possible by the second grade. Music classes are taught by classroom teachers until the fifth grade; then trained music educators lead students in the performance of more complex music, in composition, and in listening experiences. Schools frequently supply recorders, "wind pianos" (wind instruments with piano keyboards), harmonicas, and small electronic keyboards for each student. Singing in four-part harmony may begin as early as fourth grade and continues through the junior high school (Abdoo, 1984).

Performing ensembles are viewed as extracurricular clubs. They are usually well funded and enthusiastically supported by administrators and parents, but no academic credit is given to students for participation. Ensembles are generally student operated, although a teacher serves as director and adviser—many of them with no formal training in music education. Students manage, set up, and tune bands, for example, and hold sectionals in addition to the almost daily rehearsals. Still, the band adviser is revered in traditional ways, as students bow, listen silently to his words, and call him by the honorific title of *sensei* (Wilson, 1986, 46–47).

Music instruction in Japan is both traditional and Western oriented. Just as Western art and popular music have been widely accepted while traditional genres are carefully preserved, public school music resembles a Western curriculum but with a distinctly Japanese flavor. Western art and folk music, staff notation, and instructional strategies are widely practiced in Japan, just as the phenomenon of contests and festivals are commonplace. Still, the work ethic of the Japanese, their intensive study and practice habits, their respect for authority, and their preservation of certain ceremonial behaviors emerge to make music learning a Japanese experience.

Korea

Like Japan, Korea opened its doors to the West in the middle of the nineteenth century. Protestant Christian missionaries arrived in

1885, and by 1900, the Yi dynasty had replaced the traditional court orchestra with a Western-style military band. In less than a century, Korean taste in music and music education practices have become nearly identical to those of the West.

The training of secondary school music teachers in Korea is conducted at schools of music in eleven universities and in music education departments at twenty government-subsidized national universities (Sung, 1986, 149–150). As in American programs of study, prospective teachers complete courses in general education and professional education. Music courses include applied study, sightreading (of Western staff notation) and aural skills, keyboard harmony, Western music history and literature, and music education methods. There is one required class in the theory and performance of traditional Korean music for secondary teachers, and none for elementary classroom teachers.* Considering the content of teacher education programs, it would appear that Western techniques are employed by Korean music teachers in teaching Western music.

The Middle East

Music teaching and learning in the Arab Middle East is ancient. From the seventh century, music education in the memorization and recitation of the *Qur'an* contributed to the legal, ethical, and social education of adults and children (Ibsen al-Faruqi, 1986, 7). Muslim religious schools focused much of their attention on reciting the culture's most important literary work through the centuries and thereby assisted in the musical acculturation of each generation.

The arrival of European colonial powers in the nineteenth century and the wide distribution of the phonograph, radio, television, and films in the twentieth century brought major changes to the Arab Middle East. Ibsen al-Faruqi noted a number of Western influences in the school music curriculum:

> Arab children were soon learning "Auld Lang Syne" and "Frere Jacques" rather than Arab improvisational vocal techniques, Arab folk tunes, and muwashshahat [Arabic classical song]. Students were drilled in major and minor scales instead of the maqamat [Arabic system of complex melodic modes]. . . . They were taught to recognize the saxophone, the piano and the cello, but were offered no introduction to either the apprecia-

---

* There is currently no training of elementary music specialists in Korea; rather, classroom teachers with some advanced training in music during their junior and senior years offer music instruction.

tion or performance skills of the 'ud and the nay. They practiced sight singing and tried to achieve an expertise in reading Western notation, while learning nothing about improvisation and nathr al naghamat [a free-metered musical style]. (1986, 8)

While some parts of the Middle East are resisting further foreign influence today, other countries have adapted Western methods of music education intact at all levels. The current public school curriculum in Egypt, for example, consists of "singing, sol-fa according to the Curwen method, rhythmics according to the Aimé method [Paris], rhythm band with percussion instruments, appreciation, improvisation, and musical games" (Hussein, 1986, 127).

New textbooks and teachers' manuals for presenting traditional music through traditional processes have begun to appear in some countries, however, and there is a growing consensus that indigenous teacher education programs should be designed to expose teachers to the "Arab discipline [of music through] Arab materials, Arab techniques, and Arab attitudes and beliefs concerning the sound arts" (Ibsen al-Faruqi, 1986, 10). While knowledge of art music, religious chant, and folk genres in their cultural context may not always be realistic, the means by which they were traditionally transmitted and performed are deemed important by a growing number of music educators. If these educators prevail, aural learning and improvisation will be restored to their major roles in the tradition.

Performing musicians were once trained in the homes of master musicians, but gradually their instruction became a responsibility of the university. In 1968, the music department at the University of Tehran offered separate courses of study in Western and Iranian classical music. There were also two conservatories in the city, one for Western music and another that offered instruction in Iranian classical music, older Persian styles, Western, and hybrid music (Nettl, 1985, 73–74). Instructional methods vary: some teachers continue to teach vocal and instrumental music in the traditional style of aural learning, while others provide the *radif* in notated form to be learned somewhat independently by the student. Aural learning is still an important part of the musicians' training, along with experiences in improvisation that are supervised by the teacher. The proportional use of traditional and Western practices may vary, but the combination of the two is more likely now than it was a generation ago.

Nigeria

Afro-European trade and colonization brought significant changes to music education in Nigeria. Prior to European influence, the most formal music instruction in Nigeria was the apprenticeship system in which the student associated with a master musician in order to learn a particular instrument (Okafor, 1988). By the nineteenth century, the British had established private secondary schools and teacher-training colleges that offered instruction on Western instruments. Even government schools managed to offer singing classes, which were run by teachers with musical interest—but little training.

With the establishment of the first college of music in Africa at the University of Nigeria, courses in Western and traditional African music and music education methods were offered in degree programs leading to a bachelor of arts degree (B.A.) and a professorial position in one of several teachers' colleges. A certification program was also organized; it balances conservatory and academic studies and graduates both practicing musicians and school music teachers. Today, students are exposed to Western methods of music education and bring aspects of the Orff and Dalcroze methods to their teaching positions. New (1983) noted the similarities between the Orff system and traditional African methods of instruction: "Both are concerned with the direct experience of music, without the too early intervention of theory—easy for the African because he has no written notation anyway. . . . Both encourage music as a group activity" (28).

The music curriculum in elementary and secondary schools of Nigeria once almost totally reflected Western music. With the institution of studies in enthnomusicology at the University of Nigeria, there is now an awareness and a renewed interest in traditional music by the media, the schools, and the public at large. While there continues to be concern about the overwhelming effect that Western-styled schooling is having on African culture at large, there is also a belief that certain "progressive" Western methods of music instruction, for example, the Orff and Dalcroze methods, can be successfully employed in developing competent young musicians who perform and understand the older music traditions through somewhat traditional practices (New, 1983, 29).

Thailand

Western values are evident throughout Thailand. The study of English is introduced in first grade, and European influences are notable in the entire educational system. Thailand's present king is a jazz saxophonist with a music degree from Boston University. Rock concerts are major events for Thai students. While there is a general awareness of the older classical music of Thailand's royal courts, a pro-Western attitude prevails across the land.

A mandate in 1978 from the Thai Ministry of Education may eventually bring about the balance of Western and traditional music in the future. Not only did the mandate attempt to raise music to the level of a required course in elementary and secondary schools, but it recommended that an equal share of Western and Thai classical and folk songs be taught in elementary, junior, and senior high schools (Shamrock, 1988, 235). There are currently few music teachers in the Thai schools, however, and only a handful of teacher education specialists at colleges and universities. While the Ministry's mandate is encouraging, its implementation will require the training of many more teachers—particularly in the indigenous music which so few understand.

At least one music department has a carefully structured program for preparing music teachers—the Payap University Music Department in Chiang Mai. A six-semester musicianship program begins the study of Western music through Orff, singing, dictation, and Kodály-oriented ear-training. Subsequent semesters offer written theory as well. Courses in Thai music and ensemble performance are offered as electives (Shamrock, 1988, 209–210).

Although the Orff pedagogy was introduced in Thailand two decades ago, it has not been widely accepted. Orff instruments are similar to the xylophones and metallophones of Thai classical music—and may have been modeled from them—so as to make the Orff instruments somewhat superfluous. Moreover, Shamrock notes that the interaction of teacher and students in the Orff process is "out of place in the context of Thai music. Thai music is traditionally taught by rote, with the student following the teacher obediently and without question" (p. 244).

The study of traditional Thai music and musical instruments can be pursued at several universities. In Bangkok and in the provinces, applied study is offered on *ranat, pi nai, kong wong, khlui* (flute), *chakay* (zither), and several two- and three-stringed fiddles. University *pi phat, khruang sai*, and *mahori* ensembles perform several times each year, featuring students who are majoring in Thai or Western music—or both. Although they read Thai notation, these students learn their performance skills partly through demonstration, imitation, and for some instruments, chanted mnemonics (communication with K. Kantasiri, August 1987).

Vietnam

Despite a long-established Vietnamese culture, the impact of European culture brought by French colonists as early as the eighteenth century was evident in the language, dress, and educational and artistic traditions, particularly in the cities. European concerts became popular among the elite, and music education in the French style was established in many schools. Fixed Do solmization, the Chevé numerical system, and European staff notation were widely accepted in elementary schools by the early twentieth century (communication with P. Nguyen, February 1989).

Following the departure of the French, the Vietnam War, and the disintegration of the government, the Socialist Republic of Vietnam reorganized itself with an effort to return to the country's cultural traditions. In 1979, a conference of the Ministry for Culture and Information discussed the place of music education in the late twentieth century. Among the statements on approaches to the teaching of Vietnamese traditional music were these:

> For music education, we must use traditional music before taking the masterworks in world music. Music education must be in the curricula of the primary and secondary schools, the University and the specialized institutes. Every week, there must be one hour of music education as principal course and one as optional course. Music should be a compulsory subject, the marks of which are to be taken into consideration for admission to the upper class. (Giao Duc Va Pho Bien Am Nhac [Music Education and Popularization of Music], 1979, 11)

As the aim of the conference was to discuss the restoration of traditional Vietnamese music to the school curriculum, specific teaching techniques were not mentioned. Nevertheless, the Western influence is evident in the establishment of schooling as the primary means of music instruction and in a list of musical styles to be offered in the music program: "masterworks . . . [and] folk and art music from the World" (p. 8).

SUMMARY

Music and music education practices in much of the world today are based on Western models. In some cultures, schooling has largely replaced the process of learning through enculturation. Elementary and secondary school curricula prescribe the teaching of Western and traditional music; in fact, the masterworks of Western art music are commonly introduced through listening and performance experiences. In the future, school music instruction may be the primary opportunity for restoring an awareness of indigenous styles that have faded from public knowledge.

As Western music has become infused into music programs, a number of Western techniques have come to be employed by teachers and students. Music literacy is considered an important aim of music education in the schools, and ensembles and general music classes are frequently organized around music reading activities. Solfége exercises are incorporated into classes to benefit the student's voice and the ear and to develop an understanding of pitch relationships in staff notation. The formation of choirs, bands, and orchestras has increased the need for conductors with a knowledge of the Western repertoire and with training in Western theory, history, and applied music. The techniques of classical methods, such as Dalcroze, Orff, and Kodály, are employed by an increasing number of elementary music teachers.

While educational systems have adopted many Western practices, change has come gradually, if at all, in the training of performing musicians in the world's cultures. Western-style conservatories provide the setting for the study of classical voice and instrumental music, as do the homes of musicians. Regardless of the setting, many musicians continue to teach their art in the traditional manner in which they learned. For some, the presence of notation has not diminished their use of oral techniques nor their expectation that students develop aural skills in order to acquire performance techniques and repertoire. The practice of vocalizing instrumental music and the use of mnemonics are still widespread. Those musical styles that require improvisation are thus nurtured through traditional teaching and learning strategies.

As international communication and travel continue to break down barriers, the features that distinguish one culture from the next may continue to grow less marked. The world of music has been subject to cross-cultural influences resulting in intriguing new forms and styles and in the wide acceptance of Western classical and popular music. Music instruction is subject to change as well; this is particularly apparent in the establishment of Western-influenced public school music programs. But even as traditions change, certain elements are retained because their continued use makes sense to people within the culture. In the training of musicians, the development of aural skills and creative expression through vocalization and memory strategies appears constant across many cultures.

PART III

Classroom and Studio Applications

PRELUDE

◆

From a historical glance at music learning in the West (Part I) to an assessment of the transmission, teaching, and learning in music traditions of several world cultures (Part II), the foundation has been laid for a curriculum that seeks to develop basic musicianship in students (Part III). The fundamental qualities of musicians across time and distance vary little, and the nurturing of aural skills and creative musical expression are at the heart of music instruction—"then," "there," and now. From the days of ancient Greece and Rome, through the evolution and adoption of staff notation during the Middle Ages and the Renaissance, in the common practice periods of the Baroque and Classical eras, and in the European-style conservatories of the nineteenth and twentieth centuries, ear-training has maintained its place as a principal goal of music instruction for both professional and amateur musicians in the West, just as the creative elements of improvisation, interpretation, or personal expression have been the ultimate performance goals. Similarly, performers of many great art and traditional music genres in Asia, Africa, and the Americas undergo extensive aural training and strive for a truly musical performance that is grounded in the teacher's (or transmitter's) musical structure and ideas but that also reflects through improvisation the performer's own personality and musical feeling. Worldwide, musicians utilize their listening capacity to learn and retain musical information and to evaluate and strengthen their own performances. In fact, the greatest performers may well be those who allow the creative element to emerge as they express the musical essence. In order to extract the best from these commonalities and differences we must ask: What can we do for our students?

As there is such enormous precedence for the development of listening and improvisation skills, ensemble directors, classroom instructors, and studio teachers would be well advised to consider the use of strategies that nurture these skills in their students. The ability to improvise comes from a long and sequential instructional process, but the development of that ability is well within the realm of activity in rehearsals, classrooms, and studios. The aural and creative capacities, like intelligence itself, require stimulation—partly through informal experiences that the environment provides, but principally through the guidance of teachers who know the students, the music, and the instructional process. While school music programs continue with the principal aim of developing students who are musically literate and capable of responding to conductors in ensemble settings, aural and creative skills need not be dismissed or left to chance. Similarly, while private lessons emphasize technique and repertoire, the teacher's approach need not exclude ear-training and opportunities for improvisation.

Parts I and II of this book presented a theoretical basis for improvisation and its aural skills complement through surveys of historical eras and cultures; Part III offers the means by which these qualities can be developed in students. The goals of this last section are to provide teachers with practical experiences for increasing their students' ability to think in musically creative ways and to increase their own aural sensitivity and aesthetic judgment about the music they perform. Through the *Focus* experiences suggested in the following chapters, instructional strategies that were prominent historically as well as those that continue to be practiced in other cultures can be introduced to classrooms and studios. Common threads of musical training can be thus woven into the school music curriculum, and the logic of listening and musical expression made practical. In particular, an awareness of improvisation as the culmination of musical development and understanding in many periods and places may stimulate an idea too compelling to resist: that improvisation—or personal expression, at the very least—is a necessary component of musicianship regardless of the instructional or performance context. The role of music as art and the human nature of musicians as creators and interpreters of art require music to be an artistic expression. Applying this concept to the classroom, however, is a challenge to be met by discerning teachers who can guide students toward their maximal level of musical development—toward listening, creating, and re-creating with sensitivity.

If the first two sections provided philosophical, historical, psychological, and sociocultural foundations for improvisation and aural skill development, Part III is the "methods text" that provides strategies for their integration into instructional practice. Observation, imitation, repetition, vocalization, solmization, and the employment of mnemonics are tools of the trade that lead toward creative thinking in music. These techniques are hardly unknown to teachers, but they are often employed sparingly, sporadically, or without a clear understanding on the teacher's part of where they may lead.

Since there is agreement throughout the profession that creative improvisation and aural sensitivity are important goals of music teaching, a more substantive, continuous, and thorough use of the "trade tools" should be contained within the instructional process. Knowing the extent to which these techniques are employed historically and culturally is the initial stage; knowing ways in which they can be used in the workaday world of lessons is the goal. The *Focus* experiences are the fabric for lessons that train the ear and stimulate the creative mind; their ideas can be used "as is," and can be repeated, developed, adapted, or combined. Part III contains the pragmatic translation of earlier discussions, the implications of the reported research. Here are the classroom realities and the applications of theory to practice.

CHAPTER

11

◆

The Music Learning
of Children

For music teachers in the West, one of the primary goals of a music education program in American schools is music literacy. Even within only the mandatory six or seven years of general music instruction at the elementary level, prime targets for development in children are the abilities to read and write the conventional symbols of music notation. Many believe that an understanding of music derives from notational skills. To an extent, this is true in the Western cultures that offer such a sophisticated system of music preservation; however, the reading and writing of music should follow a rich and prolonged period of aural experiences. It is in this combination that children can develop a more thorough musical understanding.

Music instruction might be conceived of as a balance of receptive-passive and participatory-active experiences. In the aural mode, listening to recordings and to live performances is a receptive-passive strategy in which the individual is a receiver of musical information presented by others. Chanting, singing, speaking, or playing an instrument involves the participatory-active component of the aural mode, as the student performs the music, listening to his part alone and as it combines with other parts. An example of receptive-passive learning in the visual mode is the silent reading and comprehension of symbols, words, or notation, while writing is a participatory-active behavior of the visual mode. The kinesthetic mode would appear to be entirely experiential. However, a distinction might be made between the unconscious contact a student may have by touching or holding an instrument (receptive-passive) and the conscious physical movement of conducting gestures, eurhythmics, and dance (participatory-active). The balance of experiences in these modes is present in the programs of successful music teachers (figure 11–1).

Music programs at the primary level begin with aural experiences in preparation for note-reading. By second grade, most basal series textbooks introduce symbols and labels for durational values. Staff notation that shows pitch levels and relationships is a significant part of third-grade music. In many schools that employ music teachers, fourth-grade children study recorder or song-flute in an effort to internalize musical symbols. In middle school music, the note-reading is transferred to beginning band and orchestral instruments, and part-songs are learned from scores that represent the rhythms and melodic contours of choral music; this may occur as early as fourth or fifth grade in districts with more extensive instrumental programs. Middle school general music classes in guitar, keyboard, and handbells also develop students' reading skills. As students become more proficient at note-reading, the eyes replace the

	Receptive	Participatory
Aural	Listening	Singing
Visual	Reading music	Writing music
Kinesthetic	Touching, Feeling (holding an instrument, feeling a beat)	Moving (movement, eurhythmics, dance)

FIGURE 11–1 Receptive and participatory experiences in music, in three modes.

Adapted from Sandra Stauffer.

ears as the main channels of sensory input in music instruction. The shift from ear to eye is a part of the process of developing music literacy, but the role of the ear as the natural channel of aural information can play an important part in the development of comprehensive musicianship.

In the past few decades, a growing number of music educators in the elementary and middle schools have been turning toward experiential instruction that stresses sound before sight and the pragmatic philosophy of learning by doing. An examination of music textbooks used in the general music classroom shows an increase in programs that use hands-on, participatory approaches to music. Colorful illustrations are more frequent in recent songbooks, leaving less space for notes and discussions of theoretical concepts; some illustrations are pre-reading and pre-theory in nature. Textbooks and elementary music education curricula with an activities-oriented view demonstrate the belief that playing instruments and singing are the initial rather than the end phase of the learning process. Although in its formative stages, a philosophy that supports the development of performance skills in practice before theory is gaining support.

In elementary music classes of Western-style curricular programs, a number of instructional approaches utilizing aural, oral, and creativity techniques have been proposed and practiced. The most prevalent are the methods of Émile Jaques-Dalcroze, Carl Orff, and Zoltan Kodály. Although they are best known for their musical works, each of these men developed teaching techniques that focus on introducing children to music at an early age. Their approaches emphasize the aural qualities of music first, and then its symbolic form.

By reviewing the salient features of the three prominent European approaches to music instruction, one may discover significant patterns of music teaching and learning. In comparing common elementary school practices to certain world traditions in music learning, one finds that the similarities among transmission systems are often striking. The logic of developing musicality and performance skills in ways that emphasize aural skills will once more be reinforced through a review of these approaches. The related concepts of imitation, creative improvisation, vocalization, solmization, and mnemonics will be highlighted. Further suggestions of these techniques, based on research and observation of their use in the classroom will be offered in the following section on applications.

THE TEACHINGS OF ÉMILE JAQUES-DALCROZE

Rhythmic movement and dance came into prominence as a curricular offering in schools at the turn of the century, but it was through the system of Dalcroze eurhythmics that movement, improvisation, and solfége were integrated into music education. Jaques-Dalcroze determined that musicianship could be developed without the initial rigidity of intellectual analysis. "First the instinct, and then the analysis" was his maxim. If students were capable of moving rhythmically, then a transfer to the accurate performance of musical rhythms seemed likely. Movement became not an end but rather a means of developing a sensitivity to rhythm, phrasing, melody, and form. Jaques-Dalcroze maintained that the body was connected by a complex network of muscles and nerves to the brain, and that training physical response to music was the most direct approach to rhythmic response and musical understanding. Nearly a century later, researchers in neurology and psychology continue to reveal evidence of the mind-body link, lending support to the significance of the Dalcroze techniques of ear-training through the kinesthetic approach.

Because his mother was a Pestalozzian teacher, Jaques-Dalcroze was intensely concerned with learning through experience. He was frustrated with his own classes as a student at the Conservatory of Music in Geneva where rote drills and abstract activities without explanation or relevance to musical performance were common. As a teacher of theory, he searched for ways to develop musical sensitivity as a relief from intellectual analysis and mechanical performance. His plan was to present music to students in aural, oral, and physical modes that would eventually lead to greater expressiveness and creativity in music making.

Kinesthetic Learning

The best-known facet of the Dalcroze technique is eurhythmics in which movement is employed to transform aural sensations into feeling. The kinesthetic sense connects hearing to moving, moving to feeling, and feeling to hearing, so that this rhythmic learning comes full circle. Students learn to attend to even the slightest changes and nuances of rhythm, melody, and harmony, and to evoke a muscular response that communicates the physical feeling of the rhythm to the brain for further information processing and storage in the memory centers. Eurhythmics heightens attention, develops concentration, and deeply ingrains rhythmic sounds within the brain and body in preparation for more musical performances in the future.

Aural Skills

As eurhythmics develops the ability to respond to music kinesthetically, the objective of ear-training, or solfége, is to develop an "inner hearing." Through sight-singing and ear-training experiences, students learn to internalize beat, meter, rhythm, melody, and form. Solfége exercises are used to develop accurate hearing, relative pitch, and refined intonations. Tonal memory, or the capacity to hear and remember a pitch or melodic phrase, is the result of listening and singing in that tonal area. Gestures are often combined with singing as a vehicle for training the ear to understand the relationship between pitches and among durational patterns. The inner hearing ability is attained when the student can think and hear a melody or rhythm without the aid of an instrument or voice.

Improvisation

Jaques-Dalcroze never intended to teach by direct imitation and was chiefly concerned with the student's own creative discovery of solutions to musical problems. To assist in this discovery, he advocated improvisation as an important part of the music instruction process. Dalcroze teachers use the piano in an attempt to individualize student needs, often quickly shifting tempos, rhythms, and styles to match the movement of their students. When students have explored sufficiently an array of expressive movement possibilities and have been thoroughly exposed to many musical ideas, they are encouraged to express themselves in musically creative ways on the piano and on classroom instruments. Melodic and rhythmic fragments they have discovered become the basis for students' expanded instrumental improvisation.

Jaques-Dalcroze also advocated vocal improvisation after a sufficient foundation of sight-singing and ear-training had been laid. Among some Dalcroze teachers, solfége is taught in a way that challenges the student to create musical pieces from the briefest melodic and rhythmic motifs. While the teacher's piano improvisation presents theoretical concepts of music in a way that triggers a physical response, it can also provide ideas for the student's own improvisation. The student then recombines and reconstructs these musical ideas in creative ways that demonstrate his or her understanding of musical phrasing, form, melody, and rhythm.

Imitation

No emphasis is placed on imitative learning in Dalcroze classes, and yet they demonstrate the natural tendency of the teacher to serve as a model to students. Some eurhythmics activities are performed with the teacher moving while sounding a drumbeat or rhythm, or with a student providing the music for movement; both instances give students opportunities to observe and imitate the teacher's grace, balance, and flexibility of movement. A solfége lesson may begin with a musical phrase sung by the teacher; this is repeated and then varied by students. Aside from canons, imitation in Dalcroze instruction is indirect and fleeting, for the objective is to provide students with the freedom for musical expression at the earliest opportunity.

Retention

Classroom exercises associated with the teachings of Jaques-Dalcroze require student responses such as stepping, clapping, moving the arms, conducting, singing, and playing instruments. While the exercises are perceived as games by students, an observer sensitive to teaching techniques quickly sees that "playing" well demands an acute aural capacity, intense concentration, and almost immediate reactions to the music. An exercise called the interrupted canon is an echo technique that aids the development of the student's short-term memory. For example, the teacher sounds a rhythmic pattern that is immediately echoed by the class through vocal or instrumental means or through movement. This use of imitation is intended to strengthen the student's memory capacity for hearing and performing music (figure 11–2).

The continuous canon is a more difficult memory task that directs students to follow the teacher's movement or sounds at a space of several beats or measures. The teacher begins a rhythmic pattern with the command that students begin "four beats" or "one measure" later. Again, the imitation device is a means of producing a greater capacity for memorization rather than as a means of rote-learning songs or passages for performance (figure 11–3).

Notation

Learning to read and write music is a result of the solfége training. Some who adhere to Dalcroze techniques first give students a one-line staff to help them in rhythmically speaking and singing the solfége syllables (figure 11–4). Next, they practice singing notes on a two-line staff, then on three, and finally on the full five lines.

Other Dalcroze proponents introduce mapping as a pre-reading technique, in which the melody's rising and falling pitches are de-

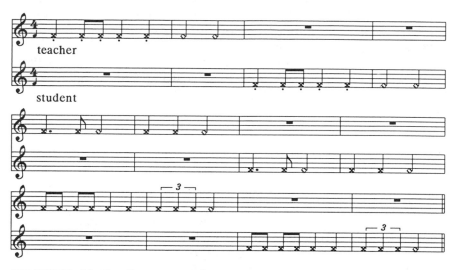

FIGURE 11–2   Interrupted canon.

FIGURE 11–3   Continuous canon.

FIGURE 11–4   One-line staff.

picted through line drawings in the air or on the chalkboard. Directions for solfége singing, eurhythmics, and improvisation are given through an economic use of words; they may be offered as well through nonverbal means such as hand gestures, facial expressions, and nods of the head. The notation of rhythmic patterns occurs after students have spent ample time moving to the rhythm. The internalized rhythm is then jotted like a telegraph message in dashes and dots across a chalkboard, and note stems are added later (figure 11–5). Music literacy is accepted as a natural complement to the Dalcroze technique, but the emphasis is on maximizing the expressive potential of the student musician.

FIGURE 11–5 Dash-a-note.

CARL ORFF'S LEGACY

The impact of Carl Orff on music instruction for children in North America is considerable. Although his approach is rich in a variety of musical experiences, the prevalence in classrooms of special-model Orff xylophones, metallophones, and glockenspiels is the clearest testimony to its popular appeal. Carl Orff acknowledged his awareness of the contemporary dance and theater scene in Europe with the development of "Schulwerk," an experiential form of music learning through creative play. Gunild Keetman, one of Orff's prize pupils, is credited by Orff himself in the application of his ideas to a pedagogy for children. From Orff's perspective, music is inseparable from movement and speech, and all were initially derived from childhood experiences. Through speech-rhythms and chants, songs, and spontaneous and structured movement, children discover and demonstrate musical concepts. While rhythm is the starting point, the ultimate aim of the Orff process is to develop creative musicianship as displayed in the ability to improvise.

Kinesthetic Learning

The untrained and natural movement of children is a significant component of the Orff process of music education. Such play activities as jumping, skipping, spinning, swinging, and running are encouraged in the interpretation of music that is played by the teacher and other students. Also, attention is drawn to the form and rhythm of children's movements, and the students are guided to improvise instrumental patterns in the rhythms and phrasing of their movement. A mirroring of movement through music, and music through movement is planned in order to capture the expressiveness of children in these forms and to nurture the natural fusion of the two.

An important step leading to the performance of Orff instruments is the introduction of preliminary body motions and gestures that one later applies to the instruments. A bordun (a repeated accompaniment pattern utilizing the first and fifth degrees of the scale) for xylophone is prepared by patting (or "patsching") both hands simultaneously on the lap. A broken ostinato pattern is first "played" with the hands in the air or on the lap. This kinesthetic learning is critical to the Orff pedagogy, a highly structured type of movement that develops the motor skills for performance.

Aural Skills

Proponents of the Orff approach agree in theory that the most expedient means of music transmission is through aural learning. Students are encouraged to explore the spectrum of environmental sounds for their musical potential, and to listen for the timbral qualities of tree leaves blowing, birds singing, and cars squealing in traffic. The aim is to develop a musical sensitivity that may eventually find its way into students' creative compositions. Focused listening is the key to learning a song; two- and three-tone chants, pentatonic folk songs, and then compositions that utilize seven—or more— pitches are likely to be learned by ear. Instrumental accompaniments as well are generally learned through observation, with the student listening repeatedly until the sounds become familiar. Music learning as advocated through the Orff approach is largely an aural experience.

Improvisation

Those who practice Orff techniques encourage children to explore space through movement, and sounds through their voices, body sounds, and instruments. Without extensive verbiage by teacher or students, the students are called upon to move expressively within spatial confines. Components of music are sampled through creative movement, with students demonstrating such qualities as short, long, smooth, choppy, light, and heavy. Separately or simultaneously with movement, students develop an awareness of sound sources, including speech, nonsense words, and environmental sounds. From sounds without organization to coherent musical sounds, students experiment with the possibilities of personal expression. Speech rhythms are assigned pitches, and the melodies then require instrumental accompaniment—often without the sounds being notated, often through spontaneous improvisation. Together, these explorations of space and sound pave the way for true musical improvisation.

Orff-trained teachers frequently interpret improvisation in a far more restricted way than that found in many Western and world musical styles. Question-and-answer activities, in which the students create brief musical responses to a teacher's musical question, are tightly controlled by the teacher and by certain rhythmic and tonal expectations. Other experiences may involve echo-style improvisation in which the teacher dictates a phrase that triggers a change of pitch or rhythm (but not both) by students. The parameters for these initial encounters with creative improvisation are sometimes quite confining, and yet they can form the basis for greater individuality and expressive freedom in the future.

Imitation

The teacher of Orff-Schulwerk is, in the purest form, a role model for musicianship and creativity. The teacher's source of model materials is based in the music of the children's native culture as well as the teacher's improvised repertoire and knowledge of composed music. Students are given the opportunity to observe and then imitate a movement, a vocal pattern, a rhythmic chant, or an instrumental passage. Canons that feature body percussion sounds and melodies sung with words or neutral syllables are common. Vocal and instrumental imitation of environmental sounds is promoted, and a vocabulary of melodic, rhythmic, and harmonic patterns becomes a reference for the invention of original music. Students build a repertoire of musical behaviors based on, but not limited to, the ideas of a well-trained teacher. As children demonstrate greater understanding of the musical elements, the role of the teacher is gradually diminished. Students eventually become models for each other. Orff techniques in children's music classes aim for the development of independent musicianship which is realized in the ability of children to create music in improvisation and composition. For children to develop chants and songs into more complete vocal and instrumental pieces, to invent their own rhythms, melodies, and accompaniment figures—these were the goals of Carl Orff's approach.

Retention

In learning rhythmic passages, a type of memory strategy is employed by Orff proponents in which speech patterns are vocalized to specific rhythms. The names of children may be attached to rhythms: John, Ma-ry, E-mi-ly, An-to-ni-ta (figure 11–6). The rhyming chants of longer phrases are eventually internalized, leaving a strong feeling for and familiarity with the rhythm, which may be

"John   Ma - ry   Em - i - ly   An - to - ni - ta"

FIGURE 11–6   Rhythmic name chants.

more easily identified in future musical pieces. Nursery rhymes, un-
pitched commercial jingles, and cheerleader chants are examples of
mnemonic devices that derive essentially from speech rhythms proposed by Orff. Indeed, nearly any spoken phrase can be set to
rhythms, including "Rain, rain, go a-way, come a-gain an-oth-er day"
and "Pe-ter, Pe-ter, pump-kin eat-er," "Beat-em, boys, beat-em" and
"You de-serve a break to-day" (figure 11–7). With ample repetition of
these speech chants, the associated rhythms become an integral part
of the young musician's knowledge of rhythmic phrases or patterns,
as in the one-measure examples.

Notation

Although the Schulwerk is based on the premise that music is a
natural part of childhood experiences and that children should experience music creatively through reading readiness activities such as
singing, moving, and playing instruments, Orff recognized that ultimately these activities should lead to music literacy. Music reading
and writing are perceived as a culmination of the various encounters
children have with the musical experience itself, and the exploration
of movement and music should precede the learning of notation.
With the introduction of the recorder, children begin reading standard notation. No prescription is ever given for teaching them how to
read music; the task is left to the teacher to develop music literacy
after a suitable period of preparation. The assumption of the Orff
approach is that children who sing, dance, and play music can readily
read notation and because of these early experiences will be more
musical in translating notes into sounds.

Pe-ter Pe-ter pump-kin Ea-ter   You de-serve   a   break to-day

FIGURE 11–7   Rhythmic speech chants.

THE SEQUENTIAL METHOD OF ZOLTAN KODÁLY

When Kodály observed the poor quality of musicianship and the extent of music illiteracy among the people in his native Hungary, he launched a powerful campaign to elevate the standards of music education. He designed a systematic method for the school curriculum, which stipulated four to six weekly periods of music instruction from kindergarten through secondary levels and a sequence of musical experiences that progressed from rhythm training through singing to instrumental lessons. The Hungarian music program emphasizes music reading and writing from an early age, through sight-singing and dictation. American-style Kodály education retains the use of pentatonic folk songs, the sol-fa approach to sight-reading with its hand signs, a rhythmic system of mnemonic syllables, and an emphasis on unaccompanied song. Kodály's conception of a national music education method has transcended geographical boundaries and the techniques are used intact or in part in many American classrooms today.

Kinesthetic Learning

In the late nineteenth century, John Curwen introduced the use of hand signs into music education practices in England, and they were later adapted by Kodály for use in Hungary. Gestures are performed from the chest to eye level by the dominant hand in an attempt to symbolize the pitches of songs and chants as they are sung. By employing the kinesthetic, the aural, and the visual senses, students are apt to learn and retain pitches and pitch relationships more quickly. In addition to hand signs, the use of folk dances is encouraged in the school music curriculum, for they are part and parcel of many children's songs in their natural form. The use of dance to illustrate concepts of rhythm and form is also recognized by proponents of Kodály.

Aural Skills

As part of the focus on music reading and writing, the Kodály method advocates a preparatory period in which the ear is trained to recognize rhythmic and melodic patterns that are eventually presented in visual form. The Tonic Sol-fa system is the foundation of pitch training, and rhythm syllables are used to establish rhythmic durations. Patterns of pitches and rhythms, rather than separate and isolated sounds, help listening students understand the relationships of notational symbols in a musical piece.

Folk songs taught by rote provide a wealth of aural experiences in pentatonic and diatonic patterns as well as common rhythmic figures. Songs are selected with specific patterns in mind, and the frequent occurrence of such patterns as la-sol-mi and mi-re-do in a variety of songs reinforces and internalizes those sounds. The repetition of patterns results in a familiarity with these basic components of music, leading to a gradual increase in the student's musical vocabulary. The development of inner hearing—the capacity to think the musical sounds without hearing them or externally voicing them—is an important thrust of Kodály training. Students acquire this skill naturally through the aural learning of traditional songs and their inherent patterns.

Improvisation

Once children have clapped rhythms, sung songs, and danced to music of folk dances, they are prepared for spontaneous and exploratory experiences at every level. In learning rhythmic skills, students are taught to respond to rhythmic phrases with their own improvised phrases. A question-and-answer activity is initiated in which the teacher (or another student) may chant or clap a four-beat rhythm that is immediately answered by the student in another four-beat pattern. Longer phrases are gradually introduced, and the student continues to respond with a similar number of beats.

In American schools, melodic improvisation is less common, although a similar question-and-answer game may be designed to allow students to express melodic ideas in a responsorial manner. Improvisation is believed by some to be more advanced than aural learning, to be preceded by extensive note-reading exercises. Improvisation is suggested as a way for students to express their vocabulary of aural patterns creatively and to interpret notated melodic and rhythmic fragments in new and musical ways.

Imitation

Teaching songs by rote is prominent in the Kodály method. As language is learned through speech before it is read or written, music is often sung before its symbols are assimilated. In the initial stages, students have a larger rote than note vocabulary; that is, they have aurally acquired many sounds and musical phrases while their ability to identify musical notation is yet limited. The teacher employs Kodály pedagogy by singing tonal patterns that are immediately repeated by the children. When a new song is introduced, it is first sung in its entirety by the teacher; the children then imitate the teacher's singing phrase by phrase. This mirroring of the song provides students an opportunity to imitate not only the song but also the correct intonation, musical phrasing, articulation, and breathing necessary for good vocal production.

The Kodály method is intended as a progressive learning sequence that begins with the preschool child and continues through secondary school; therefore, there are various levels of musical complexity that can be approached with the same philosophy and educational tools. The Tonic Sol-fa, hand signs, and rhythm duration syllables are used with ease by advanced student musicians who have learned them in their elementary school years. The use of imitation continues through the grades, and even concepts of harmony and theory may be presented aurally through rote experiences. Students may be asked to sing the individual pitches of a chord or the bass line of a harmonic progression in imitation of their teacher before progressing to exercises in harmonic analysis. Although the instructional goal of the method is a musically literate society, the system allows for rote-singing at every stage.

Retention

To help students learn and retain rhythmic patterns, Kodály offered a series of syllables first invented by Émile Chevé in the nineteenth century. The syllables, vocables with no known semantic meaning, are associated with quarter notes, eighth notes, a set of four sixteenths, triplets, and so forth. The note symbols are initially read aloud, as students vocalize the mnemonic syllables in a rhythmic chant. Note value labels are attached later, and even then, students may continue to refer to the rhythms by their vocables. Mathematical relationships are not a part of this approach to rhythm; rather, the rhythmic sound itself is internalized as a result of the students' chanting aloud. The mnemonic syllables widely practiced by Kodály teachers are shown in figure 11–8.

Students' musical memories are strengthened through activities that require them to listen to a song performed by the teacher on a neutral syllable and to identify the song. Students may focus better on learning new songs that can be added to their storage of familiar melodies; these are then retrieved during this "Name that Tune"

tah   ti-ti   ti-ri-ti-ri   syn-co-pa   too   toom   toe   tri-o-la

FIGURE 11–8 Mnemonic rhythm syllables of Kodály practice.

activity. A variation of the game provides for exercising the memory and the inner hearing capacity, as teachers give only the hand signs for the pitches of the song.

Notation

Kodály's philosophy on the music education of children is that those who are capable of lingual literacy are also capable of musical literacy. All aural experiences lead to the reading and writing of music. As reading words is a skill learned through formal training, so music reading is a learned skill. Musical understanding through literacy also generates an appreciation for music; thus, learning a musical notation system is viewed as serving a vital function in Western music education.

The learning sequence advocated by proponents of Kodály is sensitive to the psychological development of the child and is based on observations of age-dependent capabilities of children. For this reason, Kodály educators choose to teach duple meter before triple meter; minor thirds are taught before perfect fifths. The musical characteristics of the culture also determine what tonal and rhythmic materials are to be learned and when. The "childhood chant" of so-mi-la-so-mi is prevalent in European and Euro-American songs, while African and African-American songs emphasize the descending do-la-so or rising do-re-mi. The greater the frequency of melodic and rhythmic patterns in the traditional music of the culture, the greater is the use of those patterns in the music classroom.

The teaching of rhythms progresses from experiences with a steady beat, through accents and meter, to specific rhythmic durations and their patterns. Mnemonic syllables are gradually phased out as the rhythm is felt, internalized, and totally intellectualized by the student. In a similar way, common tonal patterns are presented in song, on chalkboard staves, and in the air through hand signs until the repetition (with some variety) allows the student to incorporate these melodic segments into an inner-hearing sense. The hand signs and solfége singing are sometimes replaced by the more common practice of letter names when the student reaches the stage of instrumental instruction. The ultimate goal of the Kodály sequence, however, is to develop in students the ability to hear internally and understand fully the notes on the musical staff.

PARALLELS: WITHIN THE WEST AND AROUND THE WORLD

Among the approaches currently practiced in children's elementary music classes in the West, several comparisons can be drawn. It appears that music literacy is an expectation of the three classic methods, but that their learning contents and sequences differ. Even the goals vary considerably: Jaques-Dalcroze maintained that students should develop the ability to express sound through movement before song, instrumental performance, or music reading; Orff upheld the importance of the musical experience and offered a wide variety of creative experiences for musical performance and personal expression; and Kodály supported singing as the principal mode of performance and the means for developing music reading and writing skills.

No educator can deny that the development of musical sensitivity in students requires some exposure to aural learning. One objective of Dalcroze eurhythmics and ear-training is to develop students' ability to hear musical events and phrases internally, and solfège exercises are organized to give students the ability to think and hear a melody without the use of an instrument. The Orff teacher acts as a role model, presenting potential musical phrases and providing for many experiences in song, in chant, and on instruments. An important emphasis of the Kodály system is the introduction of notation following experiences in rote-singing tonal patterns and songs and rote-chanting rhythmic phrases. All approaches advocate learning initially by ear, an experience that provides the student the relevance and musical logic necessary for understanding notation.

The emphasis on kinesthetic learning varies from method to method, but every musician-theorist-pedagogue has recognized the natural tendency of children to move to music and the importance of such movement in their realizing a fuller musical understanding. Eurhythmics is the foundation of musicianship for the Dalcroze method, and every element of music can be explored through thoughtful movement. Many Orff experiences are based on free and creative play movements that express the music, from walking to running to skipping to rocking. The Kodály process incorporates hand signals for spatial representation of pitches and their relationships, and a commitment to the folk music heritage provides opportunities for folk dancing in the Kodály curriculum.

Musical creativity as evidenced in improvisation is another common element among the elementary music practices. In the Dalcroze techniques, creativity begins with the body as an instrument, with students learning to express musical elements such as rhythm, tempo, dynamics, and melody through movement. Only later is such expression carried to improvisation vocally or on percussion instruments. Improvisation is a key aspect of the Orff approach, and students progress from free expressions of speech and movement to the building of patterns into musical pieces on xylophones. Spontaneous vocal improvisations are part of the Kodály method, as students are encouraged to provide musical answers to musical questions.

There are strategies in the various music methods for learning and retaining music and for internalizing musical sounds, a desirable outcome of musicianship. The teachings of Jaques-Dalcroze offer a number of experiences in exercising the memory capacity through canons, a practice in which the student listens and then sounds what the teacher has performed. The Orff process makes use of speech rhythms for learning and remembering particular durations, patterns, and longer rhythmic phrases; it frequently utilizes the canon as well. The use of the Chevé mnemonics and the Tonic Sol-fa among Kodály educators provides techniques for storing rhythms and tonal patterns in the memory.

As these methods of music instruction were established by composer-theorists, it is only logical that one of their primary goals is the development of music reading skills. The Dalcroze experiences provide for training in solfége and note-reading only after several years of eurhythmics training. It then uses the Fixed Do system along with mapping gestures and the introduction of a one-, two-, three-, and finally five-line staff. The Orff method does not clearly provide for a system in teaching music reading. Instead, the Schulwerk was conceived as a prereading process for developing musicianship and preparing students for future literacy through private applied study of an instrument or through more advanced music classes. The purpose of Kodály's approach is to teach music literacy, and music reading begins in the first grade—or earlier when possible—with the sol-fa system in Movable Do, progressing from tritonic (three-tone) nursery rhymes to diatonic scales by the intermediate grades.

As there are parallels among the methods, there are also parallels among these methods and learning styles found in other cultures. Features of aural learning found in the Dalcroze, Orff, and Kodály methods are related to the oral transmission process of much of the world's music. Imitation of a teacher or competent musician is a widely practiced device for learning music, from the strict use of rote singing to the more moderate view of the teacher as a role model for appropriate performance practice. Some of the greatest examples of imitation in non-Western cultures may be found among the drummers of India and Japan, who observe their teacher's performance, listening carefully for the timbral and durational values of the rhythmic patterns before attempting to play. Notation is used later only as a memory aid, but drum lessons proceed without sheet music or scores. Dalcroze, Orff, and Kodály methods also emphasize the teacher's modeling as a key pedagogical principle, with music-reading skills growing from children's earlier observations and aural experiences.

In some cultures there is a coexistence of oral and written traditions for learning music. In Thailand, teachers of ranat (xylophone) choose between presenting a piece through the phrase-by-phrase process of imitation and allowing students to glance at notation in the lesson in the hope of learning the music more rapidly. The absence of symbols indicating rhythm and phrasing in traditional Chinese notation requires the student to listen carefully to the teacher's performance so as to realize the music beyond the printed pitch symbols. Many African and Asian societies that once passed on music orally are now likely to use Western notation to some extent as a means of preserving and transmitting music.

The strict adherence to imitation in India or among jazz performers is much like the earliest learning experiences in each of the three classic European methods. The Orff process is not systematic in its presentation of specific tonal and rhythmic patterns as is the system found in India, although rhythmic chants and songs are demonstrated by the teacher as additional sound possibilities in students' creative compositions. In some sense, Orff may be more akin to the style of jazz musicians who learn their art by listening to and then emulating the great masters. The sequential Kodály method is as precise and orderly as that of Indian musicians, particularly those of the southern Karnatic traditions, and the practice of rote singing is vital to an aural understanding of patterns found in folk songs. The difference is that Kodály teachers present notation as soon as students have had ample preparation through listening and imitation experiences that will allow them to associate symbols with familiar sounds.

The use of mnemonics is widespread in music learning around the world. The rhythmic recitation of syllables is preliminary to performance and essential for learning such instruments as the Indian tabla and mṛidaṅga drums, Japanese theater and ceremonial drums, the drums of the classical court orchestra of Thailand, certain African percussion instruments, the Indonesian *kendang*, the goblet drums of Islamic influence, and the Middle Eastern tambourine. Kodály recommended that students chant rhythmic syllables before they learn notation to hasten their learning of rhythms. In practice, many Kodály teachers introduce the symbols soon after the syllables are aurally presented, with concurrent visual exercises reinforcing the mnemonic sounds of the rhythms.

Beyond the development of aural and creative skills, several other aspects of teaching style and learning behaviors emerge as significant in both music methods for children and world music traditions. A refined sense of musicianship and appropriate performance technique is shaped by teachers through techniques of successive approximation and consistent teacher approval. Verbal or not, the reinforcement of accurate pitches, precise rhythms, expressive phrasing, and creative improvisation is generously offered by effective teachers of any method in any culture. Modeling the teacher's physical behavior is another frequent occurrence, with students attending to the teacher's performance techniques on instruments of the Orff ensemble, in the demonstration of movement potential in Dalcroze, folk-dance steps in Orff and Kodály, and hand gestures in Kodály's sol-fa. Modeling is also used in formal and informal learning experiences for Japanese koto, Irish fiddle, Egyptian nay (flute), Indian sitar, Indonesian xylophone, Bulgarian gaida (bagpipe), and African kora (harp) in that students observe the performance posture of their teachers, the position of the instrument in relationship to the performer, and the preparation and follow through of the plectrum, the fingers, or the hand strokes. The interaction of aural imitation and visual modeling may be a powerful means of learning not only music but also the culture's acceptable manner of performance.

APPLICATIONS

Each of the suggested *Focus* experiences that follow is developed with the intention of strengthening the student's listening and performance skills. The experiences are designed for use in music classes for children in the elementary grades but can be easily adapted for preschool settings; several may be suitable for secondary general music classes, choral and instrumental ensembles, and private studio lessons (see chapters 12 and 13). Some may seem to be "games," as children frequently develop skills and understanding through play. The emphasis of these experiences, however, is to expand students' use of the aural faculty so as to develop their musicianship at the elementary level. Imitation, creative improvisation and the use of learning and retention strategies are associated with aural learning as means or ends of keenly developed listening skills.*

FOCUS 1: Daily Listening (aural skills)
If students are to understand the components of a musical style, they must have extensive opportunities for listening. A familiarity

* Movable Do will be employed for all *Focus* experiences that emphasize pitch and melody.

with characteristic melodies and meters and their tonal and rhythmic patterns can develop through the efforts of both music specialists and classroom teachers at the elementary level. Listening occurs as students are singing and playing instruments in the music classroom as well as through formal directed listening experiences, but casual listening can also happen as students are engaged in nonmusical activities. When children play at recess, have short breaks, and arrive at school or prepare to leave at the end of the day, sounds of a targeted musical style can be played on tapes or recordings in the classroom. This informal listening will lay the foundation for discrimination skills that will later develop from active performance and guided listening experiences. As this is not directed listening, a specialist's well-structured class sessions will be required at a later time to promote an understanding of the various music traditions or musical works.

It is the responsibility of music specialists to generate interest among classroom teachers in providing daily listening experiences for children and recommending the means for doing so. The specialist may wish to prepare a list of recommended recordings available in the library or music room for short-term loan. Suggestions to the classroom teacher for a bulletin board and development of a music listening center in the homeroom would enhance and enrich the learning that occurs in the music class. An ideal arrangement would be the provision by the music teacher of cassette tapes of musical works introduced in class or of selected examples of a particular musical style. For example, if the goal of a month-long musical unit is an understanding of Baroque style, then a tape with three- to five-minute excerpts of music by J. S. Bach, Rameau, Couperin, (Domenico) Scarlatti, Vivaldi, Telemann, and Handel would offer aural examples that could be played repeatedly during times of quiet play. Tapes might be prepared, and multiple copies produced, for music of all the Western historical periods, for the many music traditions of the world, and for particular genres, such as musical theatre, sacred vocal music, music for flutes, or percussion sounds.

This is not to say that such music should become only background accompaniment to other classroom activities; rather, the tapes will serve to supplement the music class and enable students to become more familiar with the patterns and structure of a musical style through repeated listenings. Within the limited time frame of most school music programs, the music class must be geared toward active performance, creative composition, and guided listening experiences. The music teacher leads students toward a fuller understanding of a musical style through concentrated experiences with its component parts; still, the classroom teacher may contribute to the musical growth of children outside the music class by providing informal listening experiences.

FOCUS 2: Parroting Patterns (aural skills, memory)

Teachers may begin the imitative experience by clapping, tapping, moving, chanting, or in some other way performing a rhythmic or melodic pattern. Students then imitate the teacher (see figure 11–9). They should show no change of speed, no hesitation, but rather immediate and precise imitation while keeping the same steady pulse. The phrases should be brief at first, within a four-beat framework, and then gradually lengthened to expand the students' capacity for listening and retaining. The activity can progress from the simultaneous response of the entire class to individual student responses.

A variation of this memory activity might be student imitation in a different mode: the teacher may chant a rhythm and the students may echo it in movement, on an instrument, or in sung melody. The teacher may encourage a variety of arm, leg, torso, elbow, wrist, and head movements; he or she may limit the imitation of a rhythm on pitched instruments to just two or three tones, and later expand to pentatonic and diatonic possibilities.

Melodic imitation will present a greater challenge, so that when

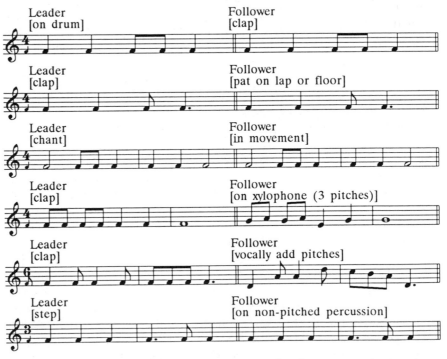

FIGURE 11–9 Sampling of phrases for listening, imitation, and recall.

the emphasis is on pitch, care should be taken at first to keep the rhythm fairly straightforward and to ensure that it consists only of beats and their simple subdivisions. The teacher may wish to use solfége or to sing on a neutral syllable, with or without hand signs or gestures to indicate pitch level. Students may echo the patterns vocally at first, but with experience they may learn to imitate them on pitched instruments.

A student may act as the leader, initiating the pattern that individual students or the class as a whole reproduces. The imitator(s) can be selected ahead of time, so that there is no lapse between the leader's pattern and the follower's imitation. Such an activity may work well with partners who can alternate between leader and follower roles. Imitation can be brief or carry across several phrases.

FOCUS 3: A System of Syllables (aural skills, memory)

Using a mnemonics system, the teacher vocally chants rhythms to students which they repeat in turn. This might be a preliminary aural activity or preparation for specific rhythm patterns in a song to be learned. The chanting of rhythms may follow any number of systems through the grade levels, but should be followed consistently after it is taught. The systems shown in Table 11–1 present possibilities for teaching rhythms:

TABLE 11–1

	Kodály	Indian*	Japanese†	Orff-chant‡	Gordon§	Label-chant
♩	ta	ta	tan	"pear"	du	quart
♫	ti-ti	ki-ta	te-ka	"ap-ple"	du-de	2-eighths
♬	ti-ri-ti-ri	ki-ta-ta-ka	—— ‖	"wa-ter-mel-on"	du-tuh-de-tuh	4-six-teen-notes
♩	too	dhum	ton [low]	"pea-each"	du	half
♪♪♪	tri-o-la	——	——	"straw-ber-ry"	du-da-di	trip-o-let

* South Indian Karnatic rhythm system; onomatopoeic sounds based on drum strokes and durations.

† Japanese *matsuri bayashi* (festival drums) sounds; require vocal inflections for accurate rendering of drum quality.

‡ Examples of word-chants rather than specific mnemonics to be used exclusively; other words and phrases can be substituted.

§ Edwin E. Gordon proposes this system, based on the suggestions of *McHose and Tibbs*, 1944.

‖ Of course, the absence of a mnemonic does not indicate the absence of the rhythm within the tradition; rather, there are many possible mnemonic labels that depend on the full musical context of the rhythm and what part of the drum is to be played.

FOCUS 4: Sing a Small Phrase (aural skills, improvisation)

By isolating a phrase of a familiar song, students can learn the pitch and intervallic structure of a melody (figure 11–10). A particular melodic pattern can be designated for the music class; this can be sung at different pitch levels using solfége. Words can be attached to the targeted phrase, preplanned by the teacher, or invented by the students using tonal inflections reflective of speech pattern. Complete dialogues can be created as students sing their conversation in a recitative-like manner. In this way, students may internalize the pattern, knowing its pitches thoroughly. They have begun the process of improvising as well, experimenting with one feature: the words.

Following exposure to particular patterns and phrases, students can be challenged to identify them in recorded music. Listening then becomes more comprehensive as isolated patterns are heard in the context of classical, folk, and popular pieces.

FOCUS 5: Patterns-in-Hiding (aural skills)

After students have learned a prescribed melodic or rhythmic pattern, songs that carry the pattern can be presented (figure 11–11). Familiar songs can be used to launch this activity; after singing them, students can search for the hidden pattern that the teacher will demonstrate for them by chanting or singing on "loo." They identify the pattern by singing the specific words of that phrase, after which the entire class sings the pattern using the solfége syllables. It may be helpful for students to hear and repeat these patterns a number of times and even to sing the entire song again before the hidden patterns are uncovered.

FOCUS 6 Questions and Answers (improvisation)

Many of the world's traditional folk songs provide examples of phrases consisting of two-measure questions and two-measure answers. When students have been adequately exposed to a repertoire of songs, and their melodic and rhythmic patterns, the teacher should encourage a fuller understanding of their use in small improvised musical phrases (figure 11–12). Vocally on "loo," with percussion instruments, or with xylophones, recorders, and keyboards, students can carry on musical conversations with the teacher or other students.

It may be necessary for students to spend time chanting and singing questions and answers together in imitation of the teacher so that the musical possibilities and the task become clear. For melodic questions and answers, solfége can be helpful (although singing on "loo" or another neutral syllable will do), with questions ending systematically on the dominant (sol), and answers on tonic (do). In a large circle, the teacher can present a question to be answered simul-

FIGURE 11–10 Melodic phrases from familiar songs for listening and later improvisation.

a. "Draw a Bucket of Water" (Anglo-American): **d-d-r-m-d-s**

b. "Spring Has Come" (Japanese): **s-l-s-m-d**

c. "Little Partridge" (Greek): **l-t-d-r-t-l**

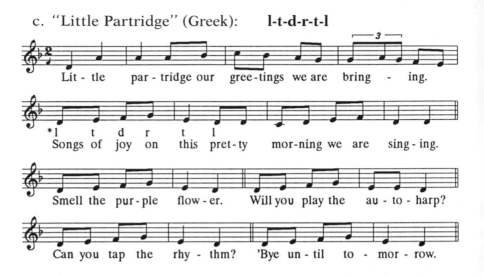

taneously by the entire group (the polyphonic texture may be an exciting musical experience in itself). Eventually, individual questions and answers can be performed. The teacher presents a rhythmic or melodic question to the child on the left who responds with an answer. That child presents a question to the child on his or her left, who responds in kind. All the while, children are keeping the pulse by conducting of lightly patting, and listening to the vocal conversations; a limit or four- or eight-beats might be initially imposed. For initial experiences, rhythmic questions and answers might be easier for students to grasp. Then when the idea is set, the pitch element of melodic dialogues is less burdensome.

FIGURE 11–11 Searching for patterns in familiar songs.

a. "Rain, Rain, Go Away" and "A Tisket, a Tasket" (Anglo-American): **s-m-l-s-m**

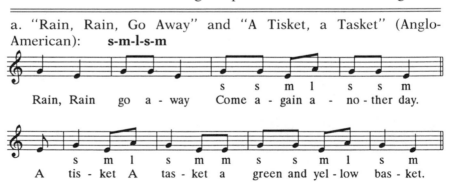

b. "School is Out" (Chinese) and "Charlie over the Ocean" (British):   **d-r-m**

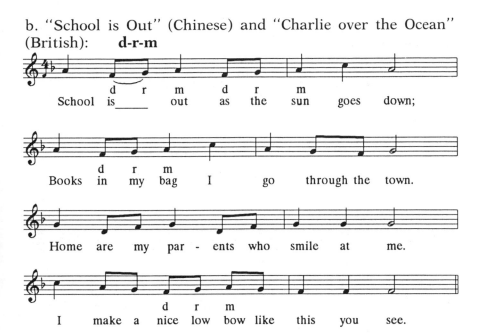

School is____ out as the sun goes down;

Books in my bag I go through the town.

Home are my par - ents who smile at me.

I make a nice low bow like this you see.

Char-lie o - ver the o - cean, Char-lie o - ver the sea,____

Char-lie caught a black - bird, he can't catch me.____

c. "Hey, Betty Martin" (Anglo-American) and "Pourquoi" (French-Canadian):

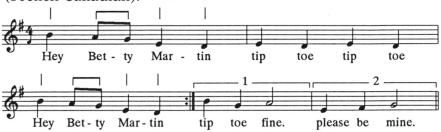

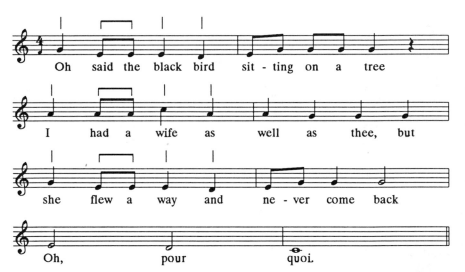

Questions should be tonally and rhythmically simple at first. They should be limited to familiar patterns, with a gradual expansion from three-tone patterns to diatonic scales, and from quarter notes to syncopations. Parameters should be clear; for example, the same phrase length (number of beats or measures) should be used for questions and answers, and the answer should end on the tonic. Question and answer improvisations can be effectively performed with partners, vocally or on instruments. This elementary experience in improvisation will allow students to use their musical knowledge in a creative and original manner as they think and hear the structure of their own music.

FOCUS 7: Name That Tune (memory)

Once a collection of songs has been learned, a challenge to students' memories is the identification of a song when only one segment of the melody or rhythm is presented (figure 11–13). The teacher may sing the melody on a neutral syllable or chant the mnemonic syllables

FIGURE 11-11 (*continued*)
d. "White Llamas" (Peruvian-Quechua Indian) and "Mary a Baby" (African-American):

for the rhythm of the melody. The presentation of a complete phrase should quite naturally lead the student to the identification of a specific song. However, it may be interesting to present only an interval or a phrase of several beats or pitches, and challenge the students to name a number of songs that contain the pattern.

FOCUS 8: Silent Singing (memory)

As students sing a familiar song together, the teacher may signal by hand clap or gesture the start of a section that will be thought instead of sung (figure 11–14). The first signal will notify the students to begin silent singing, and the second will tell them to return to singing aloud. They must respond quickly; maintaining meter and tonality during the mental singing will require concentration and exercise of memory. Internalizing the song in silent singing will give them a more personal association with it, and the return to group singing will prove to be a rewarding experience.

FOCUS 9: Play-a-Pattern (memory)

In this exercise the teacher may assign students melodic patterns to play on the xylophone, recorder, or keyboard each time the

FIGURE 11–12 Samples of musical question and answer phrases.

patterns occur in a song (figure 11–15). A selection of patterns as brief as three pitches can be played by one student, or assigned to three students to play alternating pitches of a melody, somewhat similar to the way tunes are played by a handbell choir. The use of instruments of different timbres will allow several melodic patterns to be highlighted in a single song, with each pattern distinguished by its unique timbral quality. Students who are sharing a phrase by alternating pitches should be initially encouraged to sing as they play, in an attempt to connect the individual pitches more musically. An extension of this experience is the opportunity for students to play or move to melodic or rhythmic patterns that occur in recorded instrumental works.

FOCUS 10: From Pattern to Program-Ready (improvisation)
    In examining the way music is created, a class experience in creativity may provide the sequence for future exploration by individual students (figure 11–16). As a group, the students follow the path of a composition's development, from a rhythm pattern to a melody to instrumental accompaniment. The teacher, followed by student leaders, may select an interesting rhythm (a pattern of four measures in length would work well) and develop an inner hearing and feeling for it through chanting, movement, and bodily percussion.* Next, the

---

* In fact, students should take the initiative in selecting and leading these experiences, following the teacher's modeling.

teacher sets it to melody by assigning pitches that ascend, descend, or remain the same over four repetitions of the rhythm. Last, he or she creates a simple accompaniment for xylophones or bells based on the tonic and dominant of the melody, in a similar rhythm. A few non-pitched percussion instruments may be added for rhythmic interest and the communal composition/improvisation is ready for a program performance. More important, such an exercise will allow students to become aware of the process of creating music of their own.

FOCUS 11: Creativity in Action (improvisation)

This exercise allows students the freedom to explore and express instrumentally musical ideas that they have experienced vocally and through movement. The teacher presents them with a rhythm and suggests that they use xylophones, bells, recorders, or keyboard, as they improvise melodies from their choice of pitches. Students are reminded that pitches fall into patterns, and that those patterns can repeat, be elongated (augmented) or reduced (diminished) in time, and be played sequentially at different pitch levels.

Another improvisatory experience begins with an assignment of

FIGURE 11–13 Samples of songs for "name-that-tune" challenge.

a. "There Was a Man" and "Mister Froggie Went A-Courting" (Anglo-American): **d-s**

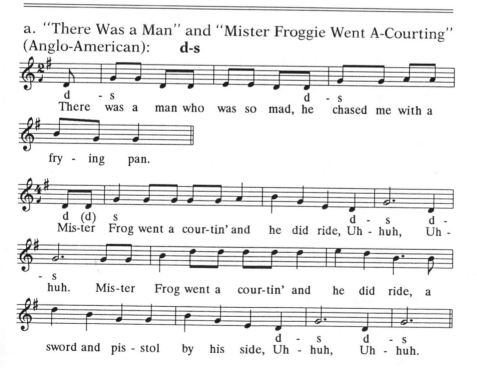

b. "Bento-Uri" (Japanese) and "Song to the Bride" (Is-raeli):

particular pitches (two, three, or four to start) and the instruction to students to provide rhythmic variety by moving pitches up or down or keeping them static. In any beginning creativity experiences, the teacher should specify a length by giving a set number of beats, mea-sures, or phrases. Fixing either the pitch or rhythm parameters will guide students in providing their music with a sense of unity and cohesion. Students should work independently sometimes, and at times with partners for feedback. The teacher should provide time for class performance and evaluation.

FOCUS 12: Many-Splendored Experiences in Song (aural skills, memory, improvisation)

After students have learned a song, they may wish to explore and experience it from different perspectives simultaneously. For a more complete internalization of a song's component parts, the

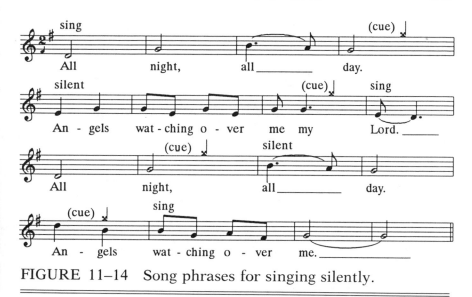

FIGURE 11–14   Song phrases for singing silently.

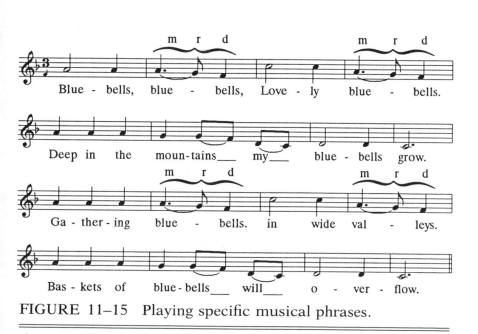

FIGURE 11–15   Playing specific musical phrases.

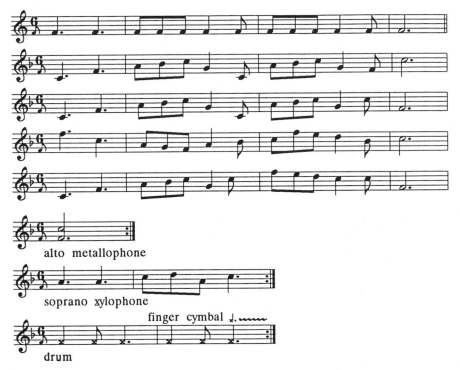

FIGURE 11–16   The evolution of rhythmic phrase to accompanied melody.

teacher should suggest that students combine several activities at once:

1. Step the beat, sing the words.
2. Step the beat, clap the rhythm of the melody (words).
3. Clap an ostinato rhythm, sing the words.Step the melodic rhythm, conduct the beat.
4. Silently sing one phrase, sing aloud the next phrase.
5. Invent a new melody for the final phrase, ending on tonic.

CHAPTER

12

◆

Music Learning in the Ensemble Setting

Ensemble performance may be viewed as a composite that is more than the sum of separate musical parts. The quality of the individual instruments or voices, the interdependence of multiple musical ideas sounding simultaneously, and even the personal interactions of performers affect the ensemble's performance. An understanding of one's own musical part as well as an awareness of its relationship to other parts may be the most distinguishing feature of ensemble music. Meaningful ensemble performances are products of individually skilled musicians with the sensitivity to respond to the greater needs of the group, and to the composition itself.

In the larger performing ensembles of Western art music, the conductor provides the musical coherence, conveying cues of appropriate tempo, dynamics, and stylistic nuances to musicians. When schools are considered reflections of mainstream American culture, the conductor-teacher is the principal influence in the growth and maintenance of the musicianship displayed by school bands, choirs, and orchestras. The choice of suitable repertoire that is musically challenging but not overly difficult for any one part is the conductor's responsibility. To maintain a balanced sound among voices or instruments is another of his or her important considerations, and as personnel changes occur from year to year in school ensembles, the conductor must put forth a great deal of effort in selecting music that can be performed in a musically expressive manner.

The school ensemble is the setting in which students refine the music skills and understanding they began to acquire at home or in elementary music classes; for some these skills are nurtured in the private studio lesson. The development of the performance techniques of individual students more frequently rests in the hands of the conductor who realizes that the musical product of his ensemble is dependent on the performance capabilities of each individual young musician. Since the process of educating students musically is the chief aim of school ensembles, ear-training, music reading skills, creative expression, and an understanding of literature, style, and interpretation are an intimate part of ensemble classes.

Music learning in ensemble classes is dependent on conductor-teachers who by necessity are first musicians. They fulfill this role as they apply a diversity of skills that focus on their own performance and aural abilities. They must be able to teach through demonstration—baritones who will sing soprano parts, or trombonists who can play phrases on the flute. They must be detectives of errors, with ears that are fine-tuned to hear an F sharp when it should be a natural or to realize that it is the sagging tenors who are causing the ensemble's intonation problems. They must possess the skill to think quickly in the resolution of problems, and should know remedies for such matters as inaccurate fingerings, poor breath control, rhythmic errors, and sloppy articulation.

The musicianship of students in ensembles can be fostered through instructional techniques similar to those employed in oral or partly oral traditions around the world. Teacher demonstration and student imitation, vocalization and solmization, memory strategies and occasions for creative improvisation are fitting devices for American school ensemble settings. When the training of musicians is bound to the written symbol, as occurs in school ensembles, the aural essence of music is sometimes diminished. To be certain, Western vocal and instrumental music of the last few centuries is preserved in symbols, and performers must learn the code for converting signs to sounds. The paradox is that the function of music as an aural and a creative art form is reduced when literacy becomes the single goal of music instruction. In truth, the inclusion of aural experiences will not only enrich the student's listening ear but will also nurture his or her creativity and musicianship. A study of the world's ensembles offers evidence that the ear leads the way in learning music. Some of the rehearsal strategies prevalent in other world societies may be relevant in teaching students in school bands, choirs, and orchestras.

The individual's aural sense is directly linked to his or her expressive abilities. In formal music instruction, creative experiences in music are largely abandoned at the sixth-grade level. Earlier aural experiences that students have received through the techniques of Dalcroze, Orff, Kodály, and various others may have encouraged their perceptual development, musicianship, and skills in creative improvisation, but the aural and creative aspects of these classic approaches are frequently abandoned when the demand for musically literate singers and instrumentalists becomes the priority. Certain aspects of the classic approaches to music instruction for children can be applied to the training of musicians in ensembles; these can complement the performance of music learned through literate means. The foundations of musicianship set in childhood through an array of ear-training games, in the spontaneous invention of songs and chants, and in the rote imitation of melodies and rhythms can be recalled periodically to ensure that music learning occurs in the rehearsal setting.

Cross-cultural teaching and learning patterns are not limited to a single setting nor are they greatly affected by the maturation of the student, the sophistication of his musical skills, or the instrument he chooses to learn. Western-style ensembles are fertile ground for the use of devices found in other music systems. Without negating the importance of music literacy, the teacher may find it useful to employ suggestions for the infusion of imitation, creative improvisation, vocalization and solmization, kinesthetic strategies, and memory devices into school ensemble classes. Historical and theoretical perspectives of American school music ensembles are highlighted to set the context for group instruction of singers and instrumentalists in the schools. A view of certain musical and social behaviors underlying many of the world's ensembles is addressed, and a number of rehearsal techniques are recommended in the section on applications for use in the classroom.

HISTORICAL PERSPECTIVES OF THE SCHOOL ENSEMBLE

The formal instruction of music in ensembles is a recent phenomenon in American schools. When one realizes that group singing was commonplace in churches by 1640 and in secular communities along the eastern seaboard soon afterward, the establishment of school choirs two centuries later seems late. The emergence of instrumental music instruction in the schools came about also in the nineteenth century, but bands and orchestras were not widespread in the schools until the early decades of the twentieth century.

Choral

From colonial times, congregational singing was an important part of the worship service in church. Singing schools were created to supply the churches with able singers who were attuned to matters of vocal production and literate in the four-note gamut, the clefs, keys, note durations, and syllables. The publishing of tune books became a major enterprise by 1750, and group singing flourished. The itinerant singing master arrived in a town with an armload of books and an enthusiasm that carried through several weeks of nightly instruction. From the singing schools adults and children alike carried back to their churches an understanding of notation and a new set of tunes.

Formal instruction in schools was organized in the colonies as early as the 1650s, but the ideal of universal public education was not realized for nearly one hundred years. It was still another century before Lowell Mason began formal instruction in vocal music—in 1838. The choir movement thus began, for the weekly lessons in tuning and developing young voices resulted quite naturally in concerts for school personnel, parents, and the general public. The singing societies in urban areas were models for choral groups in the secondary schools, which in turn fed musically experienced students into these community choirs.

From its beginnings in informal group sings and extracurricular glee clubs, the choral ensemble rose to the status of a recognized offering in the high school curriculum. Through festivals and contests, singing classes, and the improved quality of choral literature that could be performed well by young voices, a capella choirs grew steadily more favorable in the eyes of administrators, teachers, and students. The unaccompanied choral performances of European art songs and occasional arranged folk and popular songs were the principal components of choral programs by the turn of the century. The performance of Handel and Haydn oratorios became annual events attended by the entire school community. Instructional styles grew by mid-century into "schools" of choral music, and many high schools were typified as producing the St. Olaf "straight tone" and pure sound of limited vibrato or the lush and darker Westminster quality. The contemporary high school choral ensemble is ideally a result of its members' comprehensive vocal training at the elementary level, followed by their introduction to part-singing experiences and a substantial repertoire of art and folk music by the intermediate and middle school grades. The high school choir can be the premiere organization of a system's music curriculum, representing extensive training and commitment by students and teachers (Keene, 1982).

Instrumental

The establishment of bands and orchestras and the teaching of instrumental music in the schools came later than instruction in vocal music. The early colonists had little use for instruments, and prohibited their presence at worship services. When secular music was played, the first instruments used, including violins, violas, and virginals, were transported from Europe. New world instrument makers had established their craft by the eighteenth century, and public concerts of European art music were heard in centers such as Philadelphia, Boston, and Charleston. The study of instrumental music, however, was largely a tutored arrangement, as there was a long-standing belief that instruments could be taught more efficiently in a private lesson.

Isolated attempts were made to organize music academies for instruction outside the school, modeled after the European conservatory. Instruction was provided primarily on piano, strings, and instruments of the orchestra. An air of elitism hung over some of the early music academies, as only the monied and most talented individuals could participate in them.

Community bands became popular entertainment in the nineteenth century. The golden age of John Philip Sousa and Patrick Gilmore inspired many to take up the study of instruments in order to perform in the thousands of professional and amateur bands that were appearing. Although performers generally regarded their outdoor concerts in the town gazebo as a leisure activity, the sheer number of bands in the country indicated a need for formal instruction on a massive scale for instrumentalists (Larkin, 1949; Humphreys, 1987).

Instrumental programs in the schools were at first sporadic, occurring initially in the eastern and midwestern states. By the early twentieth century, however, the phenomenon of school bands and orchestras had spread widely for a number of reasons: (1) new instruments and technologies were invented, including the saxophone and the standardization of piston valves on brass instruments; (2) American companies were formed to manufacture musical instruments; (3) instrument makers hired former community band directors to teach and promote their instruments in the schools; and (4) military bands, first in the Civil War and then in World War I, produced capable musicians with extensive performing experience (some of whom became teachers after their military service).

The development of bands and orchestras whose performances were heard at school assemblies, graduations, and civic events led to instruction in instrumental music in the public schools. The changing milieu of the 1920s, including school athletics, town pride in the local schools, and competitions, nurtured the growth of school bands and orchestras. National contests were organized which not only heightened the quality of music selected for performance but also impressed the public who gained new respect for instrumental music instruction. Budgets for instruments increased, additional teachers were hired at the elementary and middle schools, and instruction books were published with the aim of educating young students in performance techniques for their instruments. The ensemble setting became a means for music learning, including music reading and expressive skills, that came about through active participation of students on their instruments.

THEORIES OF MUSIC LEARNING IN PERFORMANCE GROUPS

With the prominence assigned to performing ensembles, particularly at the secondary level, there is a gnawing suspicion held by some that the functions and processes of music learning are not being fulfilled. The large membership in the ensemble and its less than ideal ratio of students to teacher, the pressing schedule of public performances and festivals, and the frequent lack of self-initiated practice by students are valid concerns. Still, a comparison of an elementary school ensemble with its counterpart at the high school shows a more complex literature and a higher standard of performance at the secondary level—proof that music learning must be occurring. Whether this improvement is a result of students' physical and intellectual maturation, extramusical motivators, or particular learning strategies employed is not clear, but the evidence is strong that musical training in the ensemble can make for more proficient singers and players. Music learning occurs through the experience of ensemble performance, and the use of particular teaching techniques during rehearsal may be contributing to the process.

The organization of instrumental and vocal instruction is one that has repeatedly prompted the question, "Can class instruction be as effective as private lessons?" Keraus (1973) compared the performance skills of privately taught Suzuki students with those taught in a Suzuki class. Following a forty-two-week treatment, a panel of judges observed no differences among students in performance technique. Likewise, a comparison of private voice students with those in class lessons showed no difference in their performances (Sims, 1961). The instruction available through ensemble classes appears to be conducive to learning. Group instruction is viewed favorably by school administrators for reasons that include cost effectiveness and socialization factors. More important, class instruction can provide opportunities for shaping the musicianship of many students at once, through exercises in ear-training, note-reading, facility with the voice or instrument, and intellectual challenges leading to an understanding of musical style. The presence of other young people can motivate and inspire the student in an ensemble and provide listening opportunities that may subconsciously help him or her develop a more critical ear.

The Pestalozzian principle of practice before theory and sound before symbol has had a strong influence on music instruction in school ensembles. A considerable number of philosophies, theories of music learning, and derivative methods and materials applied to class instruction underscore the necessity for initial aural experiences in music before symbols are presented. Even after a study of notation, frequent returns to direct aural experiences are advised so that the meaning of symbols in their original medium can be reaffirmed. In *Teaching Band Instruments to Beginners*, Holz and Jacobi (1966) recommend numerous strategies that reflect their belief in the aural "thing before the sign," and the importance of proceeding from the "known to the unknown." Froseth's method, described in *The Individualized Instructor* (1970), asserts his interest in teaching rhythm with a mnemonics system that requires oral chanting and a keen listening sense rather than the more traditional intellectualization of durational values as a mathematics exercise. A more recent account of teaching tonality and rhythmic feeling is Schleuter's *A Sound Approach to Teaching Instrumentalists* (1984). This system is based partly on the learning theory of Edwin E. Gordon and adheres to aural/oral learning in initial stages, with a return to the imitative process throughout the instructional system. Grunow and Gordon's *Jump Right In: The Instrumental Series* (1987) is a method designed for developing aural and performance skills using chanting and singing patterns that are eventually played on recorder, percussion, wind, and brass instruments.

An aspect of aural learning commonly employed in choral and instrumental ensembles is rote imitation. Melodic and rhythmic phrases, performance techniques, phrasing, and stylistic interpretation are frequently shaped through the student imitation of the teacher. Rather than replacing literacy skills, imitation may enhance their acquisition. In an investigation of relationships among selected factors and the music reading skills of secondary school choirs, Daniels (1986) observed that the occasional use of rote procedures was a significant variable. A sight-reading test administered to members of twenty high school choral ensembles indicated that imitation of the teacher, used sparingly, appeared to be related to the development of students' ability to read notation. Thus, the singing, chanting, and playing of problem sections by the teacher, which are then echoed by students, may, in addition to providing a short-term rehearsal remedy, result in students' acquiring a more permanent understanding of the relationship of musical sound to symbol.

In learning to sing or to play, students must develop a concept of the ideal sound. Verbal descriptions are abstract and do little to convey the essence of musical quality. The literature abounds with warnings to teachers to minimize verbal instructions in rehearsals. Ernst (1978) noted that "one of the most common complaints about conductors is that they talk too much," and recommended that teachers listen to a taped rehearsal to gauge the extent to which words rather than music may dominate a rehearsal. Choral conductors are advised to "talk little, sing much," to cue parts by page, line, measure, and beat only, and to give only brief critiques before returning to further singing (Robinson and Winold, 1976).

Instead of verbose explanations, aural models should hold a prominent place in the delivery of instruction. While the teacher may serve as a model, recordings can also be commonly employed to generate interest and an understanding of ensemble performance. In attempting to determine the nature of teaching and learning performance skills, the Crane Symposium noted among its concluding statements that the most successful ensemble directors were those who combined verbalization with modeling (Fowler, 1988). Aural models aid in the development of greater expression, accuracy, intonation, balance, and general musical effect.

A number of methods recommend that students listen to and emulate aural models. Shinichi Suzuki emphasized that musical talent could be developed from careful listening, and that young violinists were like birds who "learn from experience to produce tones as beautiful as those of [their] teacher" (1982, p. 19). In a Suzuki class, children are directed to listen attentively to the teacher's performance and then to perform in like manner. This rote imitation approach is viewed as essential in developing the student's ear, bow arm, and basic finger flexibility. Only after the student has had lengthy exposure to the live aural model is he introduced to notation.

Recordings and tapes are another example of the aural-to-visual model advocated in the Suzuki method. The lack of success in the adaptation of Suzuki's method in some school settings is attributed at least partially to a "failure to use recordings as an integral part of the process" (Kendall, 1984). Parents are advised to ensure that their children hear classical music performed by outstanding artists. Recordings are recommended for informal listening during meals or at bedtime so that children may learn early on in a nonthreatening environment to identify musical styles and quality performances. They are encouraged also to listen to specially produced Suzuki method recordings at home. These are pieces learned in class that the children can try to play on their instruments during practice.

Paul Rolland's Illinois Project of string instruction, begun in the 1950s, also recommended the use of a recorded teaching repertoire. American folk songs in varying degrees of rhythmic and technical complexity were recorded in two volumes, *Tunes for the String Player* and *New Tunes for Strings*. Elementary school students were advised to listen carefully to the aural models and then to copy the sound on their instruments. Much of Rolland's approach evolved prior to the American Suzuki movement, and yet the process of listening and imitating is a shared quality in the two practices (Smith, 1987).

The use of aural models is not limited to instrumental instruction but can be found as a prominent technique in the choral ensemble as well. In *The Choral Experience: Literature, Materials and Methods*, Robinson and Winold (1976) recommended the use of a recording when introducing a new work. Students begin to internalize the musical logic and style of the piece through repeated listenings, focusing alternately on the overall style, melody, text, and expressive elements. When a recording is not available, a vocal presentation of the work by the teacher with piano accompaniment is suggested to establish style and generate enthusiasm. In *The Choral Director's Complete Handbook*, Gordon notes that "most mistakes occur because the singer does not have a mental concept of the correct solution. Often, hearing the trouble spot played or performed by a demonstrator will help. The singer should then immediately perform the music to solidify his image" (1977, 183).

Singing may be an effective learning device in both choral and instrumental classes. Individual parts can be sung by band and orchestra members in order to reacquaint students with their most personal instrument, the voice. A respite from the motoric manipulation of bows, mallets, and valves can allow greater emphasis on the connection of the ear and eye so critical to music reading. In the choral ensemble, the isolation of a particular phrase functions as an exercise in ear-training and vocal production. The use of a technical or rhythmically complex phrase as a warm-up activity can result in a better understanding of the pitches, pitch relationships, and rhythm of the problem phrase. This practice may help to overcome physiological and psychological tensions that can occur when the phrase is met in the context of a musical work. While singing is the choir's performance medium, it is also a means of learning music.

Instrumental ensembles that use singing as an instructional technique have found it to be effective in the development of intonation, perception, and a general sense of melodic and rhythmic structure. In a study of the effect of daily vocalization practice on the sense of pitch of beginning band students, Elliott (1974) found that pitch discrimination and tonal memory abilities improved among both brass and woodwind players as a result of consistent singing practice. Students who were taught to play and vocalize exercises from a methods book were better able than control groups to detect pitch errors when matching sound with notation and scored significantly higher than controls on tests of pitch perception. The effects of intonation training on secondary school wind players was studied by Harris (1977) who reported that regular vocalization in band classes improved students' intonation. The transfer of musical abilities from singing to playing is good reason to use the voice as a learning tool in instrumental ensembles.

In selecting music to advance the aural, visual, and kinesthetic senses so vital to performance, familiar melodies seem to be effective. Schleuter (1984) suggests that listening and singing are essential for establishing a sense of tonality and notes that "songs which students already know through singing are the most effective musical material for beginning instrumentalists" (p. 31). Well-known folk songs are viewed as effective for teaching beginning instrumentalists. Students who learn finger facility and performance through familiar melodies are often successful in the amount of material covered, in the level of musical complexity attained, and in the positive attitude that may result. Familiarity with songs may also be helpful to members of a choral ensemble, whose knowledge of the melodic and rhythmic components of a song can enable them to concentrate on aspects of breath support, diction, and style interpretation. The occasional use of familiar songs offers ensemble performers a certain ease, relaxation, and joy in music making that increases learning.

The presence in ensemble rehearsals of ear-training experiences in combination with notation can help students internalize sound, which is the goal of the well-trained performer of Western art music. Pedagogues Jaques-Dalcroze and Kodály noted that the phenomenon of "inner hearing" would occur as the study and performance of a musical work added patterns and phrases to the student's internalized music vocabulary. When students hear these sound components later, they not only recognize them aurally but also visualize them as notes on a staff; conversely, a glance at their notated version can summon their sound. In Gordon's music learning theory, *audiation* is the term for the process (1984). The experience of having heard, seen, and performed a phrase often leads to greater ease in processing the same phrase in future encounters, a phenomenon that increases sight-reading proficiency.

As students store the phrases of an ensemble piece in memory, they can retrieve them in the creative act of improvisation. Just as we base extemporaneous speech on the words and phrases of our prior experiences, so performers recall fragments of familiar music and fashion them into new arrangements. Even beginning students can improvise, starting with experiences in playing familiar tunes "by ear" and extracting prominent melodic or rhythmic patterns to be varied within assigned parameters of meter, phrase length, and pitch set.

The development of improvisational skills can be successfully accomplished in instrumental and choral ensembles. According to Baker (1979), whose classes in jazz improvisation often number 150 or more students, the key is "to keep everybody gainfully occupied." Despite a heterogeneous group of abilities, instruments, and voices, students learn through listening, play-along recordings, ensemble responses to the instructor's "call," silent improvisation when solos are designated, and the individual preparation and playing of transcribed improvisations. Holmes (1988) described the success of a jazz improvisation class in the middle school, illustrating the degree of creativity that can occur in an otherwise structured band class. The frequent use of teacher demonstration and student imitation, the listening and analysis of recordings, an occasional clinic by a guest artist, and the performance of standard solos begin to build in students an understanding of the nature of improvisation in the jazz idiom.

Vocal jazz can be similarly learned within group settings as singers participate through imitation and quickly sung responses to musical questions with or without text. In his method of vocal improvisation, Konowitz placed the creative experience in a prominent place in the choral curriculum. It can constitute not only a warm-up period but also a break midway in the rehearsal, or a demonstration of musical spontaneity in a performance. He encouraged instruction in vocal improvisation for stimulating "musical fluency, stylistic awareness, and creative needs" of students (1970, 2).

Despite the current emphasis on performances in choral and instrumental music programs in middle, junior, and high schools, the evidence and the increased potential of these curricular offerings as a vehicle of music learning is obvious. Even when performing schedules appear to tax the teacher and stretch the tolerance and talents of students, music learning is occurring. Contemporary learning theories, research findings, and a multitude of successful ensemble experiences guided by well-seasoned teachers support the effectiveness of group instruction. Ear-training works well with the reading ensemble. When familiar songs are used, the teacher or recordings serve as aural models, and the students use rote imitation and vocalization, listening skills are developed in the rehearsal and instruction of school bands, orchestras, and choirs. And, as in the case of many musical groups throughout the world, creative musical expression through improvisation can be nurtured in the ensembles of America's secondary schools.

MUSICAL BEHAVIORS OF THE WORLD'S ENSEMBLES

Music making is a social behavior, and thus an ensemble of performers is as human a phenomenon as music itself. Indeed, as Nettl points out, "The concept of instrumental ensemble is almost a universal phenomenon" (1985, 59). The social interactions that occur in the creation, performance, reception, and learning of music underscore the "existence of music as a social fact" (Blacking, 1977, 16). In every corner of the world, groups of singers, instrumentalists, and their combination can be heard performing for each other or for attending audiences. In many cases, the related arts of dance and theater may be infused within the music so that an ensemble performance is an interdisciplinary event that has both artistic and social meaning.

As there are distinctive sounds that characterize a society's music, there are also the near-ritual behaviors of ensemble performers and their audience that have been conditioned by their culture. Particular instruments and their combinations as well as certain vocal styles, both indigenous and adapted from other musical cultures, are preferred by a people and continued through regular performances. Well-defined "costumes," settings, and movements may be culturally prescribed for performers and audience members. The meaning of the music as a social behavior encompasses the interaction among performers of the ensemble and is reinforced by the communication of the music and its ritualistic behaviors to the listeners.

Perhaps the premiere Western art music ensemble is the orchestra. In illustration of social behaviors that belong to ensembles, the contemporary Western orchestra of European origin is one example. The orchestra is an amalgam of approximately one hundred musicians whose mission it is to create a unified and whole musical product from the contributions of many diverse timbres and often a variety of simultaneously sounded pitches and rhythms. A conductor serves as leader, coordinating the pulse and dynamics of the music and exercising his personal opinion on the correct conveyance of musical style through facial expressions and movements of the arm and its extension, the baton. The attention of the musicians is on the conductor, as all eyes shift from the sheets of notated music to the person on the podium. (One can only surmise that the musicians are heeding the sounds of their colleagues, for while the act of hearing is not an overt and observable behavior, the synchronous sound of the ensemble is undoubtedly a direct result of their listening as well.)

As a community of musicians, the members of the Western orchestra dress uniformly in black concert attire, as does the conductor. Such costumes give them a clear identity as a group of people with a shared concern, music, and many avid audience members will continue the trend in similar black formal wear, including tuxedos. The stark and uncluttered setting that many stages provide lends an ambience of formality to the concert occasion, contrasted with the Baroque-like filagree in some lobbies and seating areas, whose decoration provides a festive feeling. In performance, the movements of musicians are as controlled and subtle as their instrument will allow; there is little individual variance as bow arms move together in a synchronized choreography, and instruments of the same class and size are positioned at a uniform level when possible. All but the percussionists remain seated while performing.

The preparation for performance is marked also by standard behavior. This includes the entrance of the concertmaster after all other orchestra members are seated; the tuning procedure, with "A-440" set by the first oboe; and the entrance of the conductor to the stage in the silence that follows tuning. The stage provides a sociological separation between audience and performers. Audience response is typified by applause on the arrival of the concertmaster and the conductor, and after each work has been concluded (rather than between movements of a symphony, for example). Occasional shouts of "Bravo," "Brava," "More," and "Encore" occur following a masterful performance, often of a piece familiar to the audience. Like the music-making process of an ensemble, the extramusical procedures of musicians and audience members demonstrate social behaviors inherent in a performance. The relationship among performers and between them and their audience is a critical component in Western-style orchestras as well as in bands and choirs.

A brief examination of the North Indian concert tradition of sitar and tabla also confirms the phenomenon of social interaction onstage and in the audience. As with the Western orchestra, the logic of the duo's music and its performance practices is set by the culture. The characteristic position of performers is seated cross-legged on a carpet, the sitarist and tabla player alongside and facing slightly toward each other. A tambura player sits somewhat in the shadows behind his performing teacher, to whom he owes his respect and absolute devotion. Performers dress in loose clothing, often of silk, and wear no shoes. The women of the audience mark the concert as a special occasion with their attire, including flowing silk saris, silk punjabi suits, and the jewelry that adorns their fingers, wrists, neck, ears, and nose.

As there is no notated music in the performance tradition and no conductor, sitarist and tabla player may look instead to their instruments, to the audience, and to each other. In the improvisation that ensues, one may glance at the other to indicate the beginning of a drum solo, the start or finish of a dialogue, and the coming of a particular melodic or rhythmic flourish. At the cadence to a series of overlapping phrases, the point at which the sitar and tabla release tension that develops from the stringing together of many melodies and rhythms, it is common for the performers to exchange smiles. They are a team whose music seems independent at one moment, colliding and combining in the next. Their communication during performance is strictly nonverbal (similar to the conductor's communication with the orchestra).

The audience for North Indian music is more actively engaged than that in Western art traditions. While the music sounds, they can be seen keeping track of the tala by subtly clapping and waving their hands and counting the pulse on their fingers. For the audience to keep the tala or rhythm is frequently useful to the performers, for it allows them to follow the basic pulse even as they are performing intricate running passages and syncopations. When a virtuosic moment has occurred, members of the audience may nod their heads from side to side—which is interpreted as "yes," a certain sign of approval—or they may click their tongues to produce a "tsk-tsk" sound that Westerners might ordinarily reserve for the scolding of their children. An assortment of other vocalized sounds may be heard following climactic sections. As in the West, applause is the typical audience response at the close of a performance.

While the performance and audience behaviors of a North Indian "chamber music" concert differ greatly from those of the large Western ensembles, they comprise certain stylized actions that define the culture. Moreover, the interactions among and between factions are notable in both traditions, indicating the social nature of the ensemble and of a public performance. Throughout the world, collections of musicians attest to the place of music as a shared human phenomenon. As there are many musical dialects, instruments, genres, and customs of performance in the world's ensembles, there are also various learning and rehearsal strategies. Some are shared by a number of traditions and are particularly relevant and transferable to the teaching of music in Western choral and instrumental ensembles.

The use of notation in learning instrumental and vocal parts is frequent—although not universally employed—in the world's ensembles. Some ensemble music survives in an oral tradition and the repertoire is learned by listening. While a student can apprentice with a musician from the ensemble, as in Japan or India, his attendance at concerts and ensemble sessions is vital to his understanding of the relationship between his chosen instrument and others in the ensemble. In West Africa or Indonesia, there may be no formal apprenticeship, and the repertoire and technique is acquired through the close observation of ensemble performances and eventual immersion. Without the availability of notation in some traditions, the student must have a keen ear and careful powers of observation to gain a sense of ensemble repertoire, technique, and style.

This capacity to learn and retain melodies, rhythms, and complete musical pieces is a wonder to those who perform from the printed page. Yet, in the aural process, the memory is exercised as surely as the ear is sharpened. In the working out of musical performances, mnemonics is a prominent device for conveying rhythms. Drummers frequently have their own rhythmic language, which is known and used by performers of melody instruments in committing rhythmic melodies to memory. In a related technique, instrumentalists of an ensemble frequently sing a passage or a fixed melody and practice it repeatedly, either while playing or prior to a transfer to their instruments. From a jazz band to a classical Persian ensemble to a Thai orchestra, vocalization is a natural technique for internalizing musical parts.

The advantage of ensemble performance can be the thrill of fitting one's own part into the total ensemble, with an awareness of the parts that interweave around it. In the traditional training for performance in the Indonesian gamelan, the musician must learn all the instruments—from the gongs that provide a rhythmic structure to the fixed melody of the xylophones to the elaborating instruments. He may become specialized on a particular instrument but must be prepared to shift to other instruments at any point in a concert. This flexibility marks an awareness of the contributions of individual instruments to the musical whole. The learning is an entirely aural and kinesthetic process through which an understanding of the intricacies of gamelan music is revealed.

Improvisation is commonly practiced in the music of ensembles. While rather specific parameters are laid by the style of the culture or specific genre, especially such elements as mode, meter, and melodic contour, ensemble music becomes a spontaneously created art form when a measure of musical independence is encouraged. In a Mexican *mariachi* band, a Serbian *tamburitza* ensemble, a jazz combo, or an African xylophone orchestra, simultaneous group improvisation can be at once musically logical and ordered, expressive and spontaneous. The stylistic parameters are acquired through extensive listening and practice. The musician who first enters an improvising ensemble must develop the courage to perform in a group where the elements of competition and challenge are often present. Still, a fraternal attitude is prevalent in ensemble playing, and those who are more experienced often help the novice by showing him or her the musical secrets. Most important, the musician must learn the balance of required structural components and free expression characteristic of the style.

Of particular fascination to performers in Western ensembles is the absence of the conductor in some of the world's performing organizations, some as large as one hundred gongs and xylophones in the Indonesian gamelan. Unity and cohesion can be achieved in nonverbal ways, and following the baton is just one of them. Listening looms largely as the principal unifying factor, whether to a leading instrument or to each other. The *kendang* drum is the focal instrument for changing tempo and levels of dynamics in the gamelan; its aural cues trigger an immediate response in the gamelan players. A Maori ensemble of singers and dancers is directed by phrases that the leader will sing at the back of an ensemble of twenty or thirty singers and dancers, indicating the close of one music section and the beginning of another. In ensembles of classical Persian, Indian, and East Asian music, there is an egalitarian outlook somewhat similar to the interactions that occur in a string quartet. There is no leader but rather an even giving and taking that hinges on careful listening to individual parts and their combination. Of special note is the principle of breath rhythm that serves to give direction to the performance of the ancient Japanese *gagaku* orchestra (Malm, 1977), similar to the preparation beat used by Western conductors. The feeling for pulse can occur only through a highly developed ability to listen to other instruments while inhaling, holding, and expelling air in the performance of wind instruments. The aural sense is the critical component in maintaining musical coherence in ensembles without conductors.

Parallels between the world's traditional ensembles and those of Western art music are evident in performance and rehearsal settings. Some aspects of learning style are quite different from those currently used in school ensembles, but they possess the potential for transfer. In particular, the development of a greater aural sensitivity would seem appropriate and highly desirable. In classes of performing organizations, the members' capacity for memory can be increased, their awareness of individual musical lines within the greater ensemble can be strengthened, and their ability to create through techniques of variation and improvisation can be encouraged in occasional exercises that emphasize the listening ear. While the teacher-conductor must continue to provide the leadership in school ensemble settings, and notation must be the primary means for learning a repertoire that is preserved in written form, there are circumstances in which a number of aural techniques so common to the world's ensembles can be successfully applied. Despite the diversity of musical sounds from one culture to the next, music learning behaviors may not be as varied as we may initially think. As music is a shared human behavior, so is much of the learning process.

APPLICATIONS

In the *Focus* experiences suggested for use in the ensemble setting, aural learning is given considerable emphasis. Directed listening, imitation, and vocalization are recommended as aids to music learning, as are experiences in improvisation. The expectation is that musical invention may strengthen listening skills just as surely as aural/oral strategies will nurture creativity; the outcomes are closely related. A number of activities provide for the development of the memory, both short-term retention of musical phrases and the long-term effect of an increased capacity for storage and recall. The experiences are mostly intended as warm-ups or brief diversions in the rehearsals of large performing ensembles, including orchestras, concert bands, and choirs. They are useful for smaller ensembles as well, for section rehearsals, and for class lessons in voice and various instruments. *Focus* experiences are specifically designed for high school settings, but are relevant to assorted performing groups at the elementary level, in middle school and junior high, and at the college/university level. Refer also to the *Focus* experiences in chapters 11 and 13, as some elementary music and private studio practices are applicable to the ensemble.

FOCUS 1: Listening Preparation (aural skills)
The importance of listening cannot be overestimated in ensemble classes. In the introduction of a new work to be performed, students require an understanding of the totality of the music to which

they will contribute their part. A feeling for style, tempo, melodic themes, rhythmic quality, and dynamics as well as how the piece begins, develops, and concludes can be acquired through preliminary listening experiences. The student's knowledge of his place in the greater scheme of the music is an important result of study and rehearsal but may have greater musical meaning if it is accomplished at the beginning of instruction.

Recordings are available for many classical and contemporary works within the abilities of the secondary school ensemble. In addition to those that are commercially available, some music publishing companies produce cassette tapes and demonstration records in advertising selections available for purchase. With lesser-known compositions, it may be possible to tape a performance or rehearsal by another ensemble to share with students just beginning to study the piece. When none of these is possible, the teacher might reduce the score to a piano version for presentation to the students.

To achieve the missions of music education, which include knowledge about music as well as performance skills, the teacher should perform listening experiences that are well designed and stimulate greater attention by students to the elements of the composition. To guide their listening the instructor should present students with a list of questions that might include these: "What is the meter of the piece? Does it change?" "Can you hear a theme? In what instruments or voices? Does it repeat? How is it varied?" "What is the mode? Major, minor, modal, serial?" "What contributes to the climax?" "When might it have been written, and who might the composer be? Why?" The ears of students are the tools for determining solutions, and verbally expressing what they hear can contribute significantly to students' musical education.

A listening introduction to a composition is a valid exercise for the ears, but it might not exceed ten minutes within a single performing class. (This is not to say that every musical work should be introduced through listening; rather, the balance of listening and opportunities to sightread must be maintained in ensemble rehearsals.) Several directed listenings may be necessary, spread over several weeks' time, but with clear instructions given so as to keep students' attention focused. Students may indicate an understanding of components nonverbally by conducting in the meter, humming the theme, and attempting to sing their own part. Students can listen initially without the aid of notation; later, they can read their individual parts or the theme silently. The intent is to ease into the reading of the music and to phase out the recording.

Informal listening can occur as students enter the room, and as they pack up at the end of class. A tape of a work currently being studied by the ensemble can be prepared; this will set the mood for class and provide additional exposure to a model performance. Students who are carrying eight class periods daily, participating in extracurricular activities, handling jobs and homework, and who are bombarded by media music may find the listening a helpful reminder of the ensemble's music, an activity that may prove both reinforcing and motivating. A prepared tape is helpful as it can be quickly switched on and off for the two or three minutes between classes. Playing the tapes may need to be an intermittent strategy of aural training so that the activity does not become too procedural and grow stale. Both casual and directed listening are useful pedagogical techniques in the ensemble class.

FOCUS 2: The Truth on Tape (aural skills)

In judging the quality and progress of an ensemble in its performance of a work, the tape recorder presents the most objective view. Students are curious, too, and find the feedback as intriguing and irresistible as photographs of themselves. Tape the ensemble in its initial attempt and in later stages of performance of a musical work, and play it back for a critical comparison by students. (Videotaping is also recommended on occasion, although audiotape helps focus students' attention on the musical components—rather than the visual elements.) How has the piece improved musically? What changes can be detected in tempo and dynamics? What improvements can be noted in rhythmic accuracy, balance, and articulation?

Challenge students to sing or play their part silently, suggesting to instrumentalists that they finger along as they listen. Such an exercise leads to the detection of personal errors within the context of an ensemble, and a refinement of the ability to listen and think critically. It may build an awareness of the greater group effort at making music, and may serve in addition to motivate and instill in students a feeling of pride and teamwork and a sense of belonging to the ensemble that has both musical and social ramifications.

FOCUS 3: The Teacher as Model (aural skills)

In choral and instrumental ensembles, the teacher's position often appears administrative—and sometimes far too verbal. Teachers must talk to students about their repertoire, rehearsal goals, and performance plans, but many of the musical matters can be better handled through demonstration. Vocally in choirs, and with the teacher's primary instrument in bands and orchestras, teachers can model appropriate performance techniques and musical concerns more efficiently and effectively than through verbal means.

From single phrases to complete works, the teacher can demonstrate a mastery of music that comes from extensive training and experience.

The image of the teacher as performer sets the music class apart from all other classes, as the musical language and its communication are wordless but meaningful. Like a picture, the performance is worth many words, with a message that is both instructional and capable of arousing feeling. When the teacher performs, there is the excitement of live music that tends to motivate listeners. Since a teacher was probably drawn to the profession through a personal interest in making music, he or she can continue to nurture that interest through his performance in the classroom while also demonstrating refined musicianship for students. The performing teacher is an excellent resource in the ensemble class, as students acquire both knowledge and attitudes through the live modeling of their instructor.

FOCUS 4: Sing a Familiar Song (aural skills, memory)

From earlier exposure to folk songs in school and at home, students should have in memory a collection of familiar tunes which they can recall on cue. They can draw on their memories in producing the melodies, rhythms, and texts of the songs on request, singing without the aid of notation the songs they learned in their childhood. There are numerous collections of folk songs available, and the basal elementary textbook series provide a rich resource. Begin with songs of small range and extensive repetition such as "Hot Cross Buns," "Lightly Row," and "Kumbaya," and gradually increase the challenge to such songs as "Amazing Grace," "Scarborough Fair," and "Ode to Joy."

A familiar song can serve well as an opening warm-up for the voice in a choral rehearsal. Students can then feel comfortable with the melody and rhythm and concentrate on singing the song in full voice, with attention paid to breath support, diction, or phrasing. Students can practice associating the sound with the notational symbols by drawing the melodic contour in space as they sing, imagining the notation of the song in an assigned key as they perform, substituting solfége syllables for the text and using hand signs while singing, or notating a phrase of the melody in a melodic dictation drill following their performance. Students should be directed to listen to each other for intonation, balance, and dynamic shading, which can be cued by the teacher or a student conductor.

If they can sing a tune by ear, competent instrumentalists can play it. The transfer of a familiar song to the instruments can occur after several rounds of singing: (1) sing the song for the words and melody; (2) sing with attention focused on the melody shape and the rhythmic flow; (3) given a key, sing while imagining the song's notation or mapping its direction in the air; (4) sing while silently fingering the tune on the instrument; and (5) transfer the familiar song to the instrument. This last step may take several trials until students meet with success, but the time spent is well worth the aural training that occurs. The same tempo should be observed for singing and playing so that the rhythm will not need to be translated to a slower tempo midway through the exercise. Players of nonpitched percussion instruments can experiment with xylophone, celeste, and chimes, or can be instructed to sound the pulse or create an ostinato accompaniment.

FOCUS 5: A System of Rhythm Chant (aural skills, memory)

Students come to secondary ensembles with a knowledge of performance technique but are frequently deficient in matters of rhythm. In teaching rhythm, the teacher must select an organized system that will provide the sound, the feeling, and the way to notation. Mnemonic syllables, words, and word phrases are useful aids that are easily learned and can be applied to problematic passages with little effort. Communication with music specialists at various levels within a school district can assist the teacher in selecting a system to be utilized consistently throughout the grade levels.

Regardless of the set of syllables chosen, it should be simple, capable of being chanted, and should sound like the rhythm (i.e., naming ♩ "quar-ter" sounds more like ♫ ; a monosyllabic "ta," "du," or "ba" is closer to the rhythm itself.) Numerical systems are frequently used by instrumentalists, such as one attributed to McHose and Tibbs (1944), or a more traditional one featuring *and*s for subdivisions of the beat, and *ee*s and *ah*s for the second and fourth of four sixteenth notes. In figure 12–1, compare several common syllables, determining the one most appropriate for the ensemble that may also relate to earlier instructional experiences of the students.

Word association is another mnemonic aid for the presentation and regular practice of rhythms. Any common words or phrases can be applied to durational values and are of greater musical significance when they are extended to rhythm patterns and phrases. Compare several word association phrases with common syllable systems and determine the suitability of each. The value of the system is in how it is applied as an oral chant in learning phrases that initially appear problematic to students. The regular use of a rhythm system for vocalization should have long-term effects in the internalization of the sound, so that the future appearance of particular phrases will trigger an accurate performance.

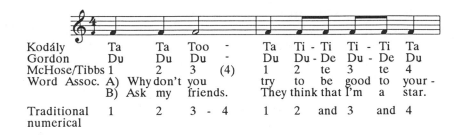

FIGURE 12–1   Systems of rhythmic chant.

FOCUS 6: For Choirs: Speak-a-Phrase in Rhythm (aural skills)

In the choral ensemble, the pitches of parts are frequently learned more easily than their rhythms. When a particular section is having rhythm difficulties with a passage, speaking the text in its assigned rhythm may be the most direct means of internalizing it. The teacher begins by chanting, followed by the section or the entire ensemble in crisp rhythmic imitation. Several repetitions may be necessary. The rhythmic chant may include gradations in tempo, dynamics, and pitch inflections, such that it has a musical quality all its own. Another rhythmic chant activity that will reinforce the problem part in relationship to other voice parts is for the full ensemble to chant the entire piece rhythmically, allowing its overlapping texts and polyphonic textures to be made clear. In addition to learning the rhythmic complexities of a work, articulation and an awareness of texture can be developed through the experience. A further result may be students' growing awareness of the relationship between rhythmic speech, chant, and song.

FOCUS 7: For Bands and Orchestras: Repertoire by Rote (aural skills, memory)

By the time students are performing in secondary school bands and orchestras, they possess a music competence that combines listening and performance skills. Those abilities can be challenged through a technique that links listening to singing to playing. Rote imitation is employed as students echo the melodic patterns and phrases of the teacher's choice, first by singing and then by playing their instruments. A musical vocabulary evolves and an aural awareness is solidified through a process that dismisses notation, at least temporarily, while it exercises the ear.

Patterns or phrases consisting of one-, two-, and four-measure melodies are introduced by the teacher, who sings them to the ensemble, using a neutral syllable (figure 12–2). Solfége syllables are also be applied to the brief melodies in order to provide an understanding of pitch relationships and to continue the foundation laid in the elementary school. Students should immediately imitate the teacher, with no time lag between the statement and its vocal or instrumental echo. The process for building a repertoire of musical patterns by rote might follow these steps for each targeted phrase: (1) teacher sings the phrase on neutral syllable "loo," students sing; (2) teacher sings phrase with solfége syllables, students sing; (3) steps 1 and 2 are repeated to reinforce the sound; (4) teacher sets the key, plays a phrase, students play.

FIGURE 12–2 Sample phrases for listening and internalizing through performance.

Phrases can be extracted from pieces currently being studied by the ensemble. They may also proceed from more obvious ascending and descending stepwise patterns, to triadic melodies, to melodies based on intervals of the fourth or fifth, or a combination of these. It may be necessary to allot many weeks or months of study with stepwise patterns alone, especially if students have no prior experience in playing by aural imitation. Patterns should at first be brief; gradually, they should increase in length as students become familiar with the process and as their capacity for immediate recall increases. Following is a sampling of phrases to be learned through imitation; these are only the beginning of the vast vocabulary that can be channeled through students' ears. Learning a repertoire of phrases by rote will help students develop their ears and add to their growing potential for improvisation.

FOCUS 8: Part-by-Part Performance (aural skills, memory)

To help students develop a sense of inner hearing, as well as a conscientiousness in following the score, sections of voices or instruments may be called upon sequentially to perform as the musical work progresses. The altos, for example, may begin the work with their part, to be replaced sixteen measures later by the basses, who are followed in ten measures by the tenors, by the sopranos and altos five measures after that, and by the full ensemble to the close of the work. The placement of the melody may be a factor in determining the order of voices or instruments, although a section may be chosen to perform its supporting part instead.

Cues for a section to continue the piece should be given one or two measures in advance, calling the name ("altos," "percussion," or "violins") or showing with the fingers a number previously assigned to a particular group. The measure number itself should not be given, for the objective is for students to follow the sound and the score independently and silently. With sufficient warning, students in the next section to participate can stand, position themselves, and prepare for attack. There should be no lag, only a steady flow from one section's performance to the next. Students need experiences in their own silent performance as others in the ensemble sound their parts aloud; this exercise may cause them to listen and to study the notation, may encourage an internal kinesthetic sense or proprioceptive response, and may help them to anticipate their sound as it fits into the greater musical picture.

FOCUS 9: Variation on a Theme (aural skills, memory, improvisation)

The transition from performing transmitted music to creating a personal music of one's own invention can occur in ensemble experiences through the use of the variation technique (figure 12–3). The teacher should select the melodic theme from a work under study or from a familiar song. The group should perform it in unison several times; as they perform, students should listen attentively to a specific musical element such as tempo, metric accents, dynamics, and mode. Their concentration on structural components will increase their awareness of the melody, and prepare them for the act of creating simultaneous variations.

Instructions for varying the theme must be specific, and only a single element should be assigned at one time for variation by the ensemble. The group can begin with those elements that readily allow unison performance, such as tempo or level of dynamics as set by the conductor. Students can be challenged as a group to perform the theme in a different mode, switching from major to minor or to Dorian mode. They can convert a melody in 2/4 to triple meter by sustaining the last sound of each measure for another beat; a similar treatment can be given to extending 4/4 to 5/4.

After a discussion with students that there can be no wrong musical response if they follow the parameters set for variation, the teacher can suggest that they consider their own personal interpre-

FIGURE 12–3   Sample familiar songs and their variations.

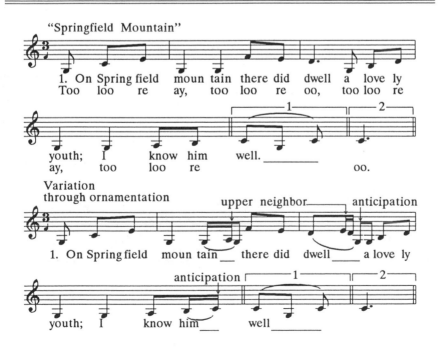

"Crawdad Hole"

Now, you get a line and I'll get a pole,__ Hon-ey. _____

you get a line and I'll get a pole, Babe.

you get a line and I'll get a pole, we'll go fish-ing in the

craw-dad hole, Hon-ey, Ba - by, mine.

Variation
through ornamentation

syncopation_____

suspension

Now, you get a line and I'll get a pole,_____ Hon-ey. _____

you get a line and I'll get a pole,____ Babe._____

trill

you get a line and I'll get a pole we'll go fish ing in the

passing

turn

craw-dad__ hole,__ Hon-ey,_____ Ba - by, mine.____

tation of the melody (figure 12–4). He or she can discuss the matter of ornamentation through devices such as passing tones, upper and lower neighbors, turns and trills, suspensions, anticipations, and syncopations. The characteristics of these decorative techniques might be best clarified through the teacher's demonstration, followed by the students' examples. As students begin to feel comfortable with the devices for melodic variation, they can be led to an exploration of variation together yet independently. The teacher will remind them that they will no longer perform in unison but that their joint effort to produce variations simultaneously is a musical event worth listening to.

The process of understanding and performing variations on a known melody unfolds over a period of time and through much practice. If students in the choral ensemble find the text cumbersome, the melody might be sung on a neutral syllable, allowing a better focus on the musical components. The invention of new ways for performing a familiar theme is an important step toward independent musicianship that can occur in an ensemble setting.*

FOCUS 10: From Rhythm Comes Melody (aural skills, improvisation)

Consider the common rhythm patterns that appear in compositions for band, orchestra, and choirs, and in the music of art, folk, and popular genres. Figure 12–5 contains frequently found rhythms. These rhythms can be presented by rote or on charts, with the teacher delivering them orally in a selected system of syllables or words, which are then imitated by the students. Some rhythms may require repetition and the teacher may wish to return to and reinforce earlier rhythms. With or without the presence of notation, the chanted phrases can be contained within a single measure and eventually be extended through repetition or the addition of contrasting rhythms to several measures. A clear visual cue from the teacher is necessary for an ensemble's imitative response, especially if meters and phrase lengths should change from one example to the next. The delivery and imitation should proceed with no hesitation or modulation of tempo.

Melody is derived through the association of pitches with rhythms. Once students are familiar with a variety of rhythms, pitch possibilities can be explored (figure 12–6). Acting as a group, stu-

---

* Some contemporary works for ensemble provide for improvisation that alternates with notated sections. Graphic pieces such as John Cage's "Notations" allow freedom within structure. Young performers may respond well to works that are mostly notated but which have small aleatoric sections for free expression.

FIGURE 12–4 Ornamentation for use in decorating a melody.

FIGURE 12–5 Sample of frequently found rhythms for listening and internalizing through performance.

dents can perform a rhythm in a scalewise or triadic progression, thus becoming oriented to the melodic potential in their voices or on their instruments. The realization of rhythm in melody can then progress through these steps: (1) teacher chants a rhythm, students chant; (2) teacher sings the same rhythm with a set of pitches based on tonal material recently reviewed; students sing; (3) teacher chants the same rhythm, students improvise their own melody based upon that rhythm. It is not necessary for students to adhere to a specific tonal scheme or pitch set; rather, the goal is to build a melody freely and spontaneously that is based on the various rhythmic patterns and phrases in study.

While students will create many and various improvisations,

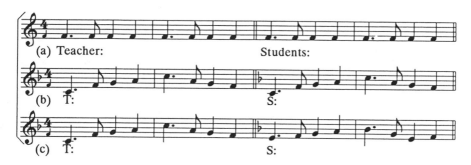

FIGURE 12–6 Rhythmic and melodic phrases for imitation (a and b) and variation (c).

when these are performed en masse, the young musicians will feel less inhibited than if they performed alone. Group practice should instill confidence so that students eventually can be called individually to improvise in step 3. The way to avoid a "musical mess" is to remind students that group improvisation is their opportunity to practice the solos they may be asked to perform. Band and orchestra students will employ their instruments in the improvisation, while choral students may wish to sing on "loo" or another neutral syllable in order to focus on the musical task more completely. A greater familiarity with the sound and sight of rhythms can result from this experience, and an opportunity for creative musical invention is also provided.

FOCUS 11: Say It with Music (aural skills, improvisation)

Improvisation is a culminating act in the music learning process. It can be used to ascertain how well beginning and more advanced students have achieved educational objectives. A student's spontaneous use of melodies and rhythms is evidence that he or she has learned and retained a music vocabulary and understands and has internalized certain aspects of style. Students can be provided occasions for improvisation in the ensemble, even if these are brief and sporadic. Music is like language, and just as one receives and understands language before expressive speech develops, a student must spend adequate time listening and imitating before he or she can improvise. With sufficient musical experience, students are capable of expressing musical ideas as spontaneously and naturally as they might participate in a conversation.

Improvised musical conversations consist of questions or statements and their responses. The teacher can begin the experience by setting limitations on phrase length, key, and meter. For example, one 4/4 measure in C major is a starting point in framing a single idea, which may later shift to a required four 3/4 measures in E minor. (At times, the performers may be given free reign in the arbitrary selection of all musical components in a stream-of-consciousness improvisation.) The teacher or a student may be designated as leader, performing questions that are answered by an individual student. The responding student can be selected prior to the dialogue's beginning, in order to allow him an opportunity to focus and prepare for an immediate response; the ensemble can conduct the beat. Alternatively, to maintain attention of the full ensemble, a student may be chosen following the question, allowing one measure to lapse before responding.

The spontaneous generation of melodies is challenging to students and is intended for ensembles that have listened to and performed discrete melodic and rhythmic patterns in isolation of a piece, as well as within songs and musical works. Using solfége syllables or a neutral "loo," vocal students may wish to remove themselves from the distraction of supplying a text as well. The possibility for developing the skill of improvising a recitative-like song from spoken dialogue, however, may also be an attractive one for singers. Another modification that can provide opportunities in improvised musical conversation is the chanting, tapping, or clapping of rhythms, which may even be used as a prelude to the invention of melodies. As students are presented with new melodic and rhythmic ideas, they will be capable of recalling them in new arrangements. The improvised musical conversations they share is one means of reviewing their knowledge.

FOCUS 12: Last Words on Creativity (aural skills, improvisation)

Some ensembles may be more favorably disposed than others toward experiences that link their aural and performance skills with their creative abilities. There may be reason to develop special-interest ensembles, particularly in vocal or instrumental jazz. Pedagogical materials by Bert Konowitz, Doug Anderson, David Baker, Jerry Coker, and Jamey Aebersold offer guidelines for ensemble organization, instructional techniques, and repertoire.

Within the large performing ensembles, strategies for developing improvisational skills are available as an end in themselves and as a means of synthesizing earlier music learning experiences. The following class experiences are recommended:

1. Choose a melodic or rhythmic motive from a piece and create a short song. Give five minutes to "working it out," and then ask for individual or small-group performances.
2. Take a theme from a work in a particular style and frame it in a new

style (i.e., perform the melody of a Bach chorale with jazz-like syncopations, or a popular song in the style of Mozart). Conduct an exploratory performance as an ensemble and provide time for individual interpretations.

3. Perform a piece in its notated style and at an appointed time, break for ensemble, section, or solo improvisation before returning to the notation. Madrigals, chorales, symphonies, suites, and folk song arrangements are examples of genres to which the experience can be applied.

4. Enliven the class with a guest performer from the community. Students may be strongly motivated by a live performance; they can also learn through observation about performance technique, style, repertoire, and even appropriate behavior as a performer. The performer may encourage the imitation by students of passages and techniques, engaging them in the transfer of listening to activity.

CHAPTER

13

◆

Music Learning in the Private Studio Lesson

The making of a performing musician in the West is the result of events that transpire between student and teacher in the privacy of the studio lesson. For a period of thirty minutes or an hour each week, the student is given the undivided personal attention of the teacher. As transmitters of their own musical heritage, teachers shape the musicianship of their students, demonstrating through their own performance the standards for tone quality and technique. They listen to students and respond to their individual needs regarding sound production, phrasing, and articulation. They offer ways to improve students' literacy skills, including sight-reading ability, and define new symbols as they occur in the notated repertoire. They recommend methods of practice, advise means for memorizing a work, and suggest opportunities for the creative expression and interpretation of a piece. Teachers are the musical agents, the models, and the motivating forces for their students. In the transmission of performance skills, the private studio lesson offers the greatest potential for intensive and highly individualized music learning.

Talented performers develop from an intricate matrix of factors that include an inherent musical talent, an interest and commitment to the development of that talent, parental encouragement, and the nurturing of talent by insightful teachers. Effective studio teachers understand the capabilities of their specific instruments for producing musical sounds. They can identify talent, offer motivational incentives, and communicate to parents the nature of their supportive

276

role. They understand the learning process, from matters of technique and note-reading to artistic interpretation. They are dedicated to teaching, as they may be to their own performance, and can alternately serve as disciplined taskmasters and compassionate allies. If students possess musical ability and interest, effective teachers will creatively seek ways to sustain and support them.

Private study in the form of the weekly session is viewed as the typical means of music instruction by both those with avocational interests and those with professional goals.* A child frequently begins Suzuki violin studies soon after he or she is walking and talking. Suzuki instruction is praised as much for its extramusical as for its musical outcomes in preschool children, including improved discipline, communication, and kinesthetic skills. With the hope of developing a certain "well-roundedness" in their children, parents frequently follow the long-established tradition of providing for piano lessons during the child's elementary years. For some, piano lessons are fleeting experiences; for others, they are a foundation for the further study and enjoyment of music; for the very few, the lessons are an initial step toward a career in piano performance. When middle school students show particular interest in orchestral and band instruments, parents may arrange for private after-school instruction for them at various academies, storefront studios, or in private homes. Students who study singing generally wait until they are in secondary school to begin this instruction as the voice needs a degree of physical maturity for lessons to be most successful. There appears to be a correlation between musical training and commitment: the longer the period of private instruction during childhood, the greater is the loyalty and dedication of the student to music and to his instrument. The commitment of the student's parents is also considerable. A student may develop professional interests; then the intensity of the individualized instruction and of the teacher-student relationship takes on paramount importance. In any case, whether the student's goal is a professional career or a pastime activity, the private studio lesson is designed for meeting unique musical needs in an efficient and effective manner.

The learning characteristics of the private lesson are an amalgam of aural, visual, and kinesthetic behaviors. The teacher provides verbal instruction through descriptions and explanations, and nonverbal instruction through his or her own performance demonstration. The student learns aurally by the modeling of the teacher and the student's imitation of what he or she hears. By watching and

---

* Group lessons are becoming more commonplace, and "partner" lessons are also increasingly popular.

listening attentively, the student learns appropriate performance po-sitions, techniques, and style. As the student's performance is evalu-ated, the teacher may provide feedback that is verbal (with comments such as "good bow arm," "much better legato sound"), musical (by replaying a particular phrase to show the student how it should be performed), visual (through smiles, nods, facial and bodily gestures), or kinesthetic (patting the back approvingly, gently shaking tension from the student's wrist). Sometimes attention is paid to developing the student's creative expression through experiences in style inter-pretation and improvisation, which are demonstrated, explained, and guided by the teacher. These behaviors form the core of the private lesson, with information channeled and received by the student through several sensory avenues.

There are more similarities than differences in the training of performing musicians throughout the world. Formal and informal instruction share a number of strategies, the most important of which is probably the communication of information through various aural, visual, and kinesthetic means. The private studio lesson, the standard forum for instruction in Western classical music, could become more effective if teachers developed an understanding of universal patterns of music teaching and learning behaviors and applied these to their teaching. A study of instructional styles of selected master musicians and teachers in the West may demonstrate the use of techniques that develop music sensitivity and expression through various verbal and nonverbal means. Several influential approaches to music learning and creativity, including Suzuki and aspects of jazz pedagogy, may offer suggestions for application in the studio. A focus on devices such as demonstration, imitation, kinesthetic awareness, improvisation and its relationship to musical expression and interpretation, and practice strategies may contribute to more meaningful learning in the music lesson.

THE WAYS OF WESTERN MASTERS

The accounts of successful teachers and their students on music teaching and the performance and practice behaviors generated by the process are enlightening to those committed to music learning in the studio. While it is commonly accepted that performance behav-iors should consume the lesson time, questions remain as to how best the teacher may guide those behaviors. Should teachers be perform-ers? Do performers make effective teachers? What should be the teacher's medium for conveying a musical idea? When are words important? Should the teacher perform the work in its entirety, or perform even a single phrase? Is vocalization important in instrumental lessons? How can the student's listening sense be engaged? Is imitation a useful device in a literate tradition? Is improvisation related to interpretation? Can either be taught in the private lesson? The perspectives of master teachers and performers on these issues suggest workable solutions.

It seems realistic to expect that teachers would continue to exercise their own musical skills, for through performance they gain information and insight into the heart of their professional life. Many private teachers, however, "retire" early from performance as soloists or as members of chamber ensembles, or even from performing for their own enjoyment. They may do little to maintain technical fitness of fingers, hands, arms, mouth, and vocal cords and may rarely stimulate themselves by reading literature beyond the capacities of their intermediate students. While teachers are often under time constraints that limit the amount of practice and performance they can cram into a crowded schedule, they should not overlook the importance of maintaining basic musicianship. The reputable karate instructor continues to practice and refine his expert martial movements, and the highly esteemed museum teacher of painting and sculpture continues to produce exhibits of art. The dancer-turned-choreographer follows a daily routine for limbering up the body, in order to maintain a personal relationship with the performing art. It follows that the music teacher would continue to make music in the lesson and perhaps for public performance as well.

Master teachers frequently perform even while on staff at universities and conservatories, because making music is their life's blood, their passion, and their original calling to the profession. They perform in solo recitals, in chamber groups, in symphony orchestras, in operas. They perform on campus and in the community, throughout the region, and sometimes internationally. At the same time, performing musicians teach because of their enthusiasm for music and their need to communicate it to aspiring young musicians. By listening to and analyzing the performance of their students, they develop a greater understanding of the music and of the techniques and interpretation inherent in its performance. There are lessons to be learned from students through the questions they ask, the problems they incur, and the answers that emerge from the combined experimentation of teacher and pupil.

Some of the finest contemporary musicians find that performing is inseparable from teaching, and that each role nurtures the other. Cellist Janos Starker underscored his commitment to education: "If I do not teach, I cannot play; if I do not play, I cannot teach. They are equally important to me" (Mullins, 1986, 18). Lynn Harrell offered a similar insight, claiming that teaching is a potential learning experience for the teacher: "In learning how to explain the cello to others, I learned myself. . . . In trying to convey the deep love I have for music, I re-encountered in my most private core that same moment of discovery" (1988, 13). Jazz musician David Baker's statements represent the ideal connection between performing and teaching: "I find that what I do as a performer reflects itself in what I do as a teacher. . . . Everything I do revolves around teaching" (Lockhart-Moss and Guregian, 1986, 12).

Similar to the way a song is handed down over time and distance in the oral tradition, teaching by performers of Western art music is often viewed by them as the transmission of a cultural and personal heritage in music. Many consider this teaching the musician's responsibility. The challenge, stimulation, and compassion of his finest teachers were recalled by oboist Bert Lucarelli, who continued with this philosophical statement: "Teaching . . . [is] a noble concept . . . [and·is] fundamentally a means of passing on a tradition" (p. 12). Harrell underscored the importance of his role as a transmitter of musical style and technique: "I have always felt that I owed others a huge musical debt and that I was to pay it through the next generation. I have always wanted to pass on at least a small part of my heritage" (1988, 13). For a surprising number of professional musicians, teaching is not a lesser occupation; rather, it is intimately linked to performance. Teaching is an honorable career path and is even exalted by those who view it as the preservation of a musical tradition.

The ability to communicate ideas nonverbally is heralded as an important attribute of the master teacher. Pianist Grant Johannesen noted that "one of Robert Casadesus' gifts as a teacher was an ability to communicate the essence of the music itself in a very few words" (1982, 25). The absence of words does not necessarily signify silence, for the message can often be conveyed more effectively when the teacher performs rather than describes the ideal performance. While fluency of word is an admirable quality, its place in the lesson is somewhat questionable. The transfer of abstract qualities of the musical language into another system is a difficult and often unsuccessful procedure. Musical ideas may be best delivered musically.

One of the most effective teaching devices in the private lesson is demonstration. The great piano pedagogue, Artur Schnabel, was known for his frequent performances in his studio lessons in order to teach stylistic nuances. Although Schnabel seldom talked much in the lesson and was unlikely to label performance techniques he delivered, his students nonetheless still communicate among themselves through such reference terms as the "Schnabel trill." His son remarked on the nonverbal impact of Schnabel's demonstrations: "How is this [term] possible, if he never talked about such things? The solution is that we were watching him. He did a lot of demonstrating" (Schnabel, 1974, 10). Schnabel's students learned the unique nature of the trill as Schnabel interpreted it by observation; they later assigned a label to it to recall the musical essence of the technique.

A teacher's demonstration may consist of a performance of a complete work to present the total musical picture, or just a phrase or melodic fragment to modify a student's inaccurate rendering. The approach used by flutist Maurice "Mo" Sharp was to play along with his student, listening intently and following up substandard phrases with his own immediate and more accurate performance. Explanations were rare, as he recognized the effectiveness of demonstration. One student noted that "Sharp didn't talk that much. If I played something he didn't like he would start making faces and then demonstrate on his instrument" (Hansen, 1986, 10).

Some of the greatest violinists studied with the master Josef Gingold, who uses demonstration and storytelling in shaping the artistry of his students. Joseph Silverstein, Jaime Laredo, Eugene Fodor, and Miriam Fried have remarked on Gingold's masterful performances within the privacy of the studio lesson, where he conveys the styles and stories of legendary performers Fritz Kreisler and Jascha Heifitz. The young violinist Joshua Bell claimed a deep admiration for his teacher, and described Gingold's approach: "Lessons include demonstration ('He still plays great') and anecdotes. . . . I hope that old style of playing has rubbed off on me, just from hearing him play a lot" (Waleson, 1988, 391).

Just as important as the teacher's demonstration is the student's reception, which usually leads to imitation. Neither role is passive, for the student is involved in aural and visual observation and the kinesthetic response that follows. The ears are listening to the expressive treatment of the musical elements as well as to performance techniques that may include breathing and tonguing; the eyes are watching for the movement of the bow, the placement of the hands on the keyboard, and the fingers on valves, frets, and keys. In an account of the training of concert pianists, Sosniak described the extent to which the master teacher served as a model to emulate:

> The young pianists studied how the teacher sat at the piano, how the teacher looked at the page of music, how the teacher prepared himself to play a particular piece or style of music, how he marked the music, and how he moved his body. They

listened for his pauses, his crescendos, his trills. They observed
his attitude toward other musicians, musical styles, performances, and competitions. (1985, 61)

Observation of the musician-teacher can be all encompassing and is
of greatest pedagogical use when followed by an imitative yet
thoughtful performance.

Imitation, then, necessitates students' heightened awareness of
what to hear, see, and feel. The teacher may direct that attention
through questions that stimulate the thought processes so that students can evaluate the sensory messages that are channeled to them.
During observations of the teacher, as well as of themselves, students
are guided toward learning what to do and why to do it. They learn
to watch the curvature of the fingers on the piano and to imitate that
position. They listen to the growing intensity of a violin's vibrato
through a sustained pitch and attempt to match that sound. They
observe the relaxed alignment of the body while the teacher performs, and through imitation and the teacher's guidance, learn to
recognize that feeling in themselves. The precision of imitation,
which can lead to an internalization of appropriate performing techniques, is dependent on the observant and aware student. Like a
scientist, the student absorbs every detail of sound, sight, and feeling
through close and careful scrutiny and evaluation.

A keen listening sense is a principal trait of the performing musician, one that master teachers emphasize in their teaching. Although notation conveys those components that can be written, the
fuller meaning of music as an expressive art can be ascertained only
through careful listening. It is for this reason that seasoned performers still return to their teachers or are coached by other performers:
they want to listen for the expressive content, the flow between the
notes, the rise and fall of dynamics and accent markings, the interpretation that the composer intends or the genre requires. The lesson
provides opportunities for training the ear, and when the student has
learned to listen to himself, he can then progress in the practice
room. He checks himself for an evenness of tone, the appropriate
extent of vibrato, phrasing, articulation, and expression. Producing
performers who learn to listen is one of the major tasks of studio
teachers.

For some musicians, their ear has been their foremost guide to
performance. Gingold recalled first listening to his brother on the
violin, and the keen ear he had even at an early age: "I kept listening
and assimilating all the Kreutzer Etudes, which my brother used to
practice—and later in life I knew them so well that every wrong note
he played, I played also, by ear" (Kent, 1988, 478). Several years

later, while in a German war camp, his instruction was proceeding informally under the tutelage of his brother. Gingold learned notation haphazardly, but continued to develop musically as he listened to his brother, to himself, and, when the family moved to New York, to artists at Carnegie Hall: "I went to school, but if there was a great fiddler or Philharmonic concert in Carnegie Hall I wanted to hear particularly, there was no school that afternoon for me! It was something that I needed for my soul, for my education, you see?" (pp. 478–479). The concerts were also good for his listening ears.

Schnabel's musical hearing was considered his central gift, which was then further refined through conscious training when he was young. His listening went beyond the melodic layers and harmonic progressions. He heard the music before he played it, and was able to transfer it to the piano with great expressiveness. Schnabel's genius was explained in this manner: "His ear governed his movements at all times. He described the process of playing in all its complexity by pointing out that he always heard every bit in advance mentally, and then in retrospect physically" (Wolff, 1974, 38). If there were musical flaws in Schnabel's public performances, they were usually due to poor acoustics. His finely tuned listening sense required adjustment time, especially to the inferior acoustics of a piano or concert hall (Wolff, 1974). Schnabel's ear and imagination rather than his visual or kinesthetic senses were his main guides to the music.

Vocalization, the technique of singing an instrumental line, is a common practice of master musicians in their teaching and in their own independent rehearsal. In a chronicle of conservatory culture at the fictitious Midland University, Kingsbury described the use of singing by a master clarinet teacher (known by the pseudonym of Goldmann) as a means of teaching musical feeling:

> One strategy frequently used by Goldmann was that of asking a student to sing a particular passage, an exercise that compels the student to experience a musical phrase in terms of a finite amount of exhaling breath, and to clarify beginnings and endings of phrases, experienced physically as points where a singer can inhale. When Goldmann told a young clarinetist to "take a breath, there" he was making a comment that was at once technical and interpretive, and he was doing this by giving a physical, bodily directive (1988, page 96).

The expression to "make it breathe," along with occasions for singing a musical phrase that is supported by deep breathing, is commonly employed by teachers in private instrumental lessons in an attempt to render the phrase more musical and filled with feeling.

Vocalization allows for an intimate association of the musician with the musical phrase. Lucarelli elevated the importance of the singing voice for instrumentalists, concluding that "in the medium of instrumental music it is generally conceded that the highest goal of all instrumentalists is to mirror the beauty and mystery of the human voice" (p. 14). To help a musician develop an understanding of lyricism in performance and to know the meaning of *cantabile* and *legato*, singing is a recommended activity. When asked whether he had any advice for student musicians, trombonist Philip Jones remarked: "If you want to be a good musician, you must go and listen to singers and to fiddle players. From them you can learn about line, about joining up notes in interesting ways, which we are not taught on our instruments" (Jones, 1986, 15). Starker's frequent use of singing as a teaching device is illustrated in this story of a student struggling with the correct bowing: " 'Sing the opening theme,' Starker bellowed. 'I can't, I'm too embarrassed,' the student admitted. 'An artist cannot afford to be embarrassed—SING!' The student sang and discovered the mistake, and her playing improved immediately" (p. 17). As vocalization requires the use of the musician's most personal instrument, the voice, the singer takes possession of the music. After he or she has internalized the music through singing, the musician can easily transfer it to the instrument.

Performance mastery is far more than an accurate reading of notated music; it requires musical expressiveness that the teacher should begin encouraging as a part of independent practice early in a musician's training. To help a musician develop the musical expression and interpretation so essential to outstanding performance, coaching by the teacher is indispensable and should occupy most of the lesson. To be memorable, a performance must be alive and seemingly spontaneous. Such performing is a product of free, flexible, and personal delivery within the boundaries of style. The master teacher advises on the balance between tradition and personal expression.

As a part of teaching for expression, experiences in improvisation can provide the opportunity to combine technical skills with fragments of musical ideas gleaned from pieces under study. The knowledge of how to build melodic motifs into phrases, and to connect phrases into complete musical forms is an important skill for performers. Not only does the process of recalling, ordering, and developing ideas aid in the analysis of previously composed music, but the skill may be helpful for the inevitable memory lapses that occur in performance. Gingold related an incident in which Kreisler improvised on the "Star-Spangled Banner" so that it sounded like "a Viennese waltz, complete with runs and double-stops." In the "Kreutzer" Sonata later in the program, Kreisler suffered a memory lapse "but he kept on playing and improvised perfectly, so a person who wasn't musically minded would never have known" (1988, 481). Memory slips are unavoidable, but the skill of improvisation can help the performer cover the error and move on to a place in the piece he or she remembers securely.

The ways of master musician-teachers can serve as models of the learning process in the studio lesson. As performing artists in their own right and as craftsmen committed to raising students to their potential as performers, these Western masters share many of the concerns of music systems in the oral tradition. Notated music does not necessitate a whole new set of learning techniques; conversely, an oral tradition is not antithetical to a literate one. The aural learning process is at work in the private studio lesson through its various nonverbal components of demonstration, imitation, vocalization, and improvisation.

EAST GOES WEST: THE SUZUKI LESSON

Despite the image of masses of children gathered in a sports arena, their bows moving together in the performance of a Vivaldi or Mozart masterwork, the Suzuki method of instruction is fundamentally a private lesson system. Its philosophy has been applied successfully not only to violin but also to piano, cello, and other stringed and wind instruments. The method is an intermingling of European art music and performance practice with Japanese pedagogical ideas, the combined influence of Shinichi Suzuki's mother country and his training as a violinist in Germany. The adaptation of the Suzuki method to public school classes is an American phenomenon, one that retains the ideology while modifying the process. There is an extensive library of books, manuals, records, and magazines to guide the teacher who wishes to follow carefully the Suzuki curriculum although the private teacher may freely choose a merger of many materials and techniques in designing a pathway to performance for his or her students. A number of Suzuki principles, however, are worthy of attention for their potential use in the studio.

Suzuki's Talent Education is a system by which each student receives one private lesson weekly. In Japan, "private" will usually include the teacher, student, and parent, but occasionally other students may observe and even be invited to play along. The act of listening to and watching another is considered a pedagogically sound practice, as is the periodic small group performance of a work in unison for parents every few months. Still, most of the student's instruction consists of the individualized attention of the teacher and the parent.

Suzuki is an aural learning process in which the student learns by listening: to his teacher, to recordings, to himself. Recordings of great artists are brought into the home and played so that the student can be aurally enriched and motivated by such models. Guidance from a teacher and from parents at home who have participated in the lessons further shape the student's discriminating ear. Eventually, the student develops the ability to listen to his or her own performance and compare it to performances of the teacher and artists he or she has heard.

Notation is introduced after considerable time spent listening. Note-reading is initiated following sufficient experience in listening and developing the kinesthetic skills of performance, usually by the end of two years of instruction (less if the student is older than the recommended preschool age). As is typical in the training of the Japanese musician, even when a system of notation is understood, the Suzuki method encourages its use only as a cue to recall music that was presented aurally at the lesson. "Playing by ear" is highly esteemed by proponents of Suzuki, and should not only precede but also accompany the use of notation.

A key component in Suzuki's Talent Education is the emphasis given to repetition. Students are expected to listen repeatedly to recordings of artists as well as to the recorded pedagogical pieces offered by the method. Repetition, review, and revision are important; they occur in the lesson and ideally at home, where parents may monitor and provide feedback to the student. Repetition leads to memorization, a natural occurrence in the sequence of listening and repeating. Beginning with eight-measure phrases and progressing to songs twice that length, the student's memory develops gradually and steadily. Ever longer pieces are introduced until the student has been trained to listen to, analyze, and memorize a complete three-movement sonata.

The transition from rote imitation to notation is a gradual process in the Suzuki method. The process of music reading is essentially one of association, as the student "watches the notes while he plays a piece he has already learned by memory, so that the logic of notation becomes apparent, not as a struggle to produce music from difficult symbols, but as a natural means of visualizing what he has already learned" (Kendall, 1984, 11).

Advocates of Suzuki defend the delay in presenting notation. Rote-learning need not lead to automatic and inexpressive performance, they reason, because students listen to the recordings of musicians whose own interpretation and creative expression has led to their designations as masters of their music. Imitation is linked to listening, music is internalized through the combined efforts of the aural and kinesthetic senses, and the potential for expression is fostered. Suzuki teachers view notation as an important visual aid and one of enormous value to the young musician who hopes to acquire an extensive performance repertoire. Notation is an efficient learning device, but one to be relegated to its proper place in the teaching of an aural art.

As the Suzuki method has met with enthusiastic acceptance in the West, the key factors of private instruction have been maintained. Teachers of Suzuki violin, cello, piano, flute, and guitar, among other instruments, adhere to Suzuki's maxims: (1) the beginning of instruction in early childhood; (2) the importance of the teacher-child-parent triangle; (3) the use of recordings for home listening; (4) a rote approach to learning; (5) the primary importance of repetition; (6) a development of the capacity to memorize; (7) the use of music from the repertoire of Western art music; and (8) the occasional recital for solo and ensemble performance. Principles of Suzuki pedagogy continue to be successful in the West, and whether applied completely or in conjunction with other techniques, the matter of sound—and kinesthetic feeling—before sight remains its most influential factor.

JAZZ PEDAGOGY: IMPLICATIONS FOR ALL STYLES

The first sounds of jazz date to the beginning of the twentieth century; a system to train jazz musicians, however, is a more recent development. Jazz is noted for its partially oral tradition and its spontaneous improvisation. The belief at one time was that jazz could not be formally taught but that a musician could best learn it independently from records or informally from others in occasional jam sessions. In the last three decades, however, many conservatories and universities have begun to reach beyond jazz appreciation courses for listeners to formal instruction for performers. The pedagogy of jazz as presented in the private lesson today offers an approach relevant to the learning of all music styles and media.

Although there is a vast array of published materials in jazz education, most are designed chiefly for independent practice. In the private studio lesson, the teacher is likely to emphasize aural learning over note-reading. An assortment of exercises is employed for ear-training and for building a student's technical competence on an instrument. Recorded and printed materials, including transcriptions of jazz solos, are also incorporated, but to a lesser extent. Manuals published by Aebersold, Baker, and Coker offer structure and ideas for future improvisation but are not usually the focus of private instruction. The teacher can introduce exercises and "licks" from his own performance experience and shape the student's techniques and style through critical comments, but it is the student's commitment to intensive and independent practice that is most vital to his or her progress. The purpose of the lesson and study of the published materials recommended by the teacher is to guide the student's rehearsal time so that he or she may develop the capacity and ideas for the most notable feature of the style: improvisation.

In learning improvisation in the jazz lesson, the student exercises the ear and the fingers (or other body parts responsible for sound production) through the performance of scales, scale fragments, arpeggios, and melodic and rhythmic motifs or patterns. The material is introduced by the teacher, usually without notation, and the student imitates it. Scales and arpeggios are played mechanically and with increasing speed as the motor skills develop. The teacher presents three- or four-note patterns, which are learned and applied sequentially at each pitch level of a given scale. Since most students begin studying jazz in adolescence or later, they may be able to read music as a result of earlier music instruction; thus, notation serves as a memory aid for exercises learned aurally in the lesson.

Training jazz musicians in formal settings is a sophisticated process, and one that requires a broad knowledge of the art of jazz. Scales are just the beginning, for at institutions such as the Berklee College of Music in Boston, the Eastman School of Music, Indiana University, the University of North Texas, and the University of Washington, a jazz education incorporates the theories and applications of an enormous variety of scales, modes, chords and their relationships, harmonic formations and progressions, aspects of musical structure, and the complexities of rhythmic patterns that lend feeling and movement to jazz. As with any collegiate degree program in music, the aim is a comprehensive education that connects the study of theory and history to performance. The private lesson is an essential part of the degree program as it allows the student to integrate information gained from various courses into his performance style under the tutelage of the applied teacher.

The studio lesson provides a workable format for learning bebop, blues, or Brahms. The approach to jazz is characteristically an aural one; indeed, listening is at the crux of the jazz lesson. The learning of "classical" piano, voice, or violin, like jazz, is enhanced through listening experiences. Teachers of jazz and classical lessons alike frequently employ demonstration and imitation in the studio lesson. Implicit in jazz training is the extensive use of recordings for outside listening and imitation by the student as well as long hours of practice on exercises intended to improve technique and offer ideas for improvisation. Teachers of classical music would hardly protest these strategies; rather, they should encourage the student's interest in outside listening, attendance at concerts, and concentrated daily practice. While a great many Western classical music genres are not improvisatory, the development of creativity through occasional practice at improvising may influence the student's greater use of expressive devices in the re-creative process of performance. Clearly, the techniques for training jazz and classical musicians have more to unite than divide them.

A WORLD VIEW OF THE PRIVATE LESSON

The music lesson is not restricted to the West but can be found as a means of formal instruction in other world cultures. The training of musicians in the performance of Asian classical music is frequently the private affair of the student and teacher, and one which may accelerate the learning process through its one-on-one communication. Where music is transmitted informally, as in traditional European cultures or African societies where music is integrated within the culture, repertoire and performance techniques may nonetheless be acquired through the association of the student with a relative or community elder who serves as the agent for instruction. As in the Western studio lesson, the interactions of student and teacher throughout the world envelop aural, visual, and kinesthetic senses. In nearly every system of music learning, nonverbal behaviors that include demonstration, observation, and imitation are widespread.

As in the West, the performance of Asian art music is studied for reasons that include personal edification, the development of a leisure activity, and interest in a performing career. Among certain East Asian groups, women and literati have traditionally sought private instruction in order to distinguish themselves as respectable members of social and intellectual classes. Japanese women performers of koto or shamisen were perceived as attractive and marriageable, and Chinese qin players were likely to be intellectuals with a need for quiet but intense music to accompany their philosophical ponderings. Today, a music education is still an honorable acquisition, so much so that in Japan, private teachers are invited by corporations to offer lessons in noh singing or shamisen performance during the lunch hour or after work. Musical training contributes to the holistic image of a well-rounded person. The aspiring musician heeds his teacher's advice as he travels toward his goal as a professional performer. For a far greater number of students, the private teacher is central to the procurement of musical knowledge as a social grace, a guide to knowing a traditional treasure.

If a culture's music is a solo tradition, then training occurs within a lesson format. Southeast Asian music is generally performed by ensembles, including the Indonesian gamelan and Thai pi phat; thus, private lessons are less likely there than in countries such as China, India, Japan, and those in the Middle East, where solo or soloistic chamber music is standard. Among the most common Asian instruments for which private instruction is available are the Chinese qin, zheng, pipa (plucked lute), and erhu (two-stringed fiddle); the Indian sitar, sarod, vina (lutes), tabla, and mṛidaṅga (drums); the Japanese koto, shamisen, and shakuhachi; the Middle Eastern 'ud, santour, tar (plucked lute), and rebab (two- to four-stringed fiddle). Instruction in vocal music may be offered as a prerequisite to, or in conjunction with, instrumental music, as is commonly the case in India.

Asian students engage in regularly scheduled lessons in the homes of teachers or in conservatory settings. It is not unusual for the "private" lesson to consist principally of the teacher and student but also of a number of students who are present to listen and observe. Seated around the walls of a koto teacher's home studio, for example, are often students and their parents who arrive before their lesson, stay afterward, or even "make a morning of it." As in a repertoire or master class, the teacher responds to the individual needs of the student whose appointed lesson time it is, but the observers are listening, watching, and taking note of relevant comments. In the extreme case of the Indian gharana system, students living with their teachers are engulfed by music, their days surrounded by the lessons of one serious student after another. Opportunities for observation abound, and observation by ear and eye is typically expected of the student. In European-style conservatories throughout Asia, lessons are designed for greater privacy, where one can learn qānūn or pipa without an audience. The benefits of what is in actuality only a semi-private lesson—or even a group lesson resembling a master class—in certain Asian settings are notable, however, both for the performing student who needs the experience of an intimate but public performance, and for the observing student who can acquire a sense of sound quality, techniques, and style.

The continuance of oral tradition in which literate means of preservation and transmission have developed is a curious phenomenon and one that underscores the importance and irreplaceable role of the teacher. If music can be regarded as a human behavior that requires the participation of people as performers and as listeners, then a natural extension might be that music learning requires the contributions of a transmitter, or teacher, and a receiver, or student. This appears to be the case in completely oral cultures such as those in parts of Africa, where written music systems have not been invented. Despite the existence of notation in the high art cultures of Asia, the teacher is nevertheless regarded as the critical link to the music. Notation has little, if any, use within the lesson itself; instead, it functions as a reminder of the teacher's singing, chanting, playing, and commentary during the student's practice time. In Asian cultures, the teacher commands respect not typically known in the West—except for the great master teachers—which is perhaps due to his indispensable role in the transmission of music whose essence can be only partially preserved on paper.

Whether music is learned in the formalized lessons of Asia or through the more casual exchange of teacher and student in other traditional cultures throughout the world, the devices are similar. Through the ages, experience and experimentation has shown that the most effective instruction features the teacher who demonstrates rather than explains and the student who imitates rather than sits silently. Throughout the non-Western world, vocalization transcends verbalization as the quickest and most direct pathway to music learning. Systems of mnemonics for rhythm, pitch, and performance technique are found in nearly every tradition, and the aural memory is thus strengthened by exercises that require the student's concentration and ability to fit small musical fragments into the larger musical performance. In the practice of improvisation (or its related techniques of variation and interpretation), the aural learning process makes its greatest contribution to the uniqueness of music as an expressive art. The world view of the private lesson, then, presents clear evidence of the significance of the ear to the development of the total musician.

APPLICATIONS

Since the aural sense is so thoroughly linked to performance skills, the private studio lesson presents an ideal opportunity to combine training of the ear, the eye, and the physical self so vital to sound production. Aspects of the aural learning process can be implemented to meet the student's individual needs; these include such strategies as demonstration, imitation, vocalization, other learning and retention strategies, and creative improvisation. Whether directed by the teacher within the lesson, or used independently by the student during practice, the suggested *Focus* experiences will affect the performer's development of such key attributes as intonation, tone quality, diction and articulation, vibrato, interpretation, and musical expression. The overlap of *Focus* experiences from elementary classroom and ensemble settings will be evident (chapters 11 and 12), as the goal for all levels and specializations is the complete musician who listens while performing and does so with an intelligent and creative expressiveness.

FOCUS 1: From Demonstration to Imitation (aural skills)

The performing teacher provides a model for the student to observe and imitate. The effective teacher should possess more than a casual familiarity with works assigned to the student and should be able to perform them as whole entities in order to communicate the spirit, the character, and the function of or composer's intention in the music. The ability to analyze and resolve a problem is characteristic of all good teachers, but for every phrase fragment that may appear troublesome to the student, the teacher should be able to demonstrate the appropriate performance technique and to produce an accurate rendering of the sound as intended by the composer. It is not sufficient that a teacher comment verbally on the student's performance, whether lavishing praise or issuing a cautious critique. Rather, the performance behaviors modeled by the teacher provide the most direct information to the student musician.

The beginning student in particular needs to know the ways in which the body can contribute to the correct sound. How should the bow arm appear as it plays on each string? How "quiet" should the wrist be on the keyboard? Where should the fingers be when they are not on the pads of a flute? What is the appropriate angle of the mallets on a snare drum? How erect must the body be while singing? As the teacher performs, the observing student learns the function and appearance of the body in achieving a truly musical sound.

Likewise, the listening student develops a concept of accurate musical sound through the teacher's demonstration. How does breath support contribute to full vocal sound and to the *sotto voce* sections? Is there an evenness in a keyboard's scalar passage in which all sounds are equal and none is inappropriately accented? What does a change in embouchure do to a clarinet's quality? How does the vibrato contribute to the intensity of sustained sounds on the violin? What are a work's expressive elements that enliven the music? The attentive student listens and learns the aural meaning of notational symbols in performance from the teacher.

The stimulus-and-response nature of teacher demonstration and student imitation behaviors should be encouraged in the lesson. Body alignment and position of the arms, wrists, fingers, and lips can be demonstrated and immediately imitated. Performance techniques and the accurate performance of musical phrases, both melodic and rhythmic, can be delivered and received nonverbally in the lesson. Students may require numerous trials, but through ample repetition and appropriate feedback, they can be guided to see, hear, and feel the correct performance behaviors that they later reinforce in independent practice.

FOCUS 2: Tape, Listen, and Evaluate (aural skills)

The tape recorder can be an invaluable resource for the aspiring musician. Lesson time is best spent by playing or singing, along with the teacher's critiques and the student's questions on musical matters. Limitations should be placed on the proportion of the lesson allotted to writing out exercises, marking up scores (beyond fingerings, bow strokes, and phrasing), writing out word-for-word translations of a foreign text in the score, and detailing lesson assignments in a notebook. A far more efficient means of preserving the lesson is to tape it. The thirty minutes can be reviewed on tape in the car, at home, and in the practice room. The student can then recall exercises, interpretation, pronunciation, and advisory remarks regarding his or her own performance technique. The student can listen repeatedly to the correct sound of the instrument as demonstrated by the teacher, and can critically evaluate his or her own imitation.

Students' recordings of their own practice sessions, or at least portions of them, can assist them in assessing their own progress. Whether the recording is a series of warm-up exercises, or a run-through of a complete work, students will benefit by listening and comparing their performances with the more desirable performance of the teacher (or other performer). The teacher may occasionally request that a tape of a practice session be brought to the lesson so that he or she can offer suggestions regarding students' independent practice habits.

FOCUS 3: Ear-Strengthening Exercises (aural skills)

In developing total musicianship, understanding how a melody is structured can be an invaluable aid to student musicians (figure 13–1). When listening and performing by ear a set of musical patterns, students exercise their memories also and add to their ability to perceive separate components which form a complete musical work. Aural knowledge of music's organization adds to students' personal fulfillment as they perform; it is thus a factor in their internal

FIGURE 13–1   Ear-strengthening exercises for listening and internalizing through performance.

motivation. As scales and arpeggios are important in developing technical facility, so can these and other exercises contribute to the student's aural training.

The teacher may aurally introduce through demonstration phrases that can be performed as warm-ups or reviews in the lesson and practice room. These are often derived from pieces a student is currently studying. This demonstration may be followed by the simultaneous performance of the teacher and student, and eventually by the student alone. These phrases should at first be quite simple, such as three sequential pitches to be performed at every scale degree. Strive for an evenness of tone quality on each pitch level so that register and range are the only variables in sound. As the student becomes familiar with the phrase, suggest that he or she independently perform it with "real" rather than "tonal" sequences (chromatically altered to maintain intervallic structure of the pattern) and in a reversal of the initial pitch order. The challenge may continue to the student's rearranging of pitches. The teacher may wish to demonstrate the appropriate performance technique although the student's attempts at modifying the pattern will encourage his or her critical analysis and creative thinking. These phrases may eventually be presented in notated form as a reminder for the student as he or she seeks to replicate the exercises in practice.

The phrases can be expanded to include additional pitches, and pitches that utilize various rhythms and articulations. The student may recognize that such an activity is not only related to aural and technical facility but also that the phrases are fundamental ideas that have been developed through repetition, variation, and sequence to form a larger musical work. With the teacher's guidance, the student may discover them in the study of compositions and in the improvisatory music he or she may wish to create.

FOCUS 4: Playing by Ear (aural skills, memory, improvisation)

In order to foster the instrumental student's aural training and increase his or her capacity to recall music heard at an earlier time, the teacher may ask the student to improvise using a folk song or musical work. Once a certain technical competence has been attained and the student is familiar with the instrument, the potential for fingering the correct melody is increased. If efforts have been expended to strengthen the ear through sequential phrase and pattern exercises, the student may approach this experience with greater confidence and ability for translating known music to an instrument. The gains are a more intimate understanding of the requested song and the instrument of performance and a recognition of ways in which music is structured melodically and rhythmically.

Beginning with folk and popular songs such as "Skip to My Lou," "Row Your Boat," "Yankee Doodle," "This Land Is Your Land," and "For He's a Jolly Good Fellow," students can explore and experiment with the appropriate pitches and rhythms belonging to the song. The music selected may be at first melodically limited, but as the student progresses, it can include chromatic and modulating melodies of several octaves. For advanced students, to recall themes from symphonic and chamber works as well as portions of well-known solo pieces would be musically challenging. Should the student know the requested work from earlier applied study, the task would be one of memory only; familiar pieces not previously studied would require aural and memory skills and a creative logic for turning an internally heard melody into sound.

While playing by ear may not be a weekly occurrence in the studio lesson, the teacher may recommend consistent independent practice of the activity. The student can select from folk and popular songs, hymns, patriotic songs, and concert arias, concerto themes, and sonata melodies. A modified version of the experience is available for singers who can be charged with singing a familiar melody by the teacher, including an instrumental theme on a neutral "ah," with correct vocal techniques—breath control, articulation, and expression. Such a strategy will serve the memory well and will also focus on the quality of the musical product.

FOCUS 5: Repeat Performance (aural skills, memory)

The development of vocal and instrumental facility is the result of continuous effort. Every correct bow stroke, proper embouchure, solid sustained tone, and clean scale passage has been preceded by countless repetitions in order for the student to achieve and retain the necessary complement of aural and physical skills. Repetition of a motif, a phrase, a section, or a complete work should occur in the lesson. The student achieves the correct sound through a shaping process in which he or she progresses toward the ideal sound step by step through the teacher's direction and encouragement. The teacher's demonstration and the student's imitation are constant and recurring behaviors to be thoughtfully executed, so that through successive approximation the student approaches the performance of the well-trained teacher. With each endeavor, the student is given verbal and nonverbal feedback to reach beyond the previous level.

Repetition is even more vital to the student's independent practice sessions. It may take hundreds of attempts to match the professional musician's delivery and to master the rhythmic and melodic precision of a single pattern, but the persevering student will focus his or her mental and sensory abilities on such tasks. Like the athlete, the musician may require extensive repetition of motor activities to achieve a specific performance gesture, whether it be a golfer's swing or a pianist's trill. The more frequent the attempts, the more precise is the movement—but only if the student is concentrating and refining the motion; inattentive repetition can have a negative impact. When the musician uses his or her aural abilities and mental concentration to monitor and assess the outcome of each repeated effort, the result is an improvement in performance technique and in the relationship between the physical, intellectual, aural, and visual components that contribute to the performer's musical potential.

Students can avoid monotony in the use of repetition by carefully focusing on the body parts that produce the sound and by listening, watching, and feeling the sound that seems right. While the musical ideas likely emanate from an assigned piece, students can shift their eyes from the notation to their own bodies. They can also close their eyes and feel the motion of the gesture, or listen pointedly to the musical flow. Thoughtful repetition leads to skill acquisition, and eventually to memorization. The consistent attempts to perfect a sound are thought to deepen the memory "traces," the myriad neural connections necessary to recall and almost involuntarily produce the same motor response in the music-making process. Muscular memory through repetition is indispensable for performance, and when joined to aural and intellectual awareness, it leads the way to solid musicianship.

FOCUS 6: Outline for Practice (aural skills, memory, improvisation)

When left to their own devices, students may find their way over time to a systematic practice procedure. Typically, they review warm-up exercises and perform the pieces assigned to them. The matter of aural training, the development of memory skills, and the cultivation of creative interpretation and improvisation are not usually considered by students as important goals in their daily sessions. Even when such experiences are introduced in the lesson, students may not understand their relevance to development as musicians nor know how to pursue them independently. Practice periods may lack structure, may emphasize less significant facets of the lesson, and may proceed haphazardly and without purpose. The teacher can direct students in making the most efficient use of their time, whether it be a thirty-minute period for an eight-year-old beginner or four hours for the serious student.

Practice time should be a period of intense concentration in an area removed from distraction, including television, stereo, people, and even the sounds of other musicians, when possible. A mirror is helpful in observing position and for singers, facial expression. Sufficient lighting prevents eye strain and allows longer periods of practice, whether the student is reading music or not. The student's attitude should be one of complete concentration of the ears, the eyes, and the body in working out the intricacies of the music rather than just playing through it. Occurrence of the latter signals that practice should cease or that a break is due. Some master musicians follow the union rule of public performance: forty minutes of performing and twenty minutes of rest.

Daily emphasis should be given to scales and arpeggios, to be performed in different rhythms for the development and maintenance of flexibility (figure 13–2). Students should work for an evenness of sound and for speed and facility while playing pitches in quarter-note rhythms, in eighths, in triplets, and in sixteenths. The shifting of accents might introduce greater interest and challenge to what can

FIGURE 13–2 Scales and arpeggios in different rhythms.

otherwise become mechanical, routine, and capable of tuning out the performer's conscious attention. A related exercise is the performance of scales and arpeggios in specific prearranged (rather than spontaneously invented) rhythms. (Time: 10 minutes per hour.)

Prescribed patterns and phrases introduced aurally in the lesson should be practiced consistently, including those that may generate directly from musical compositions under study (figure 13–3). The experience of rearranging and developing these musical units into full-fledged compositions would test the mastery of the phrases, and offer an opportunity to develop the student's creative and expressive abilities. (Time: 10 minutes per hour.)

The two or three assigned works should form the principal part of the practice time, with adequate emphasis on excerpts that are technically or musically problematic. The scales, arpeggios, and phrase exercises should prepare students for concentrated and complete performances of works. For a new piece, some of this time must be relegated to reading the notes, while for others, the time is spent in performing at tempo, emphasizing articulation and expressive devices. If the student pays scrupulous attention to the sound, the score, and the correct physical feeling, the practice session leads also to memorization of the piece. If the student has taped the lesson, he or she may wish to repeat portions that deal with the pieces, listening to his teacher, imitating, correcting, and repeating phrases. (Time: 35 minutes per hour.)

If the teacher recommends it, the student may occasionally attempt to play a familiar (but not necessarily assigned) musical work by ear. He or she may wish to challenge his or her listening ability at times by attempting an aural transcription and performance of a particular work, or portion of it: a fugue's theme, first and second themes of a sonata, a cadenza, a jazz solo, an aria. The outcome of these experiences, especially with frequent endeavors weekly, will be

FIGURE 13–3 Extracted phrases for musical development and improvisation.

a sharpening of the student's aural and memory capacities. (Time: 5 minutes per hour; or 15 minutes every three days.)

The time allotments are only recommendations, and should not be viewed as rigid and inflexible. Depending upon the needs of the student, the time may shift in several directions. Nonetheless, the incorporation of aural learning experiences by students within their practice sessions will enhance their maturation as musicians. Mindless warm-up exercises and the playing or singing through of assigned pieces without concentration can only result in musical mediocrity. The purpose of practice must be clearly in mind so that the students' understanding will increase their motivation. There are those exercises that develop basic execution skills, intonation, style, phrasing, the maintenance of pulse, tone quality, articulation, and expression. The teacher's task is to recommend and justify the inclusion of these experiences in a structure for practice that will allow students to reach their fullest potential as performers.

FOCUS 7: Silent but Certain Music (aural skills, memory)

Sometimes, the most intensive performance can occur with no sound at all. The manipulation of keys, vales, and bows and the natural emphasis given to the kinesthetic behaviors while performing can distract the student's attention from the essence of the music itself—its sound and its structure. Inner hearing is an important attribute of the performer, who should be able to read the score and silently "hear" the music without actually performing. Imagining the music silently without the score is equally helpful as an aid to memory and to a thorough integration of the music within the performer.

In the lesson, the teacher may initiate an inner hearing experience by asking the student to respond to cues for sounded and silent music. The student begins to perform and at the snap of the teacher's fingers, for example, continues silently "singing" and imagining the music. On cue, the student again performs aloud in a later section. It may be necessary for the student to follow the score in order to keep his or her place, in particular for a new piece, but the greater challenge comes when the student is dependent upon his or her memory. The student may imagine the kinesthetic behaviors of performance as well; at least, there may be an invisible proprioceptive response that occurs. More important, the silent singing and imagining is a test of listening skill and the internalization of the music.

FOCUS 8: Singing for Instrumentalists (aural skills, memory)

There is a logic behind the common practice of singing before performance on an instrument. Vocalization necessitates the use of the most personal and readily accessible instrument, the voice.

Whether the melodies are lyrical and legato or detached, fragmented, and staccato, the voice is a useful tool for carrying the music inside the musician.

Singing specific phrases that have been extracted from the larger piece is a standard rehearsal procedure. The teacher may apply solfége or neutral syllables in singing a melody, which the student then echoes. As an alternative, the spontaneous use of syllables that capture the inflections of a pitch or set of pitches—including register, accent, dynamics, and rhythm—may be especially helpful in characterizing the music. The jazz style of scat singing is an example of this process, although such improvisation encompasses the devising not only of syllables but also of pitches and rhythms (figure 13–4). The chanting of rhythms through a standard, personal, or improvised set of mnemonics is likewise an effective means of vocalization that aids both learning and retention.

The student who sings a phrase from Mendelssohn or Mozart, Bach or Beethoven, Haydn or Hindemith is better prepared to substitute fingers for vocal cords. If the voice succeeds in sounding the music, the transfer of the phrase to an instrument is likely to be smoothly executed and the performance will be a musical rendering that is intimately understood by the musician. For some instrumentalists, including those on piano, strings, and percussion, singing may also be useful during practice to accompany playing. The voice may be the guide to phrasing and interpretation, which is eventually faded as its singing quality is internalized.

FOCUS 9: Mapping for Memory (aural skills, memory, improvisation)

The performance of music by memory is a standard procedure for solo recitals and concerts of Western art music. Moreover, memorization usually demonstrates a complete commitment and involve-

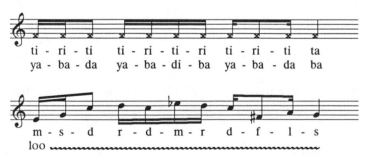

FIGURE 13–4   Melodic and rhythmic phrases using solfége, neutral, scat, and mnemonic syllables.

ment in the music. The integration of listening with reading, analysis, and inventiveness may result in memorization that is neither tedious nor painful. Fear of forgetting, a major concern and cause of performance anxiety, may be somewhat alleviated through the playful character of a mapping experience (figures 13–5 and 13–6).

The use of mapping as an aid to memorizing a musical work proceeds through the following steps: (1) Allot three minutes to look at the score. Sing, tap, clap, chant, and imagine performing while reading. Identify the mode and key, meter, texture, any recurring patterns, and the formal structure of the work. Some of this information will be immediately evident from prior study. (2) Attempt to perform the work without looking at the score, heeding information gathered through step 1. Improvise all that is not recalled, including thematic development, chordal accompaniment, embellishments, and transitions between themes and sections. (3) Return to the score for another three-minute observation. Diagram salient features on a musical map. Invent symbols to represent melodic direction, repetition, variation, and sequence. Illustrate the formal structure, or texture, or text. (4) Perform the work, using the map as a guide and a memory cue. Improvise within the character of the piece when uncertain. Repeat steps 3 and 4 as necessary, each time adding greater detail to the musical map in order to cue the memory.

A careful scrutiny of the score for its organizational components offers an opportunity for exercising analytical skills, which are tested in the student's mapping of the music. Like a sentence that is diagrammed, the elements and their relationships are ordered and notated in map form. Encouraging students to use improvised passages may not only foster in them an awareness of musical style, but may also help them develop confidence that improvisation can be useful

FIGURE 13–5 Mapping Bartok: *Mikrokosmos* VI, "March."

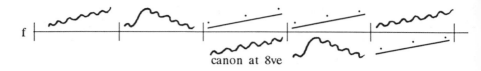

FIGURE 13–6 Mapping Bach: "Two-Part Invention," D Minor.

when they forget where they are in a piece during performance. When the inevitable memory lapse occurs, students who can improvise can maintain the continuity and character of the piece until they work their way back to a familiar point in the music.

A modification of the mapping procedure is related to aural transcription in which the music is deciphered and diagrammed without the use of a score. The key to learning is thus listening rather than reading. Such an approach to learning and remembering is applied to music not previously performed or even heard by the student; the experience is one of aural learning, memorization, and improvisation.

FOCUS 10: A Little Suzuki (aural skills, memory)

In the Suzuki method, students can perform and build a repertoire of music for performance quite naturally through the rote process, using the techniques of demonstration and imitation. Students are often introduced to notation after a period of one to two years of performing by ear when they are presented with the notation of music already learned. As students perform the familiar movements for making music and as they listen to the familiar sounds, their eyes for the first time meet the notated music and follow the symbols across the staff. This transfer from rote to note has met with much success, mainly because of the student's acquired knowledge of the ideal tonal quality and appropriate performance techniques for the execution of certain recurring musical patterns and phrases.

Such a strategy can lay the foundation for literacy on any instrument, leading from individual phrases to complete musical works. The experience need not be relegated to beginners nor solely to proponents of the Suzuki approach. The teacher may wish to provide aural encounters with complete musical works. The pieces should be reasonably brief, however; an arietta, a bouree from a suite, or a bagatelle, for example, would work well. Once the piece is aurally learned through the student's imitation of the teacher, the notation can be presented. For the more advanced student musicians who generally learn their literature by deciphering staff notation, the aural experience can be an engaging breath of fresh air.

FOCUS 11: Toward a Creative Performance (aural skills, memory, improvisation)

Improvisation is the test of a thorough musical understanding and an assurance that the student has internalized the musical patterns and phrases of a style. Whether the instrument and genre is jazz saxophone or Baroque harpsichord or nineteenth-century piano, practice in the use of musical formulas in new and unique ways is a strategy that trains the ear and the capacity for memory. Further, improvisation allows for means of personal artistic expression that may enhance the interpretation of notated music as well—in those styles that allow the performer to take some liberties in rhythm and tempo, dynamics, and accents and articulation.

In the studio lesson, the teacher may present a motif aurally. A rhythmic idea can be chanted, a melodic idea can be sung. The student listens, sings, or chants, the instrumentalist eventually transferring the motif to the instrument. The teacher directs the student in an exploration of pitches for the rhythmic motif or pitch levels for the melodic motif, perhaps performing along with the student or exchanging potential variations. The initial motif can be rhythmically expanded or reduced, melodically embellished, and treated sequentially. The student can be encouraged to create a second theme to contrast with the character of the first. By extending the musical ideas to several phrases, a structure such as binary or ternary form can be organized: The student may wish to work out other creative pieces through a similar procedure during independent practice.

The relationship between an improvised work and an expressive performance should be clarified so that the student realizes that despite the preservation of works on paper, the responsibility for a moving and artistic music performance rests with the performer. For works that have been recorded, it will be helpful for the teacher and student to follow the score while listening, noting the occasions of the performer's unwritten expressive elements. When no recording is available, the teacher can perform pieces while the student follows the notation. Analysis and discussion should lead the student to making the connection between his own freely created music and the essence of a musical work that must derive from the performer's creativity within the framework of style.

FOCUS 12: A New Style for a Known Work (memory, improvisation)

A musician needs to build an awareness of components that define musical style so that despite the use of similar symbols to notate sound, he or she will perform Mozart quite differently from Brahms, and Bartok in a way that is far removed from Bach. Stylistic knowledge results from careful listening and well-tutored performance experiences. Improvisation may offer a challenging means of demonstrating style components in a performance setting and will require considerable reliance on the listening and kinesthetic memory for specific details regarding articulation, melodic embellishment (or lack of it), rhythmic peculiarities (from hocket to syncopation to even and fluid passages), texture (monophonic, homophonic, polyphonic counterpoint, and heterophonic). All the components come into focus in defining the style of a composer, genre, or historical period. The musician who recognizes great and subtle differences and can apply them in improvisation exercises will also define those differences in future performances of composed works.

Guide students in finding a new style for a piece they have studied and performed. If they have performed a Bach invention, suggest that they attempt a Brahmsian interpretation of it. This may entail the improvisation of occasionally dense chords, the use of the hemiola technique of rhythmic alternation of duple and triple rhythm, and thus, the less constant use of quick contrapuntal passages. If the student has sung a Samuel Barber art song, recommend that he or she perform it in the style of an aria from Mozart's *The Magic Flute*, complete with trills, ornamentations, and *da capo* form. If the student has performed a Haydn sonata, ask him or her to play it like a Hindemith composition, using sequential and simultaneous intervals of a fourth while also thinning the texture.

The exercise in shifting from one style to another demands considerable musical experience. It can produce in the student a more intensive knowledge of musical style, challenging the memory and sharpening the ability to make spontaneous decisions. Furthermore, the ear is called upon to hear the style silently in advance of the performance and to monitor the sounds that are intended to define a new style.

EPILOGUE

Two themes have run through this book, both linked as vital components in the education and training of young musicians: aural skills and creative musical expression. Widely accepted as fundamental attributes of thorough musicianship, both are frequently overlooked in practice. The basic premise of aesthetic education—that formal instruction in music should provide a deeper understanding of music's artistic worth—implies the interdependence of cognition, performance, listening, and creativity in the process of teaching and learning. It follows, then, that the absence of any of these components means that a thorough aesthetic education has probably not occurred. The development of deep and personal responses to music requires the knowledge and skills that are the principal themes of this book.

"Music is an aural phenomenon, as it is also one of the creative arts." This assumption, and the notion that essential skills evolve naturally—and somehow unconsciously—through experience and instruction is a common one. A review of the contemporary curriculum, teaching materials, and the teaching-learning sequence, however, reveals an emphasis on the development of music literacy and performance skills. Ear-training and the creative process of improvisation and score interpretation are often relegated to the periphery of instruction rather than playing central roles in the making of "compleat" young musicians.

In studios, classrooms, and rehearsal halls, a comprehensive approach to the musical development of students should integrate the sensory modes and open avenues for seeing and listening, thinking and feeling, responding and expressing, and receiving. A keen listening ear complements music literacy, enhances performance ability, and stimulates improvisation and the interpretation of composed music. Just as the eye is trained to read printed notation, the ear requires a plan for monitoring what has sounded. A program for the development of comprehensive musicianship cannot separate literacy from ear-training, nor the development of performance skills

305

from the realization of the student's creative potential. Visual, aural, and kinesthetic elements should work in tandem to shape musicians who can perform musically, listen intelligently, and respond feelingly.

A study of the contemporary music teaching and learning process must encompass both historical and cultural contexts. Music is a human phenomenon, and to our knowledge, no culture has existed without it. By reviewing the the preparation of musicians in earlier historical periods and in a sampling of world cultures, broader perspectives of music transmission and education emerge. By noting the appearance of aural skills and creativity through time and across geographical boundaries, their significance as integral components of the instructional process is reinforced. Like the presence of music itself, there are music teaching and learning behaviors that appear common to many eras and peoples.

From Guido to Kodály, and from Japanese traditional music to the jazz world, rote and note processes of music learning are practiced. A few traditions espouse one perspective exclusively, as in the case of Indian classical musicians, but many offer a combination of notation and observation strategies. Traditional approaches vary from a balance of reading, watching, and listening (as in the case of the training of a Western violinist, for example), to the combination of rote teaching during the lesson and independent note learning during independent practice that follows, a prevalent procedure among some traditional teachers of Chinese qin or Japanese shamisen.

Throughout the world, there are benefits as well as limitations resulting from exclusive use of an oral or a written tradition. For performers of music in the oral tradition, the ear attends remarkably well to music as it is performed. Even in initial hearings of a musical work or song, the musician's keen listening ability can extract a general framework and specific phrases. With additional exposure, the piece is put together through the remarkable talent of a fine-tuned ear. Over time, however, the memory weakens and either creativity or degeneration of the music occurs, depending upon the cultural attitude toward change. Some music may lose its original character, or lose its essence altogether. Without the ability to read the notated music that exists in many traditions, those who "play by ear" alone can only hope that their memory will sustain them and maintain the music they have acquired.

Musicians trained in the tradition of reading notated music possess the capacity to re-create the history of music. As they read from the scores of composers before them, literate performers can recall the musical ingenuity of the masters. Their careful eye and translative skills enable them to read through manuscripts with great speed and efficiency. Without conscious attention to developing the aural sense, however, such musicians run the risk of performing in a detached and impersonal way. They may pursue their art from a linear perspective without injecting it with the refreshing and creative spirit that comes from knowing the aural essence of the music.

The development of notation was a major achievement in the history of Western art music (and in the art music traditions of many of the world's cultures), one that not only preserved music for posterity but also influenced the transmission of music for all time. Solmization practices were invented in European schools and conservatories to lead students to the logic of the staff, as well as to link their vocalizations to the development of aural skills. Still, long after staff notation was permanently in place, improvisation and expressive interpretation of the score continued to be marks of well-trained musicians. A knowledge of ornamentation and stylistic nuances was facilitated by musician-teachers who could demonstrate that which was not notated, and thus transmit to their students the unwritten essence of music so critical to a style.

An examination of musical training in a number of traditional societies supports the premise that aural and creative skills are among the fundamental traits of competent musicians. While Western influence has been considerable in the development of music instruction in these societies, many traditional practices survive. The teacher is a model of appropriate musical behavior, to be watched and listened to. In formal lessons and informal apprenticeships, in literate cultures and in those with no written notation, demonstration and imitation are important practices. Depending upon the genre and the tradition, the student's replication of what he or she hears may vary from absolute precision to free interpretation. Mnemonics are frequently employed to facilitate the learning of instrumental passages, just as the use of vocalization is a prominent strategy that often precedes instrumental performance.

Clearly, some of the world's musical traditions can only be fully realized through the creative process of improvisation. Potential material to be employed spontaneously in performance includes melodic and rhythmic phrases that are generally introduced through exercises and refined in practice. These phrases are set in the ear and in the hand, resulting in repertoires that are both aural and kinesthetic. While the spontaneity in selection of these phrases may vary from one tradition to the next, even a partially notated tradition such as jazz allows ample opportunity for the performer to personalize the music.

The interdisciplinary approach of this volume was taken to illustrate the cross-cultural similarities in music teaching and learning. Despite what may have appeared at times to be rather disparate topics, there are points of convergence. The development of the listening ear and the creative musical mind are critical goals in the contemporary curriculum, as they are central to the performance of Western art music, and to many of the world's art, folk, and popular genres. The assorted *Focus* experiences were designed to illustrate the ways in which aural and creative skills can be developed in the context of the classroom, the ensemble, and the private lesson. If there was a single message among the *Focus* experiences, it was that teachers have the potential within their daily schedules to develop a comprehensive musicianship in their students, regardless of the educational setting.

Without impeding music literacy, the use of modeling, imitative devices, improvisation, and strategies for strengthening the memory can lead to greater musical sensitivity in student musicians. This book does not advocate immediate short-cuts to music reading through excessive verbatim exercises, nor does it attempt to nurture functional illiterates who cannot realize rhythms or melodies without modeling, and who cannot think musically and creatively for themselves. Instead, the implication throughout these pages was that the key to musicianship must be a balanced diet of aural and literate exercises, with occasional opportunities for creative musical expression.

Lessons from other cultures and historical periods provide insight regarding aural and creative processes of learning and teaching. Music is clearly a shared human phenomenon, an art form to be created and listened to, and it appears to be the nature of musicians in every age and place to listen, think, and perform in musically creative ways. The realities of contemporary American society and the classroom culture require the judicious incorporation of such approaches as well as periodic evaluation to assure that students are gaining in their musical development. As we are first attracted to music for the pleasure of its sound essence, and held captive by the opportunity to express ourselves creatively through music, we cannot deny the importance of those experiences in the training we provide.

BIBLIOGRAPHY

Abdoo, Frank B. "Music Education in Japan." *Music Educators Journal* 70 (1984): 52–56.

Aebersold, Jamey. *A New Approach to Jazz Improvisation.* New Albany, Ind.: Jamey Aebersold, 1979.

Aldrich, Putnam. "Bach Techniques of Transcription and Improvised Ornamentation." *Musical Quarterly* 35 (1949): 26–35.

Alley, Rewi. *Peking Opera.* Beijing: New World Press, 1984.

Andre, Thomas, and Phye, Gary D. "Cognition, Learning, and Education." In Phye and Andre, *Cognitive Classroom Learning: Understanding, Thinking, and Problem Solving.* Orlando, Florida: Academic Press, 1986, 1–20.

Armstrong, Louis. *Satchmo: My Life in New Orleans.* Englewood Cliffs, N.J.: Prentice-Hall, 1954.

Atterbury, Betty W. "A Comparison of Rhythm Pattern Perception and Performance in Normal and Learning-Disabled Readers, Age Seven and Eight." *Journal of Research in Music Education* 31 (1983): 259–270.

Ausubel, David P. *Educational Psychology.* New York: Holt, Rinehart and Winston, 1968.

Badura-Skoda, Eva and Paul. *Interpreting Mozart on the Keyboard.* New York: St. Martin's Press, 1962.

Baker, David N. *Jazz Improvisation.* Chicago: Maher Publications, 1969.

———. *Advanced Improvisation.* Vol. 3, *Rhythmic and Harmonic Concepts.* Chicago: Maher Publications, 1974.

———. *Jazz Pedagogy.* Chicago: Maher Publications, 1979.

Bandura, Albert. "Modeling Theory: Some Traditions, Trends and Disputes." In *Recent Trends in Social Learning,* edited by R. D. Parke. London: Academic Press, 1972.

———. *Social Learning Theory.* Englewood Cliffs, N.J.: Prentice-Hall, 1977.

Barbe, Walter B., and Raymond H. Swassing. *Teaching through Modality Strengths: Concepts and Practices.* Columbus, Ohio: Zaner-Bloser, 1979.

Bartok, Bela. *Hungarian Folk Music.* London, Oxford University Press, 1931.

Bateson, Gregory. *Steps to An Ecology of Mind.* New York: Ballantine Books, 1972.

Becker, Judith. *Traditional Music in Modern Java.* Honolulu: University Press of Hawaii, 1980.

Bennett, Frank. "The Mridangam of South India." *Percussive Notes* 19 (1981): 24–29.

Berendt, Joachim E. *The Jazz Book.* Westport, Conn.: Lawrence Hill, 1981.

Berger, Donald P. "Isawa Shuji and Luther Whiting Mason: Pioneers of Music Education in Japan." *Music Educators Journal* 74 (1987): 31–36.

Bird, Charles. "Poetry in the Mande: Its Form and Meaning." *Poetics* 5 (1976): 85–97.

Birge, Edward Bailey. *History of Public School Music in the United States.* 1939. Reprint. Washington, D.C.: Music Educators National Conference, 1985.

Blacking, John. *Venda Children's Songs.* Johannesburg: Witwatersrand University, 1967.

———. *How Musical Is Man?* Seattle: University of Washington, 1973.

———. *Man and Fellow Man.* Belfast: Queens University, 1974.

———. "Can Musical Universals be Heard?" *The World of Music* 19 (1977): 14–22.

———. "Versus Gradus Novos ad Parnassam Musicum: Exemplum Africanum." In *Becoming Human Through Music,* edited by David P. McAllester. Reston, Va.: Music Educators National Conference, 1985.

Blum, Stephen. "Musics in Contact, the Cultivation of Oral Repertories in Meshed, Iran." Doctoral diss., University of Illinois, Urbana-Champaign, 1972.

———. "Changing Roles of Performances in Meshed and Bojnurd, Iran." In *Eight Urban Musical Cultures,* edited by Bruno Nettl, 19–95. Urbana: University of Illinois Press, 1978.

Bohlman, Philip V. *The Study of Folk Music in the Modern World.* Bloomington: Indiana University Press, 1988.

Booth, Gregory D. "The Teaching of North Indian Music: Three Case Studies." *Contributions to Music Education* 10 (1983): 1–8.

———. "The North Indian Oral Tradition: Lessons for Music Education." *International Journal of Music Education* 9 (1987): 7–10.

Bourne, Lyle E., Jr., R. L. Dominowski, and E. F. Loftus. *Cognitive Processes.* Englewood Cliffs, N.J.: Prentice-Hall, 1979.

Bower, Calvin M. "Boethius's 'The Principles of Music': An Introduction, Translation, and Commentary." Doctoral diss., Vanderbilt University, 1967.

Bower, Gordon H. "Analysis of a Mnemonic Device." In *Readings in Cognitive Psychology,* edited by M. Colhard. Minneapolis: Winston Press, 1972.

Bower, Gordon H., and Ernest Hilgard. *Theories of Learning.* 5th ed. Englewood Cliffs, N.J.: Prentice-Hall, 1981.

Boyd, William. *The History of Western Education.* London: Adam and Charles Black, 1952.

Brand, Manny. "Relationship between Home Musical Environment and Selected Musical Attributes of Second-Grade Children." *Journal of Research in Music Education* 34 (1986): 111–120.

Bridges, Doreen. "Fixed and Movable Doh in Historical Perspective." *Australian Journal of Music Education* 30 (1982): 2–9.

Britton, Allen P. "Music in Early American Public Education: A Historical Critique." In *Basic Concepts in Music Education.* Fifty-Seventh Year-

book of the National Society for the Study of Education. Chicago: University of Chicago Press, 1958.

Bronfenbrenner, Urie. *The Ecology of Human Development.* Cambridge, Mass.: Harvard University Press, 1979.

Bronson, Bertrand H. *The Ballad as Song.* Berkeley: University of California Press, 1967.

———. *The Singing Tradition of Child's Popular Ballads.* Princeton, N.J.: Princeton University Press, 1976.

Bruner, Jerome S. *The Process of Education.* New York: Vintage, 1960.

———. *Toward a Theory of Instruction.* Cambridge, Mass.: Harvard University Press, 1966.

Buckton, Roger. *Sing a Song of Six-Year-Olds.* Wellington: New Zealand Council for Educational Research, 1983.

Campbell, Patricia Shehan "Rhythmic Movement and Public School Education: Progressive Views in the Formative Years." *Journal of Research in Music Education* 39 (1991).

Carmack, M., and K. Skagen. *Voices from India.* New York: Praeger Press, 1972.

Carpenter, Nan Cook. *Music in the Medieval and Renaissance Universities.* Norman: University of Oklahoma Press, 1958.

Chianis, Sam. "Aspects of Melodic Ornamentation in the Folk Music of Central Greece." *Selected Reports in Ethnomusicology* 1 (1966): 89–119.

Choate, Robert A. *Documentary Report of the Tanglewood Symposium.* Washington, D.C.: Music Educators National Conference, 1968.

Choksy, Lois. *The Kodály Method.* 2nd ed. Englewood Cliffs, N.J.: Prentice-Hall, 1988.

Cobb, Buell. *The Sacred Harp: A Tradition and Its Music.* Athens: University of Georgia Press, 1978.

Coker, Jerry. *Improvising Jazz.* Englewood Cliffs, N.J.: Prentice-Hall, 1964.

Colley, Bernadette. A Comparison of Syllabic Methods for Improving Rhythm Literacy. *Journal of Research in Music Education* 35 (1988): 221–236.

Cope, David H. *New Directions in Music.* Dubuque, Iowa: William C. Brown, 1976.

Cudjoe, S. D. "The Technique of Ewe Drumming and the Social Importance of Music in Africa." *Phylon* 14 (1953): 280–294.

Curwen, John. *The Standard Course in the Tonic Sol-fa Method of Teaching Music.* London: Curwen and Son, 1901.

Cutter, Paul. "Politics of Music in Mali." *African Arts* 1 (1968): 81–95.

Daniels, Rose Dwiggins. "Relationships among Selected Factors and the Sight-Reading Ability of High School Mixed Choirs." *Journal of Research in Music Education* 34 (1986): 279–289.

Davidson, Lyle, P. McKernon, and Howard Gardner. "The Acquisition of Song: A Development Approach." In *Documentary Report of the Ann Arbor Symposium on the Applications of Psychology to the Teaching and Learning of Music.* Reston, Va.: Music Educator's National Conference, 1981.

Degh, Linda. *Folktales and Society: Story-Telling in a Hungarian Peasant Community.* Bloomington: Indiana University Press, 1969.

Dickel, Michael J. "Principles of Encoding Mnemonics." *Perceptual and Motor Skills* 57 (1983): 111–118.

Donnington, Robert. *The Interpretation of Early Music.* New York: St. Martin's Press, 1974.

Dowling, W. Jay. "Melodic Information Processing and Its Development." In Deutsch, D., *The Psychology of Music.* New York: Academic Press, 1982, 413–430.

———. "Development of Musical Schemata in Children's Spontaneous Singing." In *Cognitive Processes in the Perception of Art*, edited by W. R. Crozier and A. J. Chapman. New York, Elsevier Science Publishing Co., 1984.

Dowling, W. Jay, and Dane L. Harwood. *Music Cognition.* Orlando: Academic Press, 1986.

Dunbar, Ted. *A System of Tonal Convergence for Improvisors, Composers, and Arrangers.* Kendall Park, N.J.: Dunte, 1976.

Duriyanga, Phra Chen. *Thai Music.* Bangkok: Fine Arts Department, Thai Culture, 1973.

———. "Siamese Music in Theory and Practice." *Asian Music* 8 (1982): 55–90.

Eaklor, Vicki L. "Roots of an Ambivalent Culture: Music, Education, and Music Education in Antebellum America." *Journal of Research in Music Education* 33 1985: 86–99.

Efland, Arthur. "Art and Music in the Pestalozzian Tradition." *Journal of Research in Music Education* 31 (1983): 165–178.

Ellingson, Ter. "Buddhist Musical Notations." In *The Oral and the Literate in Music*, edited by Tokumaru Yosihiko and Yamaguti Osamu. Tokyo: Academia Music, 1986.

Elliott, Charles. Effect of Vocalization on the Sense of Pitch of Beginning Band Class Students." *Journal of Research in Music Education* 22 (1974): 120–128.

Ellis, Catherine J. *The Musician, the University and the Community: Conflict or Concord?* Armidale, New South Wales, Australia: University of New England, 1986.

Ellis, Howard E. "The Influence of Pestalozzianism on Instruction in Music." Doctoral diss., University of Michigan, 1957.

El-Shawan, Salwa. "The Role of Mediators in the Transmission of al-Musika al-Arabiyyah in Twentieth-Century Cairo." *Yearbook for Traditional Music* 14 (1982): 55–74.

Ernst, Roy E. *Development of Competence in Teaching Instrumental Music.* Fairport, N.Y.: N.P., 1978.

Ferand, Ernest T. "What is 'Res Facta'?" *Journal of the American Musicological Society* 10 (1957): 141–150.

———. "Didactic Embellishment Literature in the Late Renaissance: A Survey of Sources." In *Aspects of Medieval and Renaissance Music: A Birthday Offering to Gustave Reese*, edited by Jan La Rue. New York: W. W. Norton, 1966.

Flohr, John W., and Jacqueline Brown. "The Influence of Peer Imitation on Expressive Movement to Music. *Journal of Research in Music Education* 27 (1979): 143–148.

Fowler, Charles B. *Arts in Education/Education in Arts*. Washington, D.C.: National Endowment for the Arts, 1984.

———. "What We Know about the Teaching and Learning of Performance." *Music Educators Journal* 73 (1987): 24–32.

———. *The Crane Symposium: Toward an Understanding of the Teaching and Learning of Music Performance*. Potsdam, N.Y.: Potsdam College of the State University of New York, 1988.

Fraser, Wilmot A. "Jazzology: A Study of the Tradition in Which Jazz Musicians Learn to Improvise." Doctoral diss., University of Pennsylvania, 1983.

Froseth, James. *The Individualized Instructor*. Chicago: G. I. A. Publications, 1970.

Gagné, Robert M. *Conditions of Learning*. 3rd ed. New York: Holt, Rinehart, and Winston, 1977.

Gardner, Howard. *To Open Minds*. Basic Books, Inc., Publishers, 1989.

Garfias, Robert. "Music: Thinking Globally, Acting Locally." In *Becoming Human through Music*, edited by David P. McAllester. Reston, Va.: Music Educators National Conference, 1985.

Gaston, E. Thayer. "Man and Music." In *Music in Therapy*, edited by Thayer Gaston. New York: Macmillan, 1968.

Gates, J. Terry. "A Comparison of the Tune Books of Tufts and Walter." *Journal of Research in Music Education* 36 (1988): 169–193

Gillespie, Dizzy, and Al Fraser. *To Be or Not to Bop*. Garden City: Doubleday, 1979.

Glover, Sarah. *Scheme for Rendering Psalmody Congregational*. 1835. Reprinted with *The Sol-fa Tune Book* [1839]. Clarabricken, Republic of Ireland: Boethius Press, 1982.

Gordon, Edwin E. *Learning Sequences in Music*. Chicago: G. I. A. Publications, 1984.

Gordon, Lewis. *Choral Director's Complete Handbook*. West Nyack, N.Y.: Parker Publishing Co., 1977.

Greenfield, Patricia, and Jean Lave. "Cognitive Aspects of Informal Education." In *Cultural Perspectives on Child Development*, edited by Daniel Wegner and Harold W. Stevenson. San Francisco: W. F. Freeman, 1982.

Greenhoe, Mary Louise. "Parameters of Creativity in Music Education: An Exploratory Study." Doctoral diss., University of Tennessee, 1972.

Grunow, Richard, and Edwin Gordon. *Jump Right In: The Instrumental Series*. Chicago: G. I. A. Publications, 1987.

Grutzmacher, Patricia A. "The Effect of Tonal Pattern Training on the Aural Perception, Reading Recognition, and Melodic Sight-Reading Achievement of First-Year Music Students." Journal of Research in Music Education 35 (1987): 171–181.

Guilford, J. P. "Traits of Creativity." In *Creativity and Its Cultivation*, edited by H. H. Anderson. New York: Harper & Row, 1959.

———. "Creativity: Yesterday, Today and Tomorrow." *Journal of Creative Behavior* 1 (1967): 3–14.

Guilford, J. P., and Ralph Hoepener. *The Analysis of Intelligence*. New York: McGraw-Hill, 1971.

Hamilton, Edith, and Huntington Cairns, eds. *The Collected Dialogues of Plato.* New York: Pantheon Books, 1961.

Handy, Antoinette. "Conversations with Mary Lou Williams, First Lady of the Jazz Keyboard." *The Black Perspective in Music* 8 (1980): 195–203.

Hansen, Polly. "Maurice Sharp: Fifty Years with Cleveland." *Flute Talk* 31 (1986): 8–12.

Hara, Toshiyuki. "Education in Japan." In *Perspectives on World Education,* edited by Carltone E. Beck. Dubuque, Iowa: William C. Brown, 1970.

Hargreaves, David J. *The Developmental Psychology of Music.* Cambridge: Cambridge University Press, 1986.

Harich-Schneider, Eta. *A History of Japanese Music.* London: Oxford University Press, 1973.

Harrell, Lynn. "Coming Home as a Teacher." *The Instrumentalist* 42 (1988): 12–14.

Harris, Tomas J. "An Investigation of the Effectiveness of an Intonation Training Program upon Junior and Senior High School Wind Instrumentalists." Doctoral diss., University of Illinois, 1977.

Heller, George. "Fray Pedro De Gante, Pioneer American Music Educator." *Journal of Research in Music Education* 27 (1979): 21–28.

Hill, Jackson. "Ritual Music in Japanese Esoteric Buddhism: Shiungon Shomyo." *Ethnomusicology* 26 (1982): 27–39.

Hitchcock, H. Wiley. *Music in the United States.* Englewood Cliffs, N.J.: Prentice-Hall, 1974.

Holmes, Charles. "Bringing Jazz to the Middle School." *The Instrumentalist* 42 (1988): 20–23.

Holz, Emil A. and Roger E. Jacobi. *Teaching Band Instruments to Beginners.* Englewood Cliffs, N.J.: Prentice-Hall, 1966.

Hood, Mantle. "Aspects of Group Improvisation in the Javanese Gamelan." In *The Music of Asia,* edited by Jose Maceda, 16–23. Manila: National Music Council of the Philippines, 1966.

———. "Improvisation in the Stratified Ensembles of Southeast Asia." *Selected Reports in Ethnomusicology* 2 (1975): 25–33.

Hopkins, Pandora. "The Lore of the Hardingfele." Doctoral diss., University of Pennsylvania, 1978.

———. *Aural Thinking in Norway.* New York: Human Sciences Press, 1986.

Houtchens, Lawrence H. and Carolyn W., eds. *Leigh Hunt's Dramatic Criticism: 1808–1831.* New York: Columbia University Press, 1969.

Humphreys, Jere T. "The Child-Study Movement and Public School Music Education." *Journal of Research in Music Education* 33 (1985): 79–86.

———. "Strike Up the Band! The Legacy of Patrick S. Gilmore." *Music Educators Journal* 74 (1987): 22–26.

Hussein, Awatef Abdel Kerim. "Music Education in the Arab Republic of Egypt." *International Society of Music Education Yearbook* 13 (1986): 126–235.

Ibsen al-Faruqi, Lois. "Problems of Music Education in the Arab World: New and Old Solutions. *International Journal of Music Education* 8 (1986): 7–11.

Institute of Musicology. *Music Education and Popularization of Music.* Music

Research no. 3. Ho Chi Minh City, South Vietnam: Institute of Musicology, 1979.

Johannesen, Grant. "The Lesson." *Piano Quarterly* 119 (1982): 24–26.

Johnson, Irmgard. "The Role of Amateur Participants in the Arts of Nō in Contemporary Japan." *Asian Music* 13 (1982): 56–68.

Jones, A. M. *Studies in African Music.* London: Oxford University Press, 1959.

Jones, Phillip. "The Prince of Brass." *The Instrumentalist* 41 (1986): 10–16.

Jones, Trevor A. "The Traditional Music of the Australian Aborigines." In Elizabeth May, *Musics of Many Cultures.* Berkeley: University of California Press, 1980.

Jorgensen, Estelle R. "Philosophy and the Music Teacher: Challenging the Way We Think". *Music Educators Journal* 76 (1990): 17–23.

Jules-Rossette, Benetta. "Ecstatic Singing: Music and Social Integration in an African Church." In *More than Drumming: Essays on African and Afro-Latin American Music and Musicians,* edited by Irene V. Jackson, 119–144. Westport, Conn.: Greenwood Press, 1985.

Kalmar, Magda, and Balasko, Gitta. " 'Musical Mother Tongue' and Creativity in Preschool Children's Melodic Improvisations." *Council for Research in Music Education* 91 (1987): 77–86.

Kassler, Jamie C. "Burney's Sketch of a Plan for a Public Music-School." *Musical Quarterly* 63 (1972): 210–234.

Kaufmann, Walter. *Musical Notations of the Orient: Notational Systems of East, South and Central Asia.* Bloomington: Indiana University Press, 1967.

———. *Tibetan Buddhist Chant: Musical Notations and Interpretations of a Song Book by the Bkah Brgyud and Sa Skya Pa Sects.* Bloomington: Indiana University Press, 1975.

Keene, James. *A History of Music Education in the United States.* Hanover, N.H.: University of New England Press, 1982.

Kellas, George, Clark McCauley, and Carl E. McFarland, Jr. "Reexamination of Externalized Rehearsal." *Journal of Experimental Psychology: Human Learning and Memory* 104 (1979): 84–90.

Keller, Marcello Source. "Folk Music in Trentino: Oral Transmission and the Use of Vernacular Languages." *Ethnomusicology* 28 (1984): 75–90.

Kendall, John D. *The Suzuki Violin Method in American Music Education.* Washington, D.C.: Music Educators National Conference, 1984.

Kent, Julia. "Golden Memories." *The Strad* 99 (1988): 478–481.

Keraus, Ruth. "An Achievement Study of Private and Class Suzuki Violin Instruction." Doctoral diss., 1973.

Kingsbury, Henry. *Music, Talent, and Performance.* Philadelphia: Temple University Press, 1988.

Kiyoko, Motegi. "Aural Learning in Gidayu-Bushi: Music of the Japanese Puppet Theatre." *Yearbook for Traditional Music* 16 (1984): 97–108.

Knight, Roderic. "Music in Africa: The Manding Contexts." In *Performance Practice/Ethnomusicological Perspectives,* edited by Gerard Behague, 53–90. Westport, Conn.: Greenwood Press, 1984.

Kodály, Zoltan. *Folk Music of Hungary.* Budapest: Carvina Press, 1971.

Komiya, Toyotaka. *Japanese Music and Drama in the Meiji Era.* Tokyo: Obunsha, 1956.

Koning, Joseph. "The Fieldworker as Performer: Fieldwork Objectives and Social Roles in County Clare, Ireland." *Ethnomusicology* 24 (1980): 417–429.

Konowitz, Bert. *Vocal Improvisation Method.* New York: Alfred Music Co., 1970.

Kratus, John. "A Time Analysis of the Compositional Processes used by Children Ages 7 to 11." *Journal of Research in Music Education* 37 (1989): 5–20.

Kubik, Gerhard. *Malawian Music: A Framework for Analysis.* Malawi: Montfort Press, 1987.

Larkin, Curtis H. "Gilmore and Sousa: As I Remember Them." *The Instrumentalist* 3 (1949): 38–39.

Lartat-Jacob, Bernard. "Community Music and the Rise of Professionalism: A Sardinian Example." *Ethnomusicology* 25 (1981): 185–198.

Lawn, R. *Jazz Ensemble Director's Manual.* Oskaloosa, Iowa: Barnhouse, 1981.

Lepherd, Laurence. *Music Education in International Perspective: The People's Republic of China.* Darling Heights, Australia: Music International, 1988.

Lewin, Kurt. *Field Theory in Social Science.* New York: Harper & Brothers, 1951.

Lockhart-Moss, Eunice, and Elaine Guregian. "David Baker, Jazz Advocate." *The Instrumentalist* 41 (1986): 11–14.

Lord, Albert B. *The Singer of Tales.* Cambridge, Mass.: Harvard University Press, 1960.

Lowens, Irving. " 'Music,' Juilliard Repertory Project and the Schools." *Sunday Star* (Washington, D.C.) 30 May 1971, Sec. E:4.

Lucarelli, Humbert J. "No Easy Answers." *The Instrumentalist* 42 (1988): 12–16.

Malm, William P. *Japanese Music and Musical Instruments.* Rutland, Vt.: Tuttle, 1959.

———. *Music Cultures of the Pacific, the Near East, and Asia.* Englewood Cliffs, N.J.: Prentice-Hall, 1977.

———. "Personal Approaches to the Study of Japanese Art Music." *Asian Music* 3 (1979) 35–39.

———. *Six Views of Noh.* Berkeley: University of California Press, 1986.

Mann, Horace. *Life and Works of Horace Mann: Annual Reports of the Secretary of the Board of Education of Massachusetts for the Year 1839–1844.* Boston: Lee and Shepherd Publishers, 1891.

Mark, Michael. *Source Readings in Music Education History.* New York: Schirmer Books, 1982.

———. *Contemporary Music Education.* New York: Schirmer Books, 1986.

Maslow, Abraham. *Motivation and Personality.* New York: Harper & Brothers, 1954.

Mason, Lowell. *Manual of the Boston Academy of Music, for Instruction in the Elements of Vocal Music on the System of Pestalozzi.* Boston: Carter, Hendree and Co., 1834.

Mason, Luther Whiting. *Second Music Reader.* New York: Ginn, Heath and Co., 1870.

May, Elizabeth. *The Influence of the Meiji Period on Japanese Children's Music.* Berkeley: University of California Press, 1963.

Mazrui, Ali A. *The Africans; A Triple Heritage.* Boston: Little, Brown, 1986.

McGee, Timothy J. *The Music of Canada.* New York: W. W. Norton, 1985.

McHose, Allen I., and Ruth N. Tibbs. New York: F. S. Crofts & Co., 1944.

McKeachie, Wilbert J. *Summary, Documentary Report of the Ann Arbor Symposium on the Applications of Psychology to the Teaching and Learning of Music: Session III.* Reston, Va.: Music Educators National Conference, 1983.

McPhee, Colin. *Children and Music in Bali.* N.P., 1938.

———. *Music in Bali.* New Haven, Conn.: Yale University Press, 1966.

Mead, Margaret. "An Investigation of the Thought of Primitive Children with Special Reference to Animism." *Journal of the Royal Anthropological Institute* 62 (1932): 173–189.

———. "Children and Ritual in Bali." In *Traditional Balinese Culture,* edited by Jane Belo. New York: Columbia University Press, 1970.

Merriam, Alan P. *The Anthropology of Music.* Evanston, Ill.: Northwestern University Press, 1964.

Miller, George A. "The Magical Number Seven plus or minus Two: Some Limits on Our Capacity for Processing Information." *Psychological Review* 63 (1956): 81–97.

Miller, Samuel D. "Guido d'Arezzo: Medieval Musician and Educator." *Journal of Research in Music Education* 21 (1973): 239–245.

Miller, Terry E. *Traditional Music of the Lao.* Westport, Conn.: Greenwood Press, 1985.

Mingus, Charles. *Beneath the Underdog.* New York: Knopf, 1972.

Ministry of Education. *A Collection of Teaching Programmes for Music Education in Primary and Secondary Schools Issued from 1949–1985.* Beijing, China: Ministry of Education, 1985.

Mogdil, Sohan. *Piagetian Research: A Handbook of Recent Studies.* Windsor, Ontario: NFER Publishing Co., 1974.

Moorhead, Gladys E., and Donald Pond. *Music of Young Children.* 1941–1951. Reprint. Santa Barbara, Calif.: Pillsbury Foundation, 1978.

Morley, Thomas. *A Plaine and Easie Introduction to Practicall Musicke.* London, 1597.

Morton, David. "The Traditional Instrumental Music of Thailand." In *The Music of Asia,* edited by Jose Maceda, 90–106. Manila: National Music Council of the Philippines, 1966.

———. *The Traditional Music of Thailand.* Los Angeles: University of California Press, 1976.

Mullins, Shirley S. "The Intriguing World of Janos Starker." *The Instrumentalist* 41 (1986): 13–19.

Mursell, James L. "A Balanced Curriculum in Music Education." *Education* 56 (May 1936): 519–527.

Music Educators National Conference. *Documentary Report of the Ann Arbor Symposium: Applications of Psychology to the Teaching and Learning of Music.* Reston, Va.: Music Educators National Conference, 1981.

Nettl, Bruno. *Folk and Traditional Music of the Western Continents.* Englewood Cliffs, N.J.: Prentice-Hall, 1973.

———. "Thoughts on Improvisation: A Comparative Approach." *Musical Quarterly* 60 (1974) 1–19.

———. "Persian Classical Music in Tehran: The Processes of Change. In *Eight Urban Musical Cultures*, edited by Bruno Nettl. Urbana: University of Illinois Press, 1978.

———. "In Honor of Our Principal Teachers." *Ethnomusicology* 28 (1984) 173–186.

———. *The Western Impact on World Music*. New York: Schirmer Books, 1985.

Nettl, Bruno, and Bela Foltin. *Daramad of Chahargah: A Study in The Performance Practice of Persian Music*. Detroit: Information Coordinators, 1972.

Neuman, Daniel M. *The Life of Music in North India*. Detroit: Wayne State University Press, 1980.

Neumann, Frederick. "A New Look at Bach's Ornamentation." *Music and Letters* 46 (1965) 4–15.

———. *Ornamentation and Improvisation in Mozart*. Princeton, N.J.: Princeton University Press, 1986.

New, J. H. "Progressive Western Methods and Traditional African Methods of Teaching Music: A Comparison." *International Journal of Music Education* 1 (1983): 25–29.

Nketia, J. H. Kwabena. "The Role of the Drummer in Akan Society." *African Music* 1 (1954): 34–43.

———. *The Music of Africa*. London: Bollancz, 1975.

O'Canainn, Tomas. *Traditional Music in Ireland*. London: Routledge and Kegan Paul, 1978.

Okafor, Richard C. "Focus on Music Education in Nigeria." *International Journal of Music Education* 12 (1988): 9–17.

Palisca, Claude V. *Music in Our Schools: A Search for Improvement*. Bulletin no. 28. U.S. Department of Health, Education, and Welfare. Washington, D.C.: U.S. Government Printing Office, 1964.

Palmer, Mary. "Relative Effectiveness of Two Approaches to Rhythm Reading for Fourth-Grade Students." *Journal of Research in Music Education* 24 (1976) 110–118.

Parker, Horatio, Osbourne McConathy, Edward Bailey Birge, and Otto Miessner. *The Progressive Music Series, Teacher's Manual*, vol. 2. Boston: Silver-Burdett, 1916.

Parr, Jerry D. "Essential and Desirable Music and Music-Teaching Competencies for First-Year Band Instructors in the Public Schools." Doctoral dissertation, University of Iowa, 1976.

Parrish, Carl. "A Renaissance Music Manual for Choir Boys." In *Aspects of Medieval and Renaissance Music: A Birthday Offering to Gustave Reese*, edited by Jan La Rue, 649–654. New York: W. W. Norton & Co, 1966.

Parry, Milton. *The Making of Homeric Verse: The Collected Papers of Milman Parry*. Edited by Adam Parry. Oxford: Clarendon Press, 1971.

Pemberton, Carol. *Lowell Mason: His Life and Work*. Ann Arbor, Mich.: UMI Research Press, 1985.

Pestalozzi, Johann Heinrich. *How Gertrude Teaches Her Children*. Edited by E.

Cooks, translated by Lucy Holland and Francis Turner. London: Son-
nenschein, 1894.

Pflederer, Marilyn. "Conservation Law as Applied to the Development of
Musical Intelligence." *Journal of Research in Music Education* 15
(1967): 215–223.

Piaget, Jean. *The Origins of Intelligence in Children.* New York: International
University Press, 1952.

Pian, Rulan Chao. *Song Dynasty Musical Sources and Their Interpretation.*
Cambridge: Harvard University Press, 1967.

Picken, Laurence. "The Music of China." *The New Oxford History of Music,*
vol. 1. London: Oxford University Press, 1957.

Pond, Donald. "A Composer's Study of Young Children's Innate Musicality."
Council of Research in Music Education 68 (1981): 1–12.

Pronko, Leonard. *Theater East and West.* Berkeley: University of California,
1967.

Raiman, Melvin. "The Identification and Hierarchical Classification of Competencies and Objectives of Student Teaching Through a Partial Delphi
Survey." Doctoral Dissertation, University of Connecticut, 1975.

Rainbow, Bernarr. *The Land without Music.* London: Novello, 1967.

———. *English Psalmody Prefaces.* Kilkeyyn, Ireland: Boethius Press, 1982.

Ramanathan, S. "The Indian Sarigama Notation." *Journal of the Music Academy, Madras* 32 (1981): 84–85.

Ramsey, Johnny H. "The Effects of Age, Singing Ability, and Instrumental
Experiences on Preschool Children's Melodic Perception." *Journal of
Research in Music Education* 32 (1983): 133–145.

Rastell, Richard. *The Notation of Western Europe.* London: J. M. Dent & Sons,
1983.

Read, Gardner. *Source Book of Proposed Music Notation Reforms.* New York:
Greenwood Press, 1987.

Reck, David B. "India/South India." In *Worlds of Music,* edited by Jeff Todd.
New York: Schirmer Books, 1984.

Reimer, Bennett. *A Philosophy of Music Education.* Englewood Cliffs, N.J.:
Prentice-Hall, 1970.

———. *A Philosophy of Music Education.* 2nd ed. Englewood Cliffs, N.J.:
Prentice-Hall, 1989.

———. "Music Education as Aesthetic Education: Toward the Future." *Music Educators Journal* 75 (1989): 26–32

Reisner, Edward H. *The Evolution of the Common School.* New York: Macmillan, 1930.

Rice, Timothy. "Music Learned but Not Taught: The Bulgarian Case." In
Becoming Human through Music, edited by David P. McAllester. Reston, Va.: Music Educators National Conference, 1985.

Rideout, Roger R. "On Early Applications of Psychology in Music Education." *Journal of Research in Music Education* 31 (1982): 141–150.

Robinson, Ray, and Ray Winold. *The Choral Experience: Literature, Materials
and Methods.* New York: Harper's College Press, 1976.

Rose, Gloria. "Agazzari and the Improvising Orchestra." *Journal of the American Musicological Society* 18 (1965): 382–393.

Rosenthal, Roseanne K. "The Relative Effects of Guided Model, Model Only,

Guide Only, and Practice Only Treatments on the Accuracy of Advanced
Instrumentalists' Musical Performance." *Journal of Research in Music
Education* 34 (1986): 265–273.

Sang, Richard C. "A Study of the Relationship Between Instrumental Teachers' Modeling Skills and Pupil Performance Behaviors." *Council for
Research in Music Education* 91 (1987): 155–159.

Saunders, Trevor J., ed. Aristotle, *The Politics*, trans T. A. Sinclair, Harmonds-
worth: Penguin Classics, revised ed., 1984.

Sawa, George D. "The Survival of Some Aspects of Medieval Arabic Performance Practice." *Ethnomusicology* 25 (1981): 73–86.

———. 1989a. *Music Performance Practice in the Early Abbasid Era, 132–320
A.H./750 A.D.–932 A.D.* Toronto: Pontifical Institute of Medieval Studies.

———. 1989b. "Oral Transmission in Arabic Music, Past and Present." *Oral
Tradition* 4:254-266.

Schleuter, Stanley J. *A Sound Approach to Teaching Instrumentalists*. Kent,
Ohio: Kent State University, 1984.

Schmidt-Wrenger, Barbara. "Tshiyanda Na Ululi—Boundaries of Indepen-
dence, Life, Music, and Education in Tshokwe Society, Angola, Zaire."
In *Becoming Human through Music*, edited by David P. McAllester.
Reston, Va.: Music Educator's National Conference, 1985, 77–86.

Schnabel, Karl U., "My Father." *Piano Quarterly* 84 (1974): 10–18.

Schwartz, Elliott, and Barney Childs. *Contemporary Composers on Contemporary Music*. New York: Holt, Rinehart, and Winston, 1967.

Scott, A. C. "The Performance of Classical Theatre. In *Chinese Theater*, edited
by Colin Mackerras. Honolulu: University Press of Hawaii, 1983.

Serafine, Mary Louise. *Music as Cognition, the Development of Thought in
Sound*. New York: Columbia University Press, 1988.

Shamrock, Mary. "Applications and Adaptations of Orff-Schulwerk in Japan,
Taiwan, and Thailand." Doctoral diss., UCLA, 1988.

Shankar, Ravi. *My Music, My Life*. New York: Simon and Schuster, 1968.

Shapiro, Nat, and Nat Hentoff, eds. *Hear Me Talkin' to Ya*. New York: Rinehart and Co., 1955.

Shaw, George W. "Relationships between Experimental Factors and Pre-
cepts of Selected Professional Musicians in the United States Who Are
Adept at Jazz Improvisation." Doctoral diss., University of Oklahoma,
1979.

Shehan, Patricia K. "Balkan Women as Preservers of Traditional Music and
Culture." In Koskoff, E., *Women and Music in Cross-Cultural Perspective*.
New York: Greenwood Press, 45–54, 1987.

———. Effects of Rote versus Note Presentations on Rhythm Learning and
Retention. *Journal of Research in Music Education* 35 (1987): 117–26

Shuter-Dyson, Rosemary, and Clive Gabriel. *The Psychology of Music Ability*.
2nd ed. London: Methuen Press, 1981.

Signell, Karl L. *Makam: Modal Practice in Turkish Art Music*. Seattle: Asian
Music Publications, 1977.

Silver, Brian. "On Becoming an Ustad: Six Life Sketches in the Evolution of
a Gharana. *Asian Music* 7 (1976): 27–50.

Sims, Francis J. "An Experimental Investigation of Group and Individual

Voice Instruction at the Beginning Level to High School Students."
Doctoral diss., University of Oklahoma, 1961.

"A Sketch of the Principal Features of Contemporary Musical Life in Vienna." *Allgemeine musikalische Zeitung* III (1800): cols. 41–50, 65–68. Translated by P. Weiss. In Peter Weiss and Richard Tarushkin, *Music in the Western World*. New York, Schirmer Books, 1984, pp. 321–325.

Skinner, B. F. *Beyond Freedom and Dignity*. New York: Knopf, 1971.

Sloboda, John A. *The Musical Mind*. Oxford: Clarendon Press, 1985.

Smith, Barbara. "Learning, Variability and Change." *Ethnomusicology* 31 (1987): 201–220.

Smith, G. Jean. "The Legacy of Paul Rolland." *The Instrumentalist* 42 (1987): 25–29.

Sosniak, Lauren A. "Learning to Be a Concert Pianist." In *Developing Talent in Young People*, edited by Benjamin S. Bloom, 28–54. New York: Ballantine Books, 1985.

Southern, Eileen. *Readings in Black American Music*. 2d ed. New York: W. W. Norton & Co., 1983.

Sternfeld, Frederick W. "Music in the Schools of the Reformation." *Musica Disciplina*, vol. 2, fascicles 1 & 2, 1948, 9–122.

Stravinsky, Igor. *Selected Correspondence*, Vol. 1. Edited by Robert Craft. New York: Alfred A. Knopf, 1985.

Strunk, Oliver. *Source Readings in Music History*. New York: W. W. Norton, 1950.

Sudnow, David. *Ways of the Hand*. Cambridge, Mass.: Harvard University Press, 1978.

Sung, Kyung He. "Professional Education of the Music Teacher in Korea." *International Society for Music Education Yearbook, 1986*. 148–153. Nedlands, Western Australia: International Society for Music Education, 1986.

Suryabrata, Bernard. "Some Thoughts on Music and Music Education for Indonesia." In *Challenges in Music Education*. Perth: University of Western Australia, 1976.

Sutton, Brett. "Shape-Note Tune Books and Primitive Hymns. *Ethnomusicology* 26 (1982): 11–26.

Suzuki, Shinichi. *Nurtured by Love*. New York: Exposition Press, 1982.

Tanizaki, Jinichiro. "A Portrait of Shunkin." In *Seven Japanese Tales*. New York: Knopf, 1963.

Thomas, Ronald, *MMCP Synthesis: A Structure for Music Education*. Elnora, N.Y.: Media, Inc., 1970.

Torrance, E. Paul. *Torrance Tests of Creative Thinking*. Lexington, Mass.: Personnel Press, 1966.

———. *Understanding the Fourth Grade Slump in Creative Thinking*. U.S. Office of Education Report, 1967.

Tracey, Hugh. *Chopi Musicians*. 2nd ed. London: Oxford University Press for the International African Institute, 1970.

Treitler, Leo. "Homer and Gregory: The Transmission of Epic Poetry and Plainchant." *Musicology Quarterly* 40 (1974): 333–372.

———. "The Early History of Music Writing in the West." *Journal of the American Musicological Society* 35 (1982): 237–279.

Van der Werf, Hendrik. *The Extant Troubadour Melodies: Transcriptions and Essays for Performers and Scholars.* Rochester, N.Y.: Published by author, 1984.

Van Gulik, Robert H. *The Lore of the Chinese Lute.* Rutland, Vt.: Tuttle, 1969.

Wade, Bonnie C. "Performance Practice in Indian Classical Music." In *Performance Practice/Ethnomusicological Perspectives*, edited by Gerard Behague. Westport, Conn.: Greenwood Press, 1986.

Waleson, Heidi. "Bel canto." *The Strad* 99 (1988): 391–393.

Wallas, Graham.*The Art of Thought.* New York: Harcourt, Brace and World, 1926.

Waterman, Christopheer. *Juju.* Chicago: University of Chicago Press, 1990.

Waterman, Richard. "Music in Australian Aboriginal Cultures—Some Sociological and Psychological Implications." In *Readings in Ethnomusicology*, edited by David P. McAllester. New York: Johnson Reprint Corporation, 1971, 353–356.

Webster, Peter R. 1988a. "Creative Thinking in Music: Approaches to Research. In *Music, Society and Education in the United States*, edited by J. Gates. Tuscaloosa: University of Alabama Press.

———. 1988b. "A Model for Creative Thinking in Music with Implications for Music Education." Paper presented at the Music Educators National Conference meeting in Indianapolis, Ind., 1988b.

———. "Creative Thinking in Music: The Assessment Question." In Richmond, John W., ed., *The Proceedings of the Suncoast Music Education Forum on Creativity*. Tampa: University of South Florida, 1989.

Wertheimer, Max. *Productive Thinking.* Rev. ed. New York: Harper & Sons.

Wickes, Linda. *The Genius of Simplicity.* Princeton, N.J.: Summy Birchard, 1982.

Wilson, Tim. "Japanese Bands: What Makes Them So Good?" *Music Educators Journal* 72 (1986): 41–47.

Witmer, Robert, and Robbins, James. "A Historical and Critical Survey of Recent Pedagogical Materials for the Teaching and Learning of Jazz." *Council for Research in Music Education* 96 (1988): 7–29.

Wolff, Konrad. "Artur Schnabel." *Piano Quarterly* 84 (1974): 36–40.

Woodfill, Walter L. *Musicians in English Society from Elizabeth to Charles I.* Princeton, N.J.: Princeton University Press, 1953.

Wu, Zuguang, Huang, Zuolin, and Mei, Shaowu. *Peking Opera and Mei Lanfang.* Beijing: New World Press, 1981.

Yando, Regina, Victoria Seitz, and Edward Zigler. *Imitation: A Developmental Perspective.* Hillsdale, N.J.: Lawrence Erlbaum, 1978.

Yang, Mu. "Some Problems of Music Education in the People's Republic of China." *International Journal of Music Education* 11 (1988): 25–32.

Yung, Bell. "Choreographic and Kinesthetic Elements in Performance on the Chinese Seven-String Zither." *Ethnomusicology* 28 (1984): 505–517.

———. "Da Pu: The Recreative Process for the Music of the Seven-String Zither." In *Music and Context: Essays in Honor of John Ward*, edited by Anne Dhu Shapiro. Cambridge, Mass.: Harvard University Press, 1985.

———. "Historical Interdependency of Music: A Case Study of the Chinese

Seven-String Zither." *Journal of the American Musicological Society* 401 (1987): 82–91.

Zimmerman, M., and L. Sechrest. "How Children Conceptually Oganize Musical Sounds." Cooperative Research Project no. 5-0256, Northwestern University, 1967.

Zonis, Ella. *Classical Persian Music*. Cambridge, Mass.: Harvard University Press, 1973.

Zurcher, William. "The Effect of Model-Supportive Practice on Beginning Brass Instrumentalists." In *Research in Music Behavior*, edited by C. K. Madsen, R. D. Greer, and C. H. Madsen, Jr., 1975, 131–138. New York: Teachers College Press.

INDEX